Pakistan's Counterterrorism Challenge

South Asia in World Affairs Series

T. V. Paul, *Series Editor*

Titles in the Series

Afghan Endgames: Strategy and Policy Choices for America's Longest War
Hy Rothstein and John Arquilla, editors

Vying for Allah's Vote: Understanding Islamic Parties, Political Violence, and Extremism in Pakistan
Haroon K. Ullah

PAKISTAN'S
COUNTERTERRORISM CHALLENGE

Edited by
Moeed Yusuf

GEORGETOWN UNIVERSITY PRESS
Washington, DC

UNITED STATES INSTITUTE OF PEACE
Washington, DC

FOUNDATION
BOOKS

FOUNDATION
BOOKS

Foundation Books is an imprint of Cambridge University Press, India.

Cambridge House, 4381/4 Ansari Road, Daryaganj, New Delhi 110 002

www.cambridgeindia.org

This edition is published by Cambridge University Press India Pvt Ltd. by arrangement with Georgetown University Press, Washington DC, USA

First South Asia edition 2014

Printed in India at Shree Maitrey Printech Pvt. Ltd., Noida

ISBN 978-93-82993-91-9 Hardback

To all Pakistani and global citizens
who have fallen victim to the evil of terrorism,
and to those working to fight the menace
with dedication and sincerity

Contents

Illustrations

Maps

Tables

Acknowledgments

This book marks the culmination of over three years of efforts by the United States Institute of Peace (USIP) Pakistan program to examine and analyze various aspects of the terrorism challenge the Pakistani state has been facing for the better part of a decade. The project would not have been possible without the resources made available by the Institute's Pakistan program. I especially wish to thank Tara Sonenshine, Abi Williams, Alex Thier, and Andrew Wilder, who saw merit in this project and remained supportive in their respective capacities at USIP.

The inspiration for this volume came from the plethora of conversations and debates about terrorism and counterterrorism efforts in Pakistan that have been ongoing in Washington (and Pakistan) for some years. USIP's Pakistan program managers felt that insufficient space and opportunity existed for a practitioner's perspective on the problem from the ground in Pakistan. Therefore, foremost, I am grateful to all the authors who agreed to contribute to this volume and persevered in producing quality chapters. The journey of this volume has been an intense one, given the fast-changing environment in Pakistan and the consequent need for regular updates. The authors have all been extremely patient and forthcoming.

I was very fortunate to have excellent research and administrative assistance throughout the life of this project. Special gratitude is due to my very able and diligent associates, Megan Neville, Stephanie Flamenbaum, Ayesha Chugh, and Sairah Yusuf, who not only provided research support but also contributed through substantive and conceptual inputs to the book. All of them were deeply involved in helping me streamline the volume's focus and in reviewing and editing chapters. Most importantly, they held me to task and kept the project together whenever I wavered. Emily Horin was a great help in all housekeeping matters in the final stages of the project. I also owe gratitude to Valerie Norville, Michelle Slavin, Marie Marr, Kay Hechler, and their team in the USIP publications department for all their support and to the Georgetown University Press team for bringing the volume into its final form.

Finally, I must thank my family, especially my wife, Shanza Khan, for her understanding and support as this project moved from concept to this final product.

Abbreviations

AACP	Action in Aid of Civil Power
AJK	Azad Jammu Kashmir
ANF	Anti-Narcotics Force
ANP	Awami National Party
ASF	Airport Security Force
ATA	Anti-Terrorism Act (1997)
ATB	Afghan-trained boys
ATC	Anti-Terrorism Court
BM	Al-Badar Mujahideen
CIA	Central Intelligence Agency
CID	Criminal Investigation Department
CMO	counterterrorism military operations
COIN	counterinsurgency
CrPC	Criminal Procedure Code
CT	counterterrorism
CTC	Counterterrorism Center
ECHR	European Convention on Human Rights
ETIM	Eastern Turkestan Islamic Movement
FATA	Federally Administered Tribal Areas
FBI	Federal Bureau of Investigation
FC	Frontier Corps
FCR	Frontier Crimes Regulation
FIA	Federal Investigation Agency
FIR	First Information Report
GSM	mobile-tracking systems
HM	Hizb-ul-Mujahideen
HuJI	Harakat-ul-Jihad-al-Islami
HuM	Harkat-ul-Mujahideen
HuMA	Harakat-ul-Mujahideen Al-alami

IB	Intelligence Bureau
ICCPR	International Covenant on Civil and Political Rights
ICRC	International Committee of the Red Cross
ICT	information and communication technologies
ICT	Islamabad Capital Territory
IDP	internally displaced person
IHL	international humanitarian law
IMU	Islamic Movement of Uzbekistan
ISAF	International Security Force for Afghanistan
ISI	Inter-Services Intelligence Agency
JeM	Jaish-e-Mohammed
JI	Jamaat-e-Islami
JM	Jamaat-ul-Mujahideen
JuD	Jamaat-ud-Dawa
JUI	Jamiat Ulema-e-Islam
KPK	Khyber Pakhtunkhwa Province
LeJ	Lashkar-e-Jhangvi
LEO	law enforcement organization
LeT	Lashkar-e-Taiba
LoC	line of control
LTTE	Liberation Tigers of Tamil Eelam
MI	military intelligence
MMA	Muttahida Majlis-e-Amal
MOI	Ministry of Interior
NAB	National Accountability Bureau
NACTA	National Counter Terrorism Authority
NACTES	National Counter Terrorism and Extremism Strategy
NADRA	National Database and Registration Authority
NATO	North Atlantic Treaty Organization
NIAC	noninternational armed conflict
NSC	National Security Council
PATA	Provincially Administered Tribal Areas
PEMRA	Pakistan Electronic Media Regulatory Authority
PIPS	Pakistan Institute for Peace Studies
PML-N	Pakistan Muslim League-Nawaz
PPC	Pakistan Penal Code
PPP	Pakistan People's Party
PTA	Pakistan Telecommunication Authority
PTI	Pakistan Tehrik-e-Insaf
RAP	returnees from Afghan prisons
SAFRON	Federal Ministry of States and Frontier Regions

SBP	State Bank of Pakistan
SHO	station house officer
SIG	Special Investigation Group
SIM	subscriber identity module
SMS	short messaging service
SOP	standard operating procedure
SSG	Special Services Group
SSP	Sipah-e-Sahaba Pakistan
TNSM	Tehreek-e-Nafaz-e-Shariat-e-Mohammadi
TTP	Tehrik-e-Taliban Pakistan
UNSC	United Nations Security Council
USIP	United States Institute of Peace (the Institute)

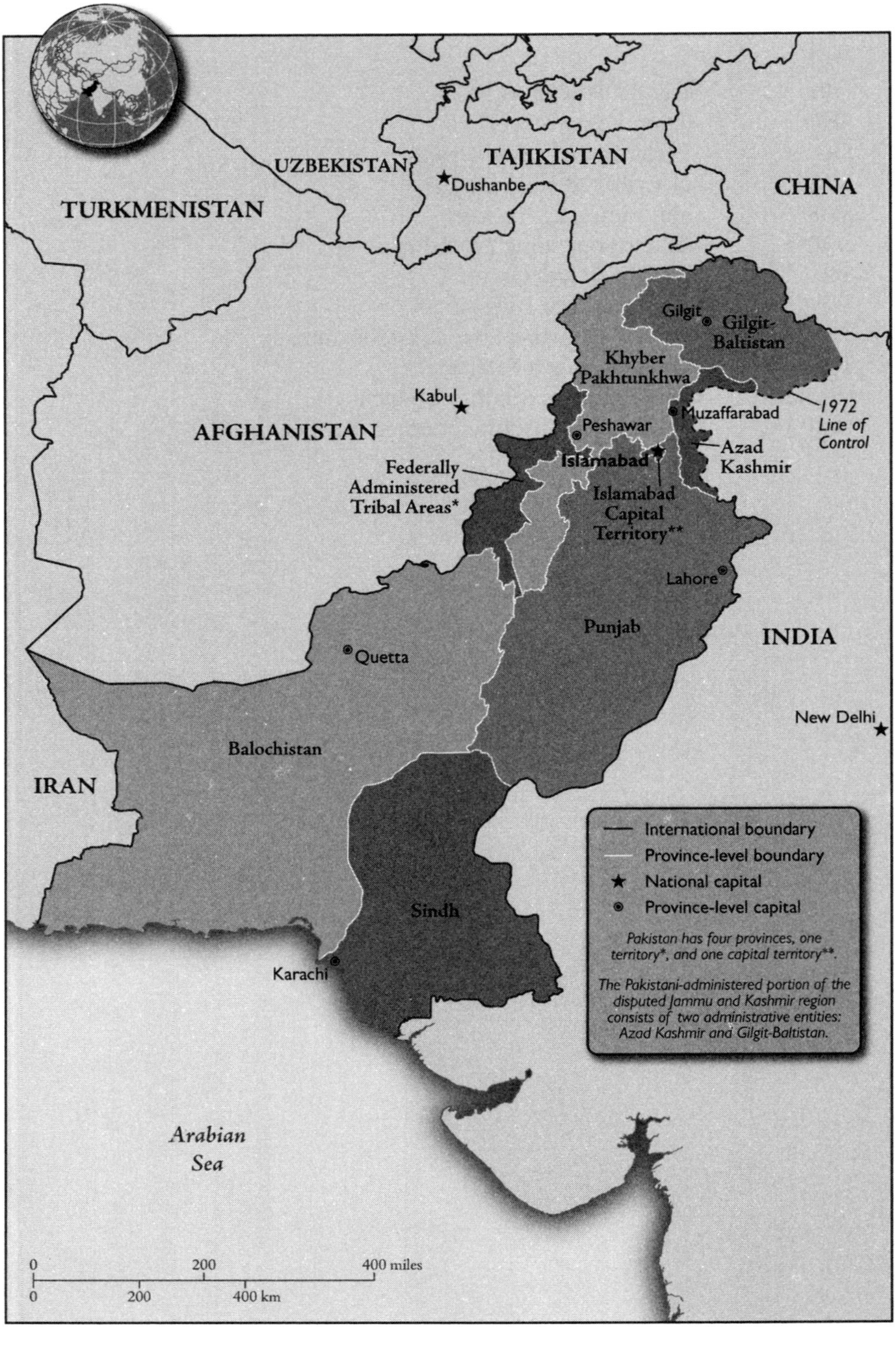

Map 1. Pakistan's Administrative Regions

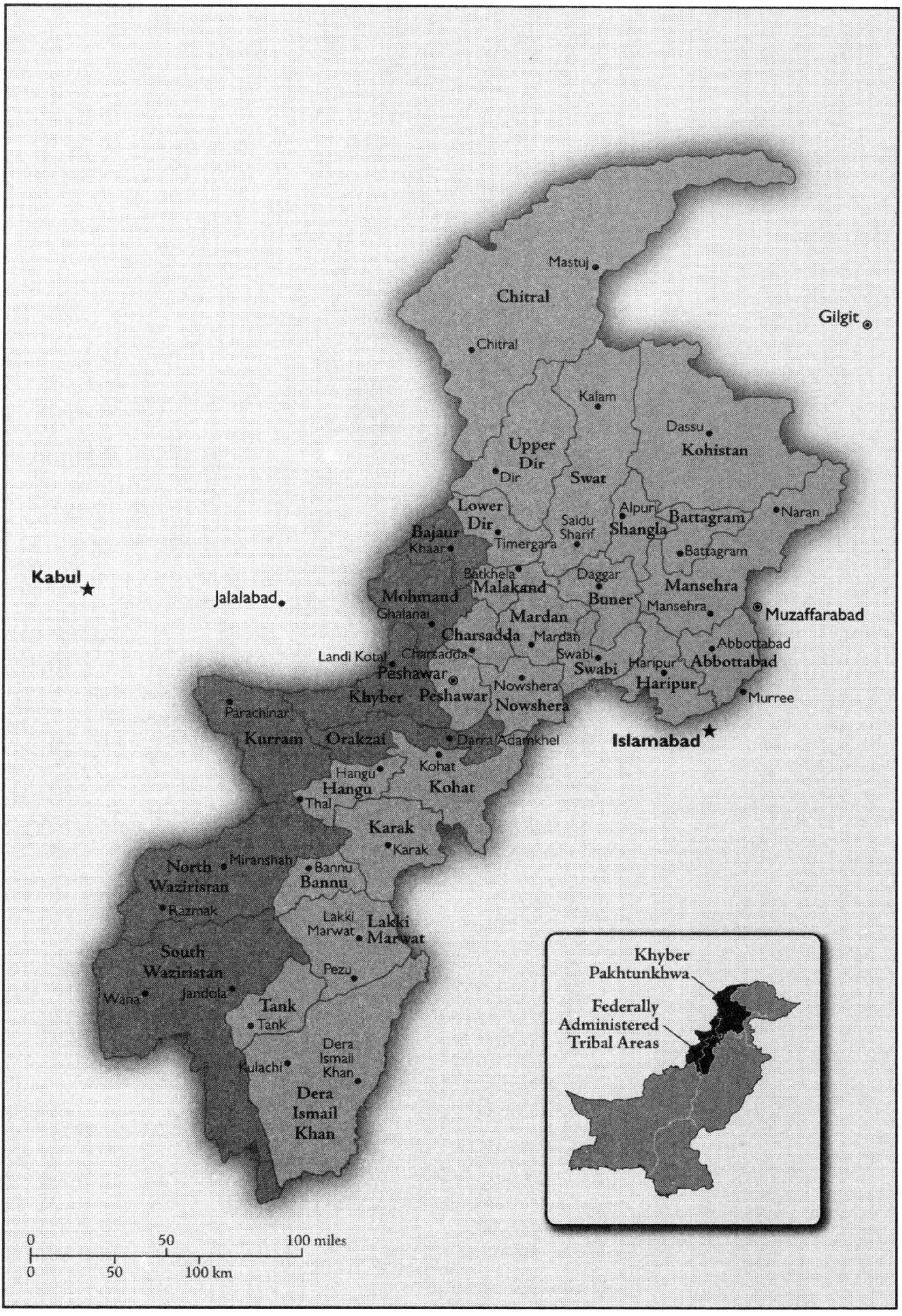

Map 2. Pakistan's Districts of Khyber Pakhtunkhwa Province and the Federally Administered Tribal Areas

Introduction

MOEED YUSUF

PAKISTAN has been in the global limelight since the 9/11 terrorist attacks on the United States. The US invasion of Afghanistan and the subsequent movement of al-Qaeda and Afghan Taliban militants into Pakistan's border regions marked the area as the "epicenter of international terrorism" (Rassler and Brown 2011, 51). Since then, Pakistan has been home to an assortment of Islamist militant groups who use Pakistani soil to target international troops stationed in Afghanistan and to threaten Western targets in general. Complicating this challenge has been the emergence of a ferocious and sustained insurgent-cum-terrorist campaign against the Pakistani state, centered in the country's Federally Administered Tribal Areas (FATA) bordering Afghanistan.

Today Pakistan is in the ironic position of being seen by outsiders as a troubling partner in the global campaign against terrorism, given its ambiguous relationship with state-sponsored militancy, while considering itself to be troubled as a result of what transpired in its neighborhood post-9/11. While Pakistan faced significant problems on the eve of the 9/11 attacks—sporadic sectarian violence (Nasr 2002), ethnic factionalism (Alavi 1988; Cohen 2004b), and poor development indicators (S. R. Khan 2013), to name a few—it remained a relatively stable country as far as the quantum of violence perpetrated within its borders was concerned. Notably, Pakistan faced no active insurgency at the turn of the century, unlike other South Asian states, including India, Nepal, and Sri Lanka. Today Pakistan features prominently on the global failed states index.[1] The combination of extreme turbulence within its borders and its possession of nuclear weapons has led many to see Pakistan as one of the most dangerous places on earth.

Much has been written about Pakistan and the myriad challenges posed by the multiplicity of local and foreign militants active on its soil. The majority of the international literature, however, focuses on the "Af-Pak" theater, given the primary interest in the counterinsurgency (COIN) campaign in Afghanistan. This focuses analyses on the Afghan Taliban movement, the dynamic between the Afghan Taliban's presence in "Af" and "Pak," and the tensions between the West and Pakistan more so than on the complexities of the myriad challenges the Pakistani state faces in countering violent extremists. Since the Af-Pak construct originated from the Obama administration's efforts to link the insurgency in Afghanistan to the growing incidence of Islamist violence in Pakistan, this construct not only created much angst between Washington and Islamabad but it also meant that Pakistan was often seen through an Afghan lens (Yusuf 2009a). Even when the focus was primarily on Pakistan, attention was paid either to narrow tactical and operational military needs (Ball 1996; Mullick 2009, 2010b; Nawaz 2011), to sweeping issues like the strategic outlook of the Pakistani state—specifically how its obsession with India colors foreign policy responses (Hanauer and Chalk 2012; Jones 2009; Yusuf 2013b)—or to long-term reform agendas linked to ideological, political, socioeconomic, and other structural reforms (Cohen 2004a; Hussain 2005; Lamb and Hameed 2012; ICG 2013).

The missing link, one that this volume seeks to address, is a comprehensive analysis of the issues that fall between these two—the tactical and the broad—extremes: an examination of the specific counterterrorism (CT) challenges facing Pakistan and how Pakistan can address them. This volume is a dedicated effort to study the threats, performance, and future opportunities for the Pakistani state strictly within the domain of CT. Special attention is paid to the nontraditional functions of force that remain central to Pakistan's ability to subdue militancy but have received the deserved attention neither from the Pakistani state in its previous experiences with insurgent and terrorist challenges nor from Western experts examining the context. In particular, the volume focuses on the weakness of political institutions, the role of policing, problems within the criminal justice system, efforts to choke financing for militancy, and regulation on the use of media and technology by militants. The direct application of military force alone, also examined in this volume, cannot solve Pakistan's Islamist challenge; until the Pakistani state can forge a political consensus on a CT vision, civilian law enforcement takes center stage, courts effectively prosecute the guilty, and militants' access to financial resources as well as to new and innovative technologies is permanently eliminated, any peace will be tenuous. Tackling these aspects does not in any way reduce the need for long-term structural reform-oriented solutions, but CT is needed to create the conditions necessary before such far-reaching reforms can begin to take effect.

The CT versus COIN Debate

For a volume of this nature, it is important to define clearly what we mean by CT, given the changes to the global outlook toward "terrorism" over the past decade. As the nature of the threat has shifted, so too have attitudes toward response options. Since 9/11 these threats have been viewed within a war framework rather than a law enforcement framework. The term "terrorism" has become part of elementary vocabulary and has been used to define a number of violent threats, mostly perpetrated by nonstate actors, whether acting on their own or at the behest of a state. The term has been employed extremely loosely as states and other powerful actors have found a political and legal incentive to declare any sustained violent opposition as terrorism, thereby gaining international sympathy and opening up an array of heavy-handed policy options otherwise unavailable or subject to international condemnation. As the currency of terrorism has become popular, so have reactions to it: "counterterrorism" and "antiterrorism." Muddying definitional matters further has been the resurgence of terms like "insurgency" and "counterinsurgency," which had faded away after the heyday of the Cold War.[2]

Both practitioners and academics have found it difficult to separate terrorism and CT from insurgency and COIN beyond the theoretical realm—to the point that Kaplan labels this confusion "counterinsurgenterrorism" (Kaplan 2009). During the Cold War, COIN was frequently used as the basis of strategy in the superpower proxy wars that took place across the third world. Terrorism was rarely the focus of COIN theorists. Today there is a great deal of debate on whether these categories can be functionally separated; some have argued that the insurgent and the terrorist have both become equally central, and where insurgencies are operational, the two are becoming intertwined (see Smith 2007). Boot (2013) links guerrillas and terrorism in a number of cases and establishes how they are used in tandem. Others point to a need to distinguish between the targets of COIN operations and CT efforts. Exum (2009) and Boyle (2010) present CT as purely a military response, while COIN is envisioned as a broader enterprise including socio-economic and governance responses. Some authors have pointed to the changing nature of insurgency itself—from the "classical" model of nonstate actors overthrowing and taking over the state to the current function of many insurgents as mere "spoilers" (Record and Terrill 2004; Cordesman 2006) as well as the increasing internationalization of what were once geographically self-contained movements (Kilcullen 2006a). Both trends have made insurgencies appear very similar to terrorist movements.

This coalescence, however, has not changed the essence of insurgency or terrorism. An insurgency seeks to erode the political authority of a recognized entity—usually the state—and replace it with the insurgent's writ.[3] Terrorism has a narrower focus: it creates extreme fear by committing violence against armed and unarmed individuals.[4] Problems in analytical clarity remain, however: where does an insurgency stop and terrorism start? In contemporary movements, does one exist without the other?

For the purposes of this book, terrorism will be considered a tactical subset of insurgency campaigns. While terrorism can exist on its own—with the creation of fear within a population seen as an end in itself—it is primarily conceived of as a tactic, a means to an end, that can be adopted by groups with diverse aims and objectives. This means that an insurgency can potentially be devoid of terrorist tactics, and that terrorism can exist without a larger strategic aim of establishing the writ of an insurgent group. However, insurgencies can and do adopt terrorist tactics in pursuit of their aims (Boot 2013), and they may do so well beyond the geographical focus of the insurgency itself. Our definition finds resonance among a number of works cited earlier; it also allows us to avoid creating an artificial distinction to isolate one phenomenon from the other. Most importantly, it most accurately depicts the situation in Pakistan. Pakistan's principal terrorist threat, the Pakistani Taliban (or Tehrik-e-Taliban Pakistan, the TTP) and its affiliates are undertaking an insurgent-cum-terrorist campaign. The insurgency is confined to the northwestern part of the country, chiefly Federally Administered Tribal Areas (FATA) and the parts of the adjacent Khyber Pakhtunkhwa (KPK) Province, but terrorism continues both there and far beyond across KPK and in Pakistan's major urban metropolis, Karachi, Lahore, Islamabad, and Quetta. Incidents of terrorism perpetrated by the TTP are not delinked from the state of the insurgency campaign at any given point in time. Developments in the insurgency cause the Pakistani Taliban to press harder or ease off as far as perpetrating terrorism is concerned. On the other hand, sectarian and other outfits operating on their own are not part of the insurgency but are active in perpetrating terrorism in the heartland of Punjab, urban Balochistan, Karachi, and parts of KPK. On the whole, there is not a single province or administered territory in Pakistan that has been totally free of Islamist violence over the past decade.[5]

Given this linkage, a narrower definition of terrorism may artificially—and inaccurately—separate insurgency from terrorism. On the other hand, too broad a definition risks widening the scope of inquiry to the structural causes—political, social, economic, and ideological—routinely cited as part of an overarching COIN framework, and missing out on the specificity of terrorist tactics employed in the insurgency. By approaching CT as a subset of COIN and paralleling terrorism as a tactical subset of insurgency campaigns, this volume strikes a balance. Through this lens, CT is viewed strictly as actions intended to *directly* prevent or respond to outfits or individuals employing terrorist tactics whether as part of an insurgency or otherwise. However, unlike the prevailing conception of CT as purely a tactical military response among some of the significant works (for example, Boyle 2010), this book adds value by examining CT more holistically. The state's policy response to the CT challenge can include military and nonmilitary aspects, provided they aim to deal directly with a terrorist's activities and actions. This is consistent with definitions of CT that see it as a set of proactive and reactive tools that enable a government to eliminate terrorism and reduce the overall capacity of terrorists to successfully carry out attacks.[6] COIN then becomes a combination of CT and broader policy actions aimed at addressing root causes of sustained insurgent violence/terrorism; the broader policy tools do not have to target the opponents perpetrating terrorism directly. For example, law enforcement or legal action against insurgents who also employ terrorist acts would constitute CT while government initiatives to introduce, say, educational reforms, or to invest economically in an insurgency-hit area, will be part of COIN but outside the purview of CT. Under this definition, military action in an insurgency-hit area will consist of CT and non-CT aspects; direct use of force would constitute CT, while aspects of a broader strategy potentially including goodwill projects carried out by the military would not. The former, not the latter, is the focus of this volume.

Scope and Rationale for the Book

Broader issues that fall within the COIN ambit are not unimportant by any means. This volume recognizes that the terrorism faced by Pakistan today is a symptom of a broader insurgent malaise with roots in state policies and regional realities all too often ignored or denied in the crafting of policy. Nonetheless, even though COIN campaigns have been conceived of having security, political, and economic pillars that form an integrated "conflict ecosystem" (Kilcullen 2006b), we have taken the choice to limit the volume to CT alone (the "security" pillar). This implies that this volume only tackles one piece, albeit an important one, of the overall militant challenge facing Pakistan. Theoretically then, Pakistan could fare well on the CT front and still lose out in the COIN realm over the long run. However, this ought not to take away from the importance of unpacking CT challenges in a self-contained analysis; rather, dealing holistically with CT issues allows for a concrete discussion on one major aspect of an overarching COIN effort that can provide realistic and implementable medium-term remedies. As a result, this book not only demonstrates the severity and specificity of the CT challenge facing Pakistan but also points to means of addressing it in a holistic manner.

This volume examines the predominant CT challenges faced by the Pakistani state from a policy perspective. Specifically, it focuses on Islamist violence being perpetrated against the Pakistani state by groups explicitly using religion as a justification for their agendas. This leaves out an important antistate nationalist movement in the southwestern province of Balochistan as well as violence related to organized crime. The scope of this undertaking is justifiable given that the separatist movement in Balochistan has an entirely different set of causes and dynamics than Islamist violence within the country. Moreover, it is the Islamist violence that has truly global implications and consequentially worries the world.

The post-9/11 context is not the first time the Pakistani state has faced violent insurgent movements or terrorist challenges. While it did not experience a concerted antistate confrontation with Islamic radical militants, it faced a massive popular uprising in East Pakistan that eventually led to the independence of Bangladesh in 1971 (Sisson and Rose 1991; Jaffrelot 2002b; Bose 2011). The separatist movement in Balochistan is an older phenomenon that had raged in the early-1970s before it reignited in 2006 (Ahmed 1992; ICG 2006a). Moreover, politically motivated and sectarian violence in Karachi has flared up repeatedly and even forced a paramilitary operation in the city during the mid-1990s (Gayer 2007; Waseem 2002).

Pakistan's past experiences notwithstanding, the Islamist insurgency-cum-terrorism that it faces today is qualitatively different. Four distinguishing features are most relevant to the focus of this volume. First, the previous incidents were geographically bound. The East Pakistan uprising was concentrated thousands of miles away from West Pakistan, the country's seat of power and often considered its heartland. Balochistan's separatism is also confined to Baloch areas of this sparsely populated province.[7] And while Karachi is the financial and commercial heart of the country, the levels of violence in the city never escalated to qualify as more than a major disruption of daily life. The present Islamist insurgent threat may be concentrated in FATA and KPK, but, as mentioned, its wave of associated terrorism has engulfed the entire length and breadth of the country; for the first time, Pakistan has experienced a metastasis of a variety of Islamist militant outfits all over the country.

The geographical limitation, at least in the case of full-fledged insurgencies in East Pakistan and Balochistan, had a direct link with the kind of response the Pakistani state sought. Since both areas were considered "peripheral" from the Pakistani security establishment's perspective, a heavy-handed military approach was adopted (Gill 2003; ICG 2006a). As a number of chapters in this volume argue, with the current threat spread around the country and the inherently complex and vast militant networks, the military's role is confined to the insurgency-hit areas in FATA and parts of KPK. The rest of the country, especially the plains of Punjab, requires a broader, nonmilitary CT effort. Also important to note, Pakistan's heavy-handed approaches of the past consistently failed to deliver: East Pakistan was lost altogether; the insurgency in Balochistan was pacified in the 1970s but grievances only grew and resulted in the resurgence of a more determined and popular separatist movement in 2006; and Karachi is again plagued with political and sectarian violence after an interlude of a few years.

To further complicate matters, the causes of violence are far more complex and amorphous than in the past. Earlier movements in Pakistan were much clearer regarding grievances that had led to violence—in most cases, these comprised a combination of socioeconomic and political disparities overlaid by ethnonational boundaries (Zaidi 1992; Jaffrelot 2002b). As discussed in chapter 1, on the state of the militancy, the current situation differs because multifaceted groups of Islamists, with aims ranging from the takeover of the Pakistani state to the elimination of minority groups, have come together to create pockets of violence all over Pakistan. Moreover, the Islamist outfits targeting the Pakistani state are not looking to break away a physical part of the state; they are in the business of seeking to transform the very ethos of the entire state and society. The desire to overthrow the current Pakistani state structures is not as much a quest for territory as it is one for ideology. The implication is that the matter cannot even be resolved by allowing a part of the country to secede.

Finally, perhaps most important is the regional and global context in which Pakistan is confronting this menace. For one, the Islamist violence knows no ideological boundaries and thus is connected to "Islamist international" in complex but tangible ways. Developments in Afghanistan and Islamic radical movements elsewhere impact the moral, support, and resources of a number of militant groups in Pakistan. Terrorist tactics have transformed completely with the induction of technology as a major part of the militant toolkit. Movement of financial transactions, use of modern technology, and legal and human rights paradigms can now be used like never before by the militants as much as by state entities. The tool of the suicide bomber is also emblematic of a major shift in the security paradigm that has informed movements and responses to them in the past (Godson and Shultz 2010). A narrow, military-heavy strategy devoid of a multifaceted approach to block all traditional and nontraditional avenues available to the nonstate perpetrators of violence can no longer succeed.

If anything, the lessons from past experiences of the Pakistani state are more about what not to do rather than what best practices may be replicated.

To be sure, a multipronged approach that factors in and is able to respond to the agenda of the Islamist enclave and the tools at their disposal is crucial. This is the prism through which contributors to this volume approach Pakistan's CT challenge. To understand what Pakistan can and cannot do in this situation requires a deeper analysis of current CT efforts that moves beyond military operations alone and takes into account understudied nonmilitary issues; specifically, the political factionalism in Pakistan that has prevented a coherent CT policy from emerging; the challenges of policing, criminal justice, and curbing militant finances; and checking the use of media and cyberspace by Islamist militants and their sympathizers.

There is voluminous literature examining Pakistan's troubled reality but none that makes this volume's focus redundant. Current analyses broadly fall in one of six categories (with considerable overlaps) in terms of their main focus: (1) those that talk about the regional Af-Pak and the broader South Asian dimension (R. Khan 2011; Markey 2009); (2) those that trace the rise of the militancy within Pakistan from the 1980s onward and the reasons behind it (Abbas 2005; Z. Hussain 2007, 2010; Jamal 2009); (3) those that focus solely on the post-9/11 period and explain Pakistan's "descent into chaos"—within this category, there are those who focus specifically on FATA (Gul 2011b; Nawaz 2009) versus those who take a broader geographical perspective (Rashid 2009); (4) those that study particular Islamist groups and their rise (Zahab and Roy 2004; Howenstein 2008; Firdous 2009; Mufti 2012; Rana 2005b); (5) those that take a more thematic approach and discuss the role of religion and the spread of the extremist ideology, its interface with politics, education, governance, and so on, without necessarily unpacking the terrorist milieu in any detail (Candland 2006; Fair 2008; Lamb and Hameed 2012); and (6) those who study the COIN challenge but with the primary lens on Afghanistan (Bergen 2011; Markey 2008). Comparatively little effort has been spent on analyzing CT as a subset of COIN, and within that, on the nonmilitary aspects. Those that do address these mostly look at one particular issue (a sector analysis) either without a focus on CT or without tying the specific aspect into the overall CT mix (see Abbas 2011; ICG 2010, 2011; World Bank and APGML 2009; Momein and Brohi 2010). This volume adds value to existing literature by focusing specifically on CT, but doing so holistically—honing in on not only traditional use of force but also nonmilitary aspects of the CT policy.

Structure of the Book

All of the chapters in this volume focus on a particular challenge and are written by Pakistani practitioners or experts who have lived amid the onslaught of Islamist violence and have continued to study or directly work to further the CT agenda. Among our contributors are a serving police officer with experience in CT, a Supreme Court lawyer who has had a role in advising and drafting CT-relevant protocols, a defense analyst who has spent time with military deployments in FATA, and experts who have spent prolonged periods analyzing Pakistani institutions, and studying militant finances and use of media and new technologies. To integrate this "inside-out" view with a more global perspective, chapters presenting broader analyses on the nature and severity of the threat to Pakistan and its ability to withstand the Islamist onslaught are written by international experts.

Five key observations emerge from the analyses provided in this volume. Together they convey extreme pessimism about the Pakistani state's ability to overcome its CT challenges successfully. First, there is lingering ambiguity even on the question of who specifically is targeted by the CT agenda. Even the state's key functionaries are often puzzled on just how widely they are to cast their CT net and with what justification. Second, and linked to the first, the overall CT effort is characterized by ambiguity and haunted by overlapping, contradictory, or dated laws, policies, and jurisdictions. Third, Pakistan lacks an overarching coordination body that can address the intrinsically linked issues addressed in this volume by bringing the state's disparate requirements and efforts together in a coherent, complementary policy framework—Ejaz Haider, Suhail Habib Tajik, Ahmer Bilal Soofi, Savail Meekal Hussain and Mehreen Zahra-Malik, and Zafarullah Khan all discuss the failure of the National Counter Terrorism Authority (NACTA) as the prime example of the absence of such an effort. Fourth, this volume argues that, despite these problems, there have been tangible improvements in the state's CT efforts in recent years—Haider and Anatol Lieven discuss this regarding the military's role in preventing an Islamist takeover; Tajik points toward the police's improved performance; Soofi demonstrates the success of specific legislation in plugging legal lacunae; and Muhammad Amir Rana writes about the impact of increased financial curbs on militant funding. That said, even combined, these cannot overshadow the fact that these are only preliminary steps when measured against the acute shortcomings still plaguing the effort. Finally, the chapters in this volume point toward two deeper changes that are required to improve the current CT effort: a meaningful correction of the civil–military imbalance that plagues relevant policymaking; and the need for continuing public support for the CT vision and strategy.

The two chapters that follow this introduction set the stage for the core CT challenges discussed later. Chapter 1 traces the rise of Islamist militancy in Pakistan, honing in on the landscape and linkages among various outfits within the militant enclave, the challenges presented by the TTP and its affiliates, and the state's response to this challenge. In order to set the scene, the chapter presents two opposing points of view on why Pakistan faces an intense challenge from Islamist militants today: the polarized debate on the lack of "capacity" versus lack of "will." The tension between these two views underlies virtually all chapters of the volume even as the focus of most of them naturally places greater emphasis on the "capacity" shortages that continue to haunt the Pakistani state.

In chapter 2, Marvin G. Weinbaum presents a threat assessment from the United States' perspective, emphasizing the lack of "will" and resolve among Pakistani decision makers to go after militancy in a holistic manner, and underscoring the mismatch in threat perceptions of Pakistani and Western decision makers. The chapter focuses on the dangers inherent in Pakistan's tendency to treat the country's militant enclave as containing "good" and "bad" elements to be targeted or supported as suits state policy. Weinbaum takes up the Lashkar-e-Taiba (LeT) as a specific case where Western and Pakistani threat perceptions diverge, with Islamabad remaining complacent to the threat despite signs of LeT's growing reach beyond Pakistan's borders. While Weinbaum and Yusuf et al. differ in the relative importance they accord to specific groups and in their emphasis on the capacity versus will issue—this is symptomatic of the divergence of indigenous Pakistani versus Western opinions on this issue—they agree that the Pakistani state is facing an extreme challenge from a variety of militant outfits. On "how" this challenge is to be addressed, Weinbaum recommends a more simultaneous effort against all militants while the Pakistani state continues to pursue a selective or sequential approach.

Having traced the rise of militancy in Pakistan and the international context within which it falls, the next six chapters each take on a particular CT challenge and unpack it to examine the various constraints and opportunities for the Pakistani state in each arena. Together these make up the core military and nonmilitary CT challenges that the state will have to deal with to be successful in its campaign against those perpetrating Islamist militancy: military strategy, political factionalism, police capacity, legal frameworks, militant financing, and cyberterrorism.

The third chapter, by Haider, is the only one in the volume dealing with the military's efforts, covering the "traditional" use of force in combating insurgency. Analyzing Pakistan's military campaigns in the northwest, he argues that after a terrible start that led to extremely high losses, the Pakistan military has learned on the job and done reasonably well in capturing physical space. It has not done nearly as well on the broader COIN concerns and on CT efforts by civilian law enforcement. His plea that the military's gains must be complemented by better civilian CT performance in urban towns underscores how intrinsically the insurgency and terrorism are linked in Pakistan's case. Specifically, he identifies three areas where the civilian effort requires strengthening: an overarching national security strategy, the institution of the police, and the legal framework under which CT is conducted. The next three chapters address the challenges in each of these areas in detail.

To frame the discussion, Hussain and Malik explain in chapter 4 why it has been so difficult to do exactly what Haider recommends: improve civilian CT performance. They argue that it is the highly factionalized nature of Pakistani politics and society as well as the corresponding absence of stable institutions that prevent coherent, overarching, and consensual policymaking. They see the absence of strong political parties that can manage differences and institutionalize uncertainty, coupled with a civil/military disconnect, as being prone to political instability and rapid institutional changes. This makes the costs of forging a national consensus on key policy issues prohibitively high. A structural weakness of this nature is therefore responsible for Pakistan's failure to come up with a comprehensive CT policy and operationalize a strong national coordinating CT body. Hussain and Malik see a dominant political faction able to sustain stable coalitions as central to forging a durable consensus on national CT policy.

In chapter 5, Tajik unpacks the role of civilian law enforcement and intelligence agencies with respect to CT. The chapter highlights the myriad constraints the police face in dealing with a threat for which they were never trained: suicide attacks and other acts of terrorism targeting civilians. Tajik argues that the police's job is hindered by "structural" and "police specific" problems, the combination of which leave the odds heavily stacked against the institution. Ironically, hotbeds of militancy such as FATA do not even allow regular police activity due to long-standing autonomies. Moreover, even in the rest of Pakistan, there are unclear and overlapping jurisdictions within the complex web of various civilian law enforcement bodies, leading to disunity and fragmentation in the CT domain. Lack of basic technology and capacity, combined with the added and growing responsibility entrusted to the police in CT, the civil/military disconnect over intelligence sharing, the absence of basic datasets to trace cases, and the multiple legal lacunae all hold the civilian law enforcement effort back from delivering positive outcomes. Looking ahead, Tajik sees the need for an overhaul of policing that would allow the remit of the police to extend across Pakistan and establish mechanisms such as a coordinated Joint Terrorism Task Force, remove military interference from civilian law enforcement, and provide police with the necessary infrastructure, technology, data, and capacity to perform CT functions.

Chapter 6, by Soofi, focuses on the legal shortcomings in the CT domain, showcasing the lack of coherence in the Pakistani state's overall CT and COIN campaigns. Soofi contests the very basics necessary for an effective campaign: there is no mission statement for Pakistan's military operations in the northwest that defines the scope and intent of ongoing operations and, subsequently, their limitations. The legality of the military's presence, its operations, and its conduct, then, are naturally suspect. The chapter traces problems with criminal justice at each step of the legal process, from poor legal cover for arrests and internment to unclear responsibilities regarding prosecutorial jurisdiction. Although improvements like the internment framework under the Action in Aid of Civil Power Regulations 2011, applicable to FATA and the Provincially Administered Tribal Areas (PATA), provides some cover for military conduct, the sum total of Soofi's analysis finds that the current criminal justice capacity and procedures create perverse incentives for military and law enforcement institutions involved in CT to sidetrack judicial processes if they hope to prevent militant acquittals due to lack of evidence or procedural flaws. His list of remedies begins with the overarching need to establish a mission statement for the state's COIN efforts, which can facilitate consensus on an antiterrorism and deradicalization strategy and address the civil/military disconnect to prevent it from undermining the state's ability to apprehend and prosecute militants. These changes must be coupled with specific improvements in the legal statutes and procedures regarding CT.

Rana's chapter on financing of militancy (chapter 7) and Khan's analysis of the growing use of cyberspace and technology by the militant enclave (chapter 8) present examples of the innovation and agility of the enemy the Pakistani state is confronting. This also points to the need for flexible and adaptive solutions. Rana details the formal and informal channels through which militants receive funding and how these have evolved in response to the Pakistani state's efforts to crack down on them. With private donations from within and outside Pakistan, receipt of alms, piracy and money laundering, and with a growing stake in formal economic sectors such as school chains, health care, housing, media houses, and the like, militants have an impressive and diverse array of funding sources. The real game-changer in their favor, however, has been militants' increasing reliance on crime, narcotrafficking, and smuggling to augment their financial base. Rana acknowledges efforts by the Pakistani state to curb financing of militants through formal channels but highlights the lack of focus on what he calls "nontraditional" sources. He sees the need for a comprehensive policy to choke militant financing; this requires a wide-ranging national effort and coordination with regional partners, both of which have, for the most part, been missing.

Khan traces the growing propensity of Islamist outfits to use cyberspace, technology, and media to spread their message and perpetrate terrorism. Given the Pakistani context, wherein right-wing rhetoric has grown and garners significant sympathy among the public, Khan sees a tangible increase in the penetration of the militant enclave in these contemporary arenas. Pakistani militants always had a presence in print media, but now they are also actively involved in "cyberactivism" and what Khan calls "hacktivism." Use of cell phones, DVDs and CDs, radio, internet, and TV channels to spread jihadi ideology and, in the case of cell phones, to directly plan, monitor, and perpetrate terrorism is now well documented. Sadly, this is one area where nascent government efforts to introduce legal regimes have met with little success; no strong laws exist at the moment to tackle the threat from use of cyberspace by militants. Militants, on the other hand, are busy employing contemporary technologies to create a conducive environment and execute terrorism.

The final chapter by Anatol Lieven brings the discussion full circle by examining the severity of the threat to the Pakistani state and whether it will be able to survive the Islamist challenge mounted through the insurgency–terrorism combine. Lieven sees Pakistan's situation as paradoxical: the primacy of local political patronage networks and the army's predominance in Pakistan both preserves the state and limits its potential for transformative positive change. Lieven argues that this status quo will prevent Pakistan from being overthrown by an Islamist revolution even as it continues to face terrorism. He perceives that this balance can be upset only if the army collapses—which, ironically enough, he contends is most likely to happen through an external trigger: a US direct action against Pakistan that galvanizes the right wing and forces a mutiny among Punjabi officers of the Pakistan Army who refuse to fight their ethnic kin in the heartland of the country.

The conclusion highlights broad observations from the discussions in the volume and enumerates the short- to medium-term policy prescriptions that contributors to this volume believe are required to address the ongoing Islamist terrorism in Pakistan. These bring home the point that Pakistan is facing an acute CT challenge that requires a multifaceted national effort if Pakistan is to emerge from its present crisis. While the challenges outlined by the authors highlight the improvements in CT efforts in recent years, the sheer magnitude of those challenges does not leave much room for optimism.

Notes

1. Pakistan has ranked thirteenth, twelfth, tenth, and tenth in 2012, 2011, and 2010, and 2009, respectively, on *Foreign Policy* magazine's global Failed States Index. For more details, see www.foreignpolicy.com/failed_states_index_2012_interactive.

2. The resurgence of COIN literature is linked to the US military campaigns in Iraq and Afghanistan. For recent works on COIN, see Galula (2006), Van Creveld (2008), and Kilcullen (2010).

3. This definition moves beyond the "classical insurgency" model that conceives of insurgencies as directed only toward the takeover of the state, or of secession in order to create a new state (Galula 2006), toward viewing an insurgency as aimed at establishing the "insurgent's writ" more broadly—whether in the form of a separate state, an area of local autonomy, or simply dispersed local influence. This follows definitions put forward by Kilcullen (2006a) and McCormick, Horton, and Harrison (2007) that conceive of contemporary insurgencies as the struggle to control a contested political space between a state and one or more nonstate actors.

4. Terrorism defined in this way uses the essence of more detailed definitions that incorporate the physical and psychological aspects of terror, the use of symbolic violence, and the broader political aims of terrorist groups, such as the definition presented in Schmid and Jongman (2005).

5. Pakistan has four constitutionally recognized provinces, one de facto province without constitutional recognition, FATA, and the autonomous administered territory of Pakistani Kashmir (Azad Jammu and Kashmir).

6. This view of CT is found in official US thinking as well. See the definition of "counterterrorism" in US Department of Defense's, "Joint Publication 1-02 Department of Defense Dictionary of Military and Associated Terms," July 12, 2007.

7. The province of Balochistan is Pakistan's largest by area and smallest by population. It has two distinct ethnic divisions; the northern part of the province is dominated by the Pashtuns while the central and southern part is dominated by ethnic Baloch.

CHAPTER 1

Pakistan's Militancy Challenge

From Where, to What?

MOEED YUSUF

with contributions from Megan Neville, Ayesha Chugh, and Stephanie Flamenbaum

THE PAKISTANI civilian and military authorities remain in a race against time to pacify Islamist militancy that is generating violent opposition to the state. However, the state is unlikely to succeed unless the military expands its operational capacity, the government addresses the many institutional weaknesses that constrain a coherent antiterrorism policy, and Pakistan's regional security calculus is reconfigured to exclude extremists. Foreign perspectives suggest that Pakistan has been insincere and duplicitous in fighting terrorists on its soil, often picking and choosing who it wishes to target. There has been a constant push by the Western world to get Pakistan to "do more." A dispassionate Pakistani view would acknowledge the merits of the Western critique, but it would also emphasize a number of genuine structural constraints that demand a more nuanced understanding of the problem.

This chapter sets the scene for the rest of the book by providing a historical overview of Pakistan's Islamist militant threat. It addresses the evolution of the militant challenge, the state's response, the major constraints—both domestic and regional—as well as critiques the Pakistani state's strategy. While the discussion encompasses the overall militant challenge, much of the description focuses on the principal anti-Pakistan outfit, the Tehrik-e-Taliban Pakistan (TTP) that has been the centripetal force for Pakistani militants in recent years. This is a function of the relatively greater attention the Pakistani state has paid to the TTP and its affiliates as compared to some of the other outfits.

The chapter begins by laying out what the problem of militancy means for Pakistan. We then present an overview of the current state of Islamist militancy and the actors involved in perpetrating it. Next, we trace the roots of militancy and explain its subsequent post-9/11 expansion, with a parallel focus on the state's responses. Finally, the chapter discusses the key constraints that continue to hinder Pakistan's ability to wipe out militancy from its soil, and critiques the Pakistani state's position.

What Is at Stake? Understanding the Challenge of Militancy

Historically, Pakistan perceived its greatest security threat as emanating from its eastern neighbor, India. However, in the past decade, the attention has been forced inward; internal militancy has increasingly become the foremost security concern. According to the Pakistan Institute for Peace Studies (PIPS) 2010 security report, the proliferation of militant groups has overwhelmed law enforcement agencies, providing small militant outfits the space to significantly increase the number of terror attacks, most notably in Punjab, Sindh, and Khyber Pakhtunkhwa (KPK) provinces (PIPS 2010). Balochistan, in the country's southwest, has also been in turmoil since 2006 courtesy of a resurgent secessionist movement and a pattern of targeted sectarian killings of Shia Hazaras.[1]

From 2003 to 2013, more than forty-seven thousand Pakistani civilians and security personnel lost their lives and many more were injured in terrorist attacks.[2] Domestically, Islamist militants violently contest the right of ordinary citizens and the nation's notable political and moderate religious leaders to reject radical Islamist ideology. In the past decade, several of Pakistan's most prominent political and religious leaders, including former prime minister Benazir Bhutto, governor of Punjab province Salmaan Taseer, and moderate Sunni clerics such as Maulana Sarfaraz Naimi, have fallen victim to militant violence; many others have only narrowly escaped assassination attempts. Militant aggression against sectarian targets has also significantly intensified, as has militant propensity to target religious minorities. Indeed, it is no exaggeration to state that a once moderately peaceful Pakistan has descended into chaos, with hardly any region of the country left immune to Islamist militant violence.

Compounding these internal dynamics, Pakistan's delicate and dysfunctional relationship with its traditional rival, India, allows militant groups to register a significant threat to Pakistan's regional security. As was the case in the December 2001 attack on the Indian parliament by the Pakistan-based militant outfit Jaish-e-Mohammed (JeM), and again in the November 2008

Mumbai carnage orchestrated by Lashkar-e-Taiba (LeT), such episodes cause Pakistan to be the object of tremendous international condemnation.[3] They also risk escalating India–Pakistan tensions. Should a similar, future attack in India occur, some Indian strategists argue that the government in New Delhi will face too much public pressure to be able to exercise the restraint it showed following the 2008 Mumbai attacks.[4] Indeed, armed nonstate organizations based in Pakistan are in the unusual, and perilous, position of being able to undermine peace between two nuclear armed neighbors.

Militants also continue to contest Pakistan's stability at the international level; they have done so in two ways. First, the presence of anti-US Afghan militants on Pakistani soil has made Pakistan one of the most important fronts in the US-led campaign in Afghanistan. When the United States invaded Afghanistan after 9/11, a large number of Afghan and foreign militants present in the country were able to seek safe havens across the porous border in Pakistan's tribal regions, the Federally Administered Tribal Areas (FATA).[5] Subsequently, these border regions have been branded as the global epicenter of terrorism and are currently a site of the controversial US predator drone attacks.[6] In essence, militants' presence in northwestern Pakistan (FATA and parts of the adjacent KPK province) and the US resolve to eliminate anti-Afghan militants has dragged Pakistan into an "international war." Second, Pakistan-based militant organizations like the TTP are beginning to find value in extending their reach globally. The failed Times Square car bomb attempt in New York by TTP-trained Pakistani-American militant Faisal Shahzad in May 2010 was a stark reminder of how easily militants in Pakistan could generate an international crisis implicating the Pakistani state.[7]

Lay of the Land: What the Pakistani State Is Dealing With

The most commonly cited Islamist militant organizations in Pakistan differ according to their ideologies, objectives, principal targets, and strength (see table 1.1). However, even as their core focus varies there are often common or overlapping objectives that position some of them in parallel or joint campaigns against the Pakistani state and citizens, as well as against regional forces. In terms of principal targets, the militant complex in Pakistan has traditionally been divided into four categories: anti-Pakistani state; anti-United States/NATO; anti-Indian; and sectarian. Some predate the 9/11 attacks in the United States while others have sprung up only since the onset of the US-led military campaign in Afghanistan.

The tendency of the Pakistan-based Islamist milieu to overlap and cooperate in their agendas and activities has increased significantly over the past

TABLE 1.1
Major Islamist Militant Groups Operating in Pakistan

Major Targets	*Predominantly Foreign*	*Predominantly Pakistani*
Anti-Pakistan	Al-Qaeda; assortment of other foreign militants based in FATA	Tehrik-e-Taliban Pakistan; Harkatul Jihad-e-Islami; Lashkar-e-Jhangvi; assortment of splinter groups of traditionally anti-India groups—the "Punjabi Taliban"
Anti-US/NATO	Al-Qaeda; Mullah Omar's "Quetta Shura" Taliban; Haqqani network; Hizb-e-Islami; assortment of other foreign militants based in FATA	Muqami Tehrik-e-Taliban; "Punjabi Taliban"
Anti-India	Hizb-ul-Mujahideen; Al-Baraq	Lashkar-e-Taiba; Jaish-e-Mohammed; Al-Badr; Harkatul Mujahideen-al-Alami; Harkatul Jihad-e-Islami
Sectarian	Jundullah	Sipah-e-Sahaba Pakistan; Laskhar-e-Jhangvi; Sunni Tehrik; Sipah-e-Muhammad; Tehrik-e-Jafria

Source: Authors' compilation. Earlier version published in Yusuf 2011a.

decade. For instance, prior to 9/11, one could afford a relatively neat division between the state-sponsored anti-India groups and the sectarian outfits that were beginning to raise their head in the 1990s despite the state's opposition. Al-Qaeda and others, like the Iran-focused Jundullah, on the other hand were absent altogether. While some of these distinctions are still intact, militancy in Pakistan is now part of the "Islamist international" whereby these groups have metastasized and found common cause, at least in terms of their opposition to the US-led presence in Afghanistan—even though not all outfits are actively involved in fighting alongside the Afghan insurgents—and in terms of imposition of Sharia, whether locally (in FATA and parts of KPK), nationally (the takeover of the Pakistani state), or internationally (in Afghanistan, or even a global caliphate). In addition, what all except the Shia militant outfits converge on is the ultraconservative, orthodox Deobandi-cum-Wahabi ideology as the basis to justify violence in the name of religion.

All Islamist militant outfits in Pakistan have also managed to rise above their ethnic and linguistic ties. This is ironic because the Pakistani state, worried about the multiple ethnic and linguistic cleavages within its society, has itself always sought to promote Islam as the unifying bond above all ethnonationalist claims.[8] Even though the issue of Pashtun nationalism has often come into play with regard to the Afghan insurgency, and the Pashtun link has helped the Afghan Taliban immensely in gaining local support in FATA, the bond of ethnicity explains little in terms of the rise of antistate militancy within Pakistan. Organizations like the TTP have attempted to portray themselves as a Pashtun outfits at times (Murphy 2012, 146) but in reality they have seen the traditional, Pashtun-dominated makeup of FATA and KPK as a major threat to their existence and have thus actively targeted the symbols of Pashtun traditions. The TTP is responsible for killing more than six hundred tribal elders, the *maliks*, over the past decade and has targeted numerous *jirgas*, the assemblies of tribal elders (Nawaz 2009, 7; Qazi 2011, 582). It is only by creating a leadership vacuum in the traditional tribal society, a process that in reality began with the Afghan jihad against the Soviet Union during the 1980s, that the radical elements of society have risen to dominate the local landscape. Other non-Pashtun outfits like the Punjab-based groups and foreign outfits like al-Qaeda have also never sought to seek support based on their ethnicities or nationalities.

Moreover, even when the primary objectives across militant groups remain different, the respective goals can often complement one another, leading to increased institutional linkages—the Afghan Taliban's desire to retain sanctuaries in Pakistan to fight in Afghanistan, for example, that fit very well with the TTP's efforts to portray itself as a force fighting in support of the Afghan insurgents even as its real agenda is nationally oriented against the Pakistani state (Rassler and Brown 2011). Similarly, even though the anti-Shia agenda of Punjab-based Sunni sectarian groups is seemingly irrelevant to the TTP's call for imposition of Sharia in FATA, the ideological affinity and desire of both groups to support the Afghan insurgency allows them to converge, offering militants useful opportunities for reinforcement. Furthermore, in a minority of cases, linkages across groups do not even reflect ideological similarities. Connections may be made purely on a pragmatic basis; they may have a great deal to do with capacity building, logistical support, or simply expediency.

In essence, the distinctions between militant groups operating in Pakistan outlined earlier can no longer be considered fixed; both the composition and the ideological orientation of these groups are constantly evolving. As a result, there is considerable fluidity in group membership and in the scope of militant operations. Shapiro and Fair (2010) and Hussain (2012) in particular point out how Punjabi militant groups have splintered and altered their objectives regarding the Pakistani state. Moreover, individual militants are no longer steadfast in their patronage to militant organizations. While militants may declare affiliation to a parent organization, they sometimes operate independently and outside the jurisdiction of their hierarchical leadership. Attempts to create a typology of terrorist groupings based on ideology or consistency of targets have consistently run into this problem (Tellis 2008; Shapiro and Fair 2010).

Specifically, there have been growing institutional linkages between the originally FATA-based TTP and a number of Punjab-based sectarian and other outfits. The TTP in turn acts as both a local franchise and coalition builder for al-Qaeda (Siddiqa 2011). For example, law enforcement accounts of raids on Punjab-based organizations report that militants from the Pakistani tribal belt are often present at the site of the raid; similarly, Punjabi members of Lashkar-e-Jhangvi (LeJ), JeM, and Sipah-e-Sahaba Pakistan (SSP) from urban centers in Pakistan's heartland are increasingly found to be operating with al-Qaeda and the TTP in the tribal belt.[9] Members of some of the Punjabi groups are also involved in sectarianism within Pakistan and in fighting international forces in Afghanistan. Even the TTP itself is not a unified entity; it operates as a decentralized web of local militias with diverging incentives, alliances, and a fair share of infighting.[10]

As far as possible, table 1.2 attempts to define the objectives and activities of various Islamist militant outfits while capturing some of the overlaps and nuances highlighted earlier. It also notes the composition of the groups based on their origins.

From Moderate Conservatism to Violent Extremism: How Did Pakistan Get Here?

Pakistan has transformed from being a relatively stable country to an excessively violent one over the past decade. However, the roots of the Islamist militant challenge that the Pakistani state is confronting today lie in the 1980s. This section traces the journey of this transformation over the past three decades.

Setting the Stage for the Emergence of Militancy: 1979–2001

As antistate violent insurgencies and terrorism go, Pakistan's case is anomalous in that the existential militant threat it is facing today originated, to a

TABLE 1.2
Objectives and Activities of Major Islamist Militant Groups in Pakistan

Major Islamist Militant Groups in Pakistan	*Objectives*	*Focus of Activities in Pakistan*	*Composition*	*Period of Presence in Pakistan*
Al-Qaeda	International: Incite Muslims to rise up against the "'infidel'" West, including through armed resistance Expel Western powers from the Middle East Extend the reach of Islam and establish an international caliphate Destroy Israel Pakistan-specific: Destroy Pakistani constitutional order (and state infrastructure) Establish sharia in Pakistan Use Pakistan as sanctuary and a physical planning and staging ground for international attacks	Attacking Pakistani state and society Acting as a franchiser for Pakistani groups Convening and coalescing Sunni militant groups willing to work with it Financial support and operational capacity building of these groups Anti-West terrorist plots	Almost strictly Arab-Afghan (some intake of Pakistanis)	2002 onward

TABLE 1.2 (Continued)
Objectives and Activities of Major Islamist Militant Groups in Pakistan

Major Islamist Militant Groups in Pakistan	*Objectives*	*Focus of Activities in Pakistan*	*Composition*	*Period of Presence in Pakistan*
Tehrik-e-Taliban Pakistan	Establish sharia in Pakistan (in specific enclaves regionally, then nationally) Hints of global aspirations and support for international terrorism "Defensive jihad" against the Pakistan Army seen as supporting the US against Afghan Taliban	Attacking Pakistani state and society Forging stronger links with Punjabi Taliban and Sunni sectarian groups conforming to the Deobandi-cum-Wahabi ideology Acting as al-Qaeda's primary Pakistan franchise Recruitment base in northwest Pakistan	Predominantly Pakistani Pashtun	2002 onward (formal creation of Tehrik-e-Taliban Pakistan in 2007)
"Punjabi Taliban"	No cohesive objective because of a lack of organizational unity. Predominantly a "generational split" from sectarian and Indian-specific militant groups in the Punjab, variously aimed at: Jihad in Indian Kashmir to remove Indian influence Jihad against the US/NATO-ISAF presence in Afghanistan	Attacking Pakistani state and society Forging stronger links with TTP (and, by extension, with al-Qaeda) Recruitment base in southern Punjab	Majority Deobandi Punjabis (as factions split from Lashkar-e-Jhangvi, Sipah-e-Sahaba Pakistan, and Jaish-e-Muhammad, as well as criminal and freelance elements)	2007 onward

TABLE 1.2 (Continued)

Objectives and Activities of Major Islamist Militant Groups in Pakistan

Major Islamist Militant Groups in Pakistan	*Objectives*	*Focus of Activities in Pakistan*	*Composition*	*Period of Presence in Pakistan*
	Marginalize Shias by declaring them non-Muslims or undertaking their active elimination Conduct campaigns against other Barelvi groups or Deobandi subsects (due to ideological disagreements)			
Lashkar-e-Taiba (and other anti-Indian groups such as Jaish-e-Muhammad and Harkatul Mujahideen-al-Alami)	Jihad in Indian Kashmir to unite Kashmir with Pakistan and undermine Indian influence Active and passive support for the insurgency in Afghanistan Some shift toward undermining Pakistani state interests (LeT is perhaps the only group that can be totally excluded from this)	Anti-Indian terrorist plots Increasingly aligned with Afghan groups fighting against US/NATO-ISAF Attacking Western interests within Pakistan Involved in some militant attacks within Pakistan Potential to attack international targets	Mostly Punjabi Pakistanis or Kashmiris (from both Pakistani and Indian-administered Kashmir), as well as international fighters (Arab, Afghan, British, Yemeni, among others)	1990s onward

TABLE 1.2 (Continued)
Objectives and Activities of Major Islamist Militant Groups in Pakistan

Major Islamist Militant Groups in Pakistan	*Objectives*	*Focus of Activities in Pakistan*	*Composition*	*Period of Presence in Pakistan*
Afghan Taliban; Haqqani network; Hizb-e-Islami; Muqami Tehrik-e-Taliban	Eliminate US/NATO-ISAF presence from Afghanistan Establish sharia in Afghanistan Reclaim their respective power centers in Afghanistan	Attacking US/NATO-ISAF presence in Afghanistan	Mostly Afghan, some Pakistani Pashtuns, and international fighters present in FATA Muqami Taliban is predominantly Pakistani	2002 onward
Sipah-e-Sahaba Pakistan; Lashkar-e-Jhangvi	Marginalize Shias by declaring them non-Muslims or active elimination Establish a Deobandi-infused, Sunni-specific sharia system in Pakistan Where ideologically overlapping, support groups involved in the Afghan insurgency and the Tehrik-e-Taliban Pakistan	Attacking rival sectarian groups Sipah-e-Sahaba Pakistan and Lashkar-e-Jhangvi expanding ties with al-Qaeda and operating in Afghanistan as well	Overwhelmingly Punjabi, with some Karachi-based membership	1980s onward
Sipah-e-Muhammad; Tehrik-e-Jafria	Counter Sunni militant targeting Create a society based on "pure Islam" (after the Iranian model)	Attacking rival Sunni militant groups within Pakistan		1990s onward

Sources: Authors' compilation based on multiple conversations with Pakistani and international experts on the subject. Other data sources: Mir 2008; Rana 2005b; Hussain 2012, Abbas 2008, 2009b; Howenstein 2008; Firdous 2009; Qazi 2011; Brandt 2010; Imran 2010a; Shapiro and Fair 2010; Fishman 2010; Bajoria and Masters 2011; Rassler and Brown 2011; Mufti 2012.

large extent, through support of, not despite, the Pakistani state. Only in the post-9/11 context has antistate militancy continued to rage, despite the state's desire and efforts to quash it. To fully comprehend Pakistan's journey from a relatively moderate polity with no noticeable presence of Islamist militancy in its mix to one deeply infested by it, it is important to understand the centrality of the "India obsession" of the Pakistani security establishment. Engaged in an acutely acrimonious relationship from the very beginning, both India and Pakistan have employed hardcore realpolitik toward each other. For Pakistan, the weaker of the two parties, this has meant an outright focus on ensuring that it remains independent of India's policy dictates (Yusuf 2013b). This security-centric desire to hold its own against India's overbearing presence in the region—not to fall in line with India's vision of South Asia—has had a number of domestic implications for Pakistan, not least among them Pakistan's understanding of its security needs, especially vis-à-vis India and Afghanistan, and the subsequent propensity of the Pakistani security establishment to use Islamist militants as tools of foreign policy over the years (Rassler and Brown 2011; Hanauer and Chalk 2012;Yusuf 2013b).

The concern about the security threat from India has also meant that the Pakistani security elite have remained desperate to avoid what they call a "two front" situation—that is, an active threat from the western border (read: Afghanistan) in addition to the eastern front. This concern in large part explains Pakistan's long-standing preference for a pliant and friendly government in Afghanistan—the other "troubling" neighbor that has had irredentist claims on the Pakistani Pashtun heartland in the northwest—and its support to hard-line Islamist Sunni Pashtun elements above all other ethnicities and even moderate Pashtuns in Afghanistan since the 1980s. Such elements were seen as being dependent on the Pakistani state for support, as opposed to India, and as less beholden to ethnically motivated claims than to religious ones (Yusuf 2013a).

Pakistan's current militancy conundrum, then, is rooted in more than three decades of questionable national and international political and security policies. Militant groups emerged as part of Pakistan's regional and international security calculus during the Soviet occupation of Afghanistan in the 1980s. To contest the Soviet presence in South Asia, American and Pakistani intelligence agencies supported irregular fighters, the mujahideen, as proxies.[11] The legacy of this strategy destabilized Pakistani society. The Afghanistan–Pakistan border became increasingly porous to allow militants to move covertly from support bases in Pakistan to operations in Afghanistan. Pakistani society was also deeply affected: infrastructure emerged to support illicit operations and armed nonstate actors; a whole generation was brought up in a promilitancy environment; "jihadi" rhetoric was introduced into educational and regional policy lexicon; FATA and the neighboring regions were infested with a gun culture; narcotics smuggling took off and still provides a major source of revenue for militants; and Pakistan became host to more than three million Afghan refugees with attendant economic and societal implications across the country.

The eventual forced withdrawal of Soviet forces convinced the Pakistani security elite of the effectiveness of the use of "jihad" as a domestic and foreign policy tool. Pakistan's Inter-Services Intelligence (ISI) extended, now without American support, promilitancy policies eastward to erode the military prowess of India—principally by backing an insurgency in Indian Kashmir that erupted in 1989.

While support for militancy—or "freedom fighters," as the Pakistani security establishment saw them—became a crucial element of Pakistan's security policy, the country's military and intelligence agencies never intended on actually radicalizing Pakistan. In fact, the military sought to shield Pakistan from the potential domestic repercussions of their aggressive use of extremists to enhance regional security. Even as the state supported them on the one hand, it constantly discredited militants and denied any active military support to the fighters in Kashmir on the other hand. Moreover, even though Gen. Muhammad Zia ul-Haq, the Pakistani ruler during the 1980s, favored Deobandi religious political parties to stem the popularity of Pakistan's more moderate political outfits, the voice of the ultraright remained relegated to the margins of Pakistan's political arena.[12] Key state institutions did not adopt an extremist character as a whole—they did, however, become increasingly conservative under General Zia—and the state supported the lines that society traditionally drew to distinguish its conservative disposition from extremism.

In retrospect, however, the policy was extremely shortsighted. Until the 9/11 attacks in the United States, the agendas of the state and nonstate jihadi groups remained relatively aligned. However, once the Pakistani state took a U-turn on the pro-Taliban policy in Afghanistan that it had followed since the mid-1990s and sought to tone down support for militancy in Indian Kashmir, the ability of the militant enclave to challenge the state became readily apparent. Militants had already penetrated Pakistani society, and they had a vast following thanks to their social service networks, with much of their recruitment coming from within Pakistan. They also gradually became financially independent of the Pakistani state courtesy of external funding sources—a mix of alms sent in good faith by Muslims abroad, indirect contributions by foreign Muslim governments, and criminal and illegal activity. Moreover, their long association with the ISI gave them a degree of functional knowledge of the agency that proved helpful when they turned against their former patrons. Fresh militant outfits were to emerge in opposition to the US invasion of Afghanistan and forge alliances with some of these traditionally prostate groups whose presence predated 9/11.

Post-9/11 Militancy and the State's Response

This section deals with the post-9/11 militancy challenge for the state and its response in two phases: 2002–7, and 2007 onward. The two phases were marked by a distinct shift in the scale of militant violence within Pakistan, the state's outlook toward the menace, and its consequent shift in strategy to fight militant enclaves.

PHASE I: 2002–7

Following the Soviet withdrawal from Afghanistan, militants did not pose a direct threat to the Pakistani state. At that time, the militant outfits (with the exception of sectarian groups focused on targeting private citizens from rival sects) were not motivated to disrupt the state that funded its operations and was largely complacent about the expanse of militancy. However, the marriage of convenience between the ISI and militant groups could not withstand the dramatic changes to the international security environment that transpired following the 9/11 attacks in the United States. Pakistan found itself caught between two fundamentally contradictory and competing forces: international pressure to recant its strategic partnerships with militant groups, and intensified jihadist fervor stirred by the invasion of Western forces in Afghanistan and the US declaration of a "global war on terror" (Ali 2009).

Islamabad faced intense international pressure to support the US-led effort in Afghanistan; the UN Security Council Resolution 1386 authorizing US military action all but necessitated that Pakistan support international efforts.[13] Not doing so may have meant international isolation or even worse—direct US military action against militants in FATA. The situation also presented then Pakistani President Gen. Pervez Musharraf an opportunity to sustain his dictatorship by taking advantage of the country's alliance with the United States.

However, the Pakistani government feared that in pledging support for US-led forces in Afghanistan, the state would be unable to weather the resulting backlash, both in terms of disapproval from citizens with decades-long resentment toward the United States for leaving Pakistan on its own to deal with the turmoil in Afghanistan after the Soviet withdrawal from the country, and in terms of a violent response from aggrieved militants. Pakistani security forces were not enthusiastic about directly turning against actors they had supported and used as policy tools for so long. Even if military actors had wanted to, they lacked the necessary capacity. In addition, along Pakistan's western border, inhabitants of the tribal regions fiercely oppose military intrusions of any sort from the central government, let alone from international forces. It was therefore inevitable that the local population in FATA would resist the introduction of Islamabad-led or authorized operations to weed out militants wishing to stand up against the United States.[14]

Shortly after the US invasion of Afghanistan, when the al-Qaeda and Afghan Taliban leadership sought refuge in FATA, they managed to rekindle the fervor for jihad that had existed in the area two decades prior. Therefore, when Afghan Taliban leaders Mullah Omar and Mullah Dadullah connected with tribal elders in the FATA to recruit Pakistani tribesmen and madrassa students and to set up a FATA chapter for the Afghan Taliban in 2002, they found significant traction (Behuria 2007). Al-Qaeda's influence and financial prowess further managed to harness the spirit of jihad. Allegedly, the group paid as much as $250 per month to Pakistani tribesmen willing to participate in the war in Afghanistan (Hussain 2007).

The Pakistani state's decision to intervene militarily in South Waziristan Agency of FATA in 2002 to target foreign militants proved to be the final blow: it antagonized the locals and the traditional rival tribes of Mehsuds and Ahmadzai Wazirs in South Waziristan rose up against the Pakistani Army, both to challenge its ingress in support of the Americans and equally to ensure that they were not weakened vis-à-vis the other.[15] Interestingly, in reviving the Soviet-era "culture of militancy," foreign and domestic radicals exploited preexisting socioeconomic, development, and misgovernance-related grievances of the tribes.

The Pakistani state compromised by appeasing both sides. Musharraf publicly pitted the state against militants, especially foreign ones—conveniently, Mullah Omar's Taliban were not considered "foreign" under this rubric—who had entered FATA to escape US military action in Afghanistan while retaining ties with the Afghan Taliban conglomerate.[16] The military therefore went after al-Qaeda operatives and other Arab and Central Asian militants but spared the Afghan Taliban conglomerate and Pakistani groups for the most part. Under pressure from the international community, the state also pulled back its support for the Kashmiri insurgency after 2003 and pressured the anti-India groups to stop infiltrating into Indian Kashmir.[17] It did not, however, use any force against these predominantly Punjab-based groups.

From 2002 to 2007, Pakistan's overall antimilitant strategy involved a mix of military action, peace deals, and relative neglect. In the northwest, Pakistan cooperated with US operations in Afghanistan by providing a logistical lifeline, access to Pakistani bases, intelligence, and more general counterterrorism support to target foreign militants. However, the effort was ultimately unable to assert control because of capacity constraints, because the militants' fighting prowess turned out to be quite remarkable, and because the state mismanaged the peace deal as the negotiating process bypassed traditional tribal elders. By the time the state realized this debacle, the militancy challenge was no longer limited to just foreign fighters. Between 2004 and 2007, a strong cohort of anti-Pakistan militant groups, later to coalesce under the TTP brand, emerged to command much of the FATA, running affairs on their own terms (Qazi 2011). These were the actors who had been the principal beneficiaries of the peace deals as they used it to strengthen their position within the local social hierarchy, to force their rivals into submission, and to better prepare themselves to challenge the state. The pretext of these groups was that Pakistani forces were proxies of the American campaign in Afghanistan and thus legitimate targets. Very shrewdly, though, they did not declare their anti-Pakistan agenda until they had gained sufficient strength.

The International Crisis Group's December 2006 report, "Pakistan's Tribal Area: Appeasing the Militants," correctly stated that military operations meant to "deny al-Qaeda and Taliban safe haven and curb cross-border militancy failed, largely due to an approach alternating between excessive force and appeasement" (ICG 2006b, 3). All along, the Pakistani security establishment believed that it ultimately could control militant groups and could selectively curtail their operational capacity of certain organizations by revoking state support or threatening retribution. Civilian and military decision makers never really grasped the extent to which the militancy in FATA had turned inward against the Pakistani state. These naïve assumptions were soon discredited as "the societal penetration of the religious-cum-militant outfits during the 1990s now allowed these organizations to create their own resource mobilization, framework independent of—in fact in opposition to—the state" (Yusuf 2011a, 91). New outfits that sprang up after 9/11 found easy access to this milieu.

The militarization of the Afghanistan–Pakistan border by foreign troops and the US strategy in Afghanistan also contributed to the remarkable destabilization of Pakistan's border regions (Innocent 2009, 7–11). Despite the significant externally led improvement in conditions in parts of Afghanistan, the post-9/11 period also created vast populations of disaffected peoples in peripheral areas. This perpetuated the rise of illicit weapons and drug economies, and ossified a prevalent notion among Pakistanis that American military strategy and a perceived pro-US government (as they saw it) in Islamabad were the primary sources of regional instability. This understanding of affairs was reinforced by the militant narrative, as militants—even those not specifically targeted by the state—cashed in on Islamabad's perceived alignment with Western forces. The state's posturing created a common sense of grievance between militants and local populations. As Yusuf and Mukherjee pointed out, "for the first time, Pakistan's varied Islamists . . . managed to transcend sectarian and ethnic boundaries and collaborate under the banner of 'Islamism'" (2007, 3). This was in large part responsible for foreign and indigenous militant groups with markedly different objectives establishing formal and informal strategic partnerships to counter the newly emerging "near enemy," the Pakistani state.

The most obvious manifestation of the state's unifying influence among Islamist groups was the formation of the TTP, a group that galvanized anti-state sentiments in the tribal belt to launch a campaign that was decidedly anti-Pakistan in its orientation and operations. Similarly, the intertwining of al-Qaeda operatives with predominantly Pakistani Islamists signified an inward shift of the militants' operational focus toward the Pakistani state.

PHASE II: 2007 AND BEYOND

The military's unsuccessful attempt to reassert control over militant groups in intermittent military campaigns from 2002 to 2007 set the stage for further internal destabilization and increased militant violence. In December 2007, the various militant chapters operating across FATA and neighboring districts of the KPK came together to form the umbrella organization TTP. Meanwhile, traditionally sectarian groups had also begun to receive succor from al-Qaeda and were beginning to expand their scope of interest. Moreover, as the Pakistani state pulled back its support to the insurgency in Kashmir, the anti-India groups found it hard to keep their outfits intact; some of them began to splinter, and these splinters—resentful of the state for giving up jihad in Kashmir at America's behest, as they saw it—were attracted to the TTP and the fight in Afghanistan. On the other hand, organizations like the LeT began sending volunteers to fight alongside the Afghan Taliban in Afghanistan, but they refrained from targeting the Pakistani state.

By late 2007, the TTP had embarked upon a violent campaign against the Pakistani government and spread its activities far beyond FATA. The watershed event was the Red Mosque siege in Islamabad in July 2007, an incident where the government launched a commando operation against a group of clerics who had openly challenged the state's authority and were holding out with hundreds of seminary students, many of them hailing from the Swat

Valley in KPK adjoining the tribal areas. This operation led to several deaths of those inside the compound. Post–Red Mosque, there was a surge in militant recruitment, especially from Swat and neighboring regions. The militant message emphasized the classic "Islam-in-danger" slogan, the religious duty to support the fight against the "infidel" American army (and more directly its proxy, the Pakistani security forces), and the hypocrisy of the Pakistani state with respect to their treatment of the Afghan Taliban conglomerate versus the TTP. These propaganda campaigns not only stimulated pledges by young males to join the fight, but it also generated substantial revenue from domestic and foreign sympathizers. The TTP and its affiliates also used intimidation to gain recruits. With the popular narrative after the Red Mosque affair presenting the state as committing atrocities against young children and women, its already weak writ in the northwest quickly eroded further. The TTP was now openly declaring its anti-Pakistan intent and putting it into action.[18] The Swat Valley soon became the first settled region outside of FATA to fall to the TTP.[19]

In this phase, the fast-deteriorating security situation in Afghanistan also added to Pakistan's woes. The Afghan Taliban conglomerate, while ideologically linked to the TTP, was very careful in maintaining its distinct identity and avoiding either sanctioning or initiating attacks against the Pakistani state. Moreover, as the Afghan Taliban resurged in Afghanistan, possible largely due to a shift in US policy to focus on Iraq after 2003, the Pakistani state's incentive to tackle them decreased even further. Islamabad, with its hands full with domestic militant challenges, was not ready to open new fronts against an entity that was still seen as favorable to Pakistan, especially when it seemed to be regaining lost ground in Afghanistan. The persistent US pressure on Pakistan to "do more" against the Afghan Taliban safe havens, now spreading from FATA and into Balochistan province's capital, Quetta, some distance south of the tribal belt, and Pakistan's ambivalent responses nonetheless further galvanized militants to coalesce to brace for a potential onslaught.[20]

Additionally, as US and Pakistani forces took out extremist leaders in FATA, militant organizations became increasingly decentralized, making it more difficult to isolate and target them. Their new leaders also tended to be more radical in their approach. For example, as a 2011 United Kingdom Home Office report states, "despite the death of Baitullah Mehsud [the TTP leader] in August 2009, security continued to deteriorate in the tribal areas as well in other parts of the country, namely Punjab . . . with the reality that militancy does not depend on individual commanders but on a grassroots network whose foundations are madrassas, mosques, and training camps scattered in villages, districts and urban centers across Pakistan."[21] Finally, mounting instability in Afghanistan and Pakistan created an environment in Pakistan hospitable to collusion between militant groups and criminal organizations. PIPS reported in 2010 that "a growing nexus between criminals and militants emerged as a serious concern for the security agencies" (2010, 29–30). Illicit drug economies provided revenues for terrorist attacks, and partnerships with weapons smugglers bolstered militants' arms stockpiles. The extent of the problem can be gauged by the fact that as much as 40 percent of Afghanistan's heroin/morphine passes through vital trade points in the FATA, KPK, and Balochistan (UNODC 2009, 15).

By late 2007, the number of TTP-orchestrated attacks was rising by the day, along with the use of suicide bombers to cause maximum damage. In vast swaths of FATA and subsequently in settled districts such as Swat, the TTP and its affiliates began to defy the state completely, and to further entrench their own governing structures. The Red Mosque incident crystallized the access of militants to the urban elite who were otherwise immune to much of what had been taking place in the northwest. Between 2007 and 2010, the military introduced an unprecedented 140,000 military troops—compared to the 80,000 deployed in 2005—in FATA and parts of KPK, complete with heavy weaponry and air support to contest the TTP's expanding territorial and support base (S. Khan 2011). After many ups and downs, and after failing at fresh attempts to secure workable peace deals, the Pakistani military finally initiated a full-fledged operation in Swat and cleared the area in July 2009 (see also chapter 3, this volume).[22] A number of other operations were launched in FATA around this time.

Urban Pakistanis faced the worst backlash during this period as the TTP sought to raise the stakes in response to military successes in the northwest. In 2009 and 2010, deaths resulting from terrorist violence—11,704 and 7,435, respectively—far surpassed the totals for any prior year (SATP).[23] The militants not only targeted urban towns regularly—in some periods even on a daily basis—but they managed to penetrate some of the most secure and high-profile locations in the country: the surgeon general of Pakistan's army was killed just outside the army's headquarters in Rawalpindi in February 2008; the visiting Sri Lankan cricket team was attacked in Lahore in March 2009, as was the Manawan police training center in the city weeks later; the army headquarters itself was attacked in October 2009; the US consulate in Peshawar was attacked in April 2010; a high-security naval base was attacked in Karachi in 2011; and five-star hotels frequented by foreigners were blown up in Islamabad and Peshawar more than once. It is only since mid-2011 that incidents of urban terrorism have gone down, credited largely to the TTP's losses in the northwest and a much-improved urban intelligence network that has managed to disrupt terrorist sleeper cells belonging to the

Punjabi Taliban groups. That said, militants keep resurfacing in the "cleared" territories and periodically launch successful attacks against the security forces. The most high-profile of these was the August 2012 attack on the Pakistan Air Force's production facility and base in Kamra, north of Islamabad (Malik 2012). Moreover, even though the military claims to have cleared most of FATA, except perhaps the North Waziristan agency where the Haqqani network and the TTP now coexist, a number of other FATA agencies also remain tense. More recently, the TTP and its affiliates have begun to use Afghan border regions to launch attacks against Pakistani security forces in FATA and KPK. The TTP has reportedly taken advantage of the 2010 US troop withdrawal from the remote eastern border regions of Afghanistan by using the newly unprotected territory as a sanctuary (I. Ahmed 2011).

Pakistan's Selective Approach: The Never-Ending "Capacity" versus "Will" Debate

Much has been written and said about why Pakistan has been unable to tackle the violent Islamist threat more effectively. All contentions center around the "capacity" versus "will" debate in one way or another. Pakistan's stance is that it lacks the capacity to "do more" while the US and NATO view maintains that the lack of will has held Pakistan back. This divergent interpretation has caused a fundamental disconnect between the two allies.

Throughout the period discussed here, the Pakistani security apparatus focused on the most immediate threat: the TTP–al-Qaeda combine and their affiliates. Accorded secondary importance were sectarian attacks across Pakistan that saw a parallel rise and continued unabated in areas like Balochistan and even Karachi, Pakistan's largest city. Factions of the Afghan Taliban using safe havens in Pakistan but not actively pursuing an anti-Pakistan agenda were ignored to a large extent; the state kept its truce in return for their noninterference in the Pakistani militancy and only used direct coercive measures to check their activities in Afghanistan when facing external pressure from the United States during crucial periods in the Afghan counterinsurgency (COIN) campaign. Moreover, the Pakistani military allowed the sparing use of US drone strikes in FATA as a quid pro quo for not being able to "do more," and for disallowing any major US boots on the ground in the tribal areas.[24] Intelligence cooperation between the two sides also continued, although it was marked by significant mistrust. Other outfits such as the traditionally anti-India groups were never seen as an urgent internal threat. Most of the anti-India groups are based in the Pakistani heartland of Punjab and continue to exist there. Levels of infiltration in Kashmir, however, have been substantially lowered since 2003, although the LeT did manage to perpetrate the massive Mumbai terrorist attacks in November 2008. From time to time, targeted law enforcement actions are undertaken against these groups, but rarely are these based on any overarching strategy to counter their existence. The Pakistani state's justification is lack of capacity to open new fronts; much of the world perceived this stance, especially with regard to the Afghan Taliban conglomerate and the LeT, as a case of lack of "will" underpinned by the Pakistan Army's view of certain militant groups as strategic assets. Table 1.3 summarizes the Pakistani state's approach against the major militant outfits since 2007.

Perhaps the reality lies somewhere in between the Pakistani and global positions. There is certainly a capacity constraint that the world has been too quick to dismiss, but there is also room for legitimate suspicions given some of the behavior exhibited by the Pakistani state. In the following discussion, we briefly lay out the thrust of both views.

It Is about Capacity

Pakistan's capacity constraints begin with the military. Islamabad has committed more than 140,000 troops to fight the TTP and its affiliates and has lost thousands of soldiers in the process. According to official data, the military launched a total of 403 major and minor operations between 2007 and 2010—mostly in FATA—and there have been more since.[25] Despite this, according to a PIPS 2010 security assessment report, there was "no major change in the militant landscape" in western Pakistan even after the military success of 2009–10 (2010, 27). The Pakistani military "is organized and trained for set-piece warfare with India, not a counterinsurgency against its own people in the forbidding physical and social geography of the Afghanistan/Pakistan border" (Thier 2008, 3). Pakistan's security forces were not adept at the kind of pitched, urban, and semiurban warfare challenging the state. They also lacked access to the right kind of equipment; basics like helicopters and night vision goggles, to name just two, were not available in sufficient quantities (Nawaz 2011). While US assistance has helped over the past few years, it has only been able to partially fill the gap. Moreover, while the military underwent significant on-the-job learning that gradually led to higher success ratios, Pakistani soldiers have found it hard to fight fellow Muslims in their own country. Desertion rates were not trivial in the early years post-9/11, but even now the lower ranks of the military are outraged at Pakistani support to the United States and feel that they are being forced to do America's bidding.[26] They are unlikely to be enthused if asked to operate

TABLE 1.3
State's Response to Islamist Militant Groups, 2007–Present

Militant Group	*State's Response*
Al-Qaeda	Military and paramilitary action in FATA Law enforcement action in the rest of Pakistan[a] US drone strikes
Tehrik-e-Taliban Pakistan	Military and paramilitary action in FATA and KPK Law enforcement action in rest of Pakistan[a] US drone strikes Broader COIN strategy (development +)[b]
"Punjabi Taliban"	Military and paramilitary action in FATA and KPK Law enforcement action in Punjab[a] Broader COIN strategy (development +)[b]
Lashkar-e-Taiba	Containment and appeasement to prevent further terror strikes
Afghan Taliban; Haqqani network; Hizb-e-Islami; Muqami Tehrik-e-Taliban	"Blind eye" Containment beyond a point Constant negotiations of deals of noninterference and deals to limit cross-border attacks into Afghanistan US drone strikes
Sipah-e-Sahaba Pakistan; Lashkar-e-Jhangvi; Sipah-e-Muhammad; Tehrik-e-Jafria Pakistan	Law enforcement[a] Broader COIN strategy (development +)[b]

[a] Law enforcement refers to police and intelligence operations and may include extrajudicial killings.

[b] Development + refers to nonmilitary aspects of counterinsurgency strategy aimed at instituting a more responsive state; usually includes rapid development, improved governance and service delivery, greater access to education and health care, and so on.

Source: Authors' compilation. Earlier version published in Yusuf 2011a.

on new militant fronts that do not directly threaten them or their fellow civilians.

Adding to the problem is Pakistan's civilian law enforcement sector. First, no overarching counterterrorism (CT) strategy links the civilian and military efforts. Moreover, police do not operate in FATA, and while they do in the rest of Pakistan, the institution is ill prepared and paralyzed by corruption. Applicable to KPK, according to the US strategy of "clear, hold, and build," law enforcement is critical to the reconstruction and rehabilitation of a region following the "clear" phase of military operations.[27] There is hardly an example of an insurgency, especially one that has a significant urban dimension, where sustainable peace ensues without putting civilian law enforcement in the lead. Unfortunately, throughout its history, Pakistan has largely relied on the military for major security challenges, and the police have been used merely as a politicized instrument of repression. As a consequence, law enforcement is unable to provide "holding" support to the military without constant military oversight in regions like Swat.

To overcome some of the weaknesses of civilian law enforcement and, indeed, its absence in FATA, the government and the military encouraged the creation of *lashkars* (village militias) to help counter the threats posed by the TTP and its partners in FATA and neighboring parts of KPK.[28] By doing so, this reduced the burden on the military but at the cost of creating new armed militias which, if history is any guide, may well become a problem for the state in the future. As for urban towns in the heartland, the Pakistani police and civilian intelligence were never equipped to deal with sustained terrorist threats and have thus experienced countless failures and personnel losses since 9/11 (see chapter 5, this volume). It is only in recent years that their ability to preemptively identify and target threats has seen visible improvement. Even then, much is left to be desired.

The weaknesses of the criminal justice system, the subject of chapter 6 in this volume, also hampered the military's efforts significantly. The military kept alleged militants in illegal detention for the fear that civilian court trials would acquit them. Indeed, the intelligence agencies recorded a number of instances where captured militants were released by courts due to insufficient evidence and subsequently rejoined the militancy and launched attacks against the security forces. Moreover, often judges and witnesses called by the court fear for their personal safety and thus hesitate to testify against alleged militants or to hand out guilty verdicts to them (Abbas 2011, 12). Pakistan also lacks high-security prisons. Keeping militants in regular jails is believed to have a radicalizing effect on other prisoners; the authorities are thus not keen on admitting more captured militants to the already overcrowded jails.

However, capacity constraints are not limited to the tangibles. Pakistan's internal political weakness, the absence of consociational models of politics in a system marked by tenuous coalitions, long-standing civil–military tensions, and the presence of right-wing political parties sympathetic to the Taliban have all hampered Pakistan's efforts over the past decade. Between 2002 and 2007, when the Pakistani Taliban gained strength in FATA and KPK, Musharraf, despite advancing significant help to the United States, never really owned up to the war as his own; he continued to conflate his government's compulsions with an American agenda and thus kept the war unpopular. Moreover, the ruling coalition in the KPK province during his tenure was an amalgamation of six religious parties, some of whom have close links to the Afghan and Pakistani Taliban. This Muttahida Majlis-e-Amal (MMA) government continued to block efforts to launch sustained operations against the TTP in Swat.[29] After the left-leaning Pakistan People's Party (PPP)–led civilian government took power in Islamabad in 2008, Pakistan was constantly beset with economic crisis, political tussles within the ruling coalition and within the opposition, and institutional tensions between the executive, judiciary, and the military. All this kept the focus away from developing a comprehensive roadmap to eliminate Islamist militancy.

Public opinion has also played an extremely important but divisive role in Pakistan's ordeal. For a host of complex reasons, Pakistan has seen a rise in intolerance and the culture of violence over the past decade that has allowed the militants to use the ideological lexicon of jihad to conflate their agenda with Islam and with the US "occupation" in Afghanistan. A combination of their efforts and the Pakistani state's reluctance to stem the growing tide of anti-Americanism in the country has meant that the average Pakistani citizen believes that American policies are the primary cause of the problems their country is facing.[30] Constant public rebuke from the United States and the "do more" mantra have only reinforced this view. Right-wing political parties have also cashed in on this rhetoric. The end result is that, for the most part, Pakistani citizens are inclined to blame the terrorist problems on external geostrategic factors rather than seeing the Pakistani Taliban for what they are (Yusuf 2009b). They have thus been opposed to prolonged military operations; on very few occasions have Pakistani citizens come out en masse in support of decisive military action—the Swat operation of 2009 was one exception.[31] They remain partial to the idea of negotiations with the TTP as a means to end the chaos. It is increasingly clear that public opinion is unlikely to back any state action that may lead to blowback akin to the period following the Red Mosque incident. The US demand for a military operation in North Waziristan against the Haqqani network has been on hold partly for this reason (Abbot 2012).

Interestingly, the United States and Pakistan have ended up with polar opposite conclusions from the experience of the past decade. Pakistani strategists and public opinion alike believe that it has been too much action, not too little, against Islamist militants that has caused havoc in Pakistan. The initial military forays into FATA under US pressure are cast as the original sin. Had Pakistan not entered the United States' war, the narrative goes, the backlash would never have come. The abrupt post-9/11 U-turn in Pakistan's promilitancy policy and curbs on cross-border activity of militants is also blamed for the multitude of splinter groups that have emerged out of existing anti-India and sectarian groups. This fracturing has left Pakistan, and by extension allies like the United States, with a much more complicated challenge. This view condones a selective-cum-sequential approach—target those who harm you first but do not antagonize those who do not until you have dealt with the more immediate threats. The United States and much of the Western world, on the other hand, believes that half-hearted actions, the selective approach, and the excessive resort to peace deals in FATA over the past decade are the core problem. They would like Pakistan to see all Islamist militants as equally threatening and tackle them in a holistic manner.

The three-decade-old infrastructure of jihad and the multitude of militant organizations operating out of Pakistan imply that the challenge of curbing the inflow of fresh militants is a truly daunting one. Literature on radicalization talks of demand-side "pull" factors as signifying the presence of a ready-made outlet for susceptible youth. A buoyant demand for Islamist militants, a ready cause to fight for, and easy access to militants all greatly increase the possibility of alienated and disgruntled youth taking to violence. Perhaps nowhere in the world is access to militant infrastructure easier than in Pakistan today. Moreover, with high levels of socioeconomic deprivation and marginalization of areas such as FATA and even Southern Punjab, with a proportion of the religious seminaries that continue to supply youth ingrained with some sympathy for the jihadist narrative, and with a burgeoning youth population with few employment opportunities, the supply side "push" factors are just as strong.[32] Even a robust CT policy can only dent demand; unless it is accompanied by a broader COIN effort to address supply side concerns, total victory is unlikely. If Pakistan were to start making a turnaround today, it will be years before its effects become visible; in the interim, any military victories may only represent tactical gains.

It Is about Will

The Pakistani state's position has been challenged by various quarters, not only its foreign partners and neighbors like India and Afghanistan but also by the strategically liberal community, however small, within Pakistan. The most obvious critique of a purely capacity-based argument is linked to Pakistan's regional security paradigm and its continuing obsession with India. There is little doubt that even as Pakistan has moved away from backing Mullah Omar's Afghan Taliban as Afghanistan's legitimate leadership, it still remains deeply concerned about Indian presence in Afghanistan and worries of a post-2014 Afghanistan that is hostile toward Islamabad and friendly to New Delhi (Yusuf, Yusuf, and Zaidi 2011). Part of the reluctance to go after the Afghan Taliban safe havens in the Pakistani border regions is reflective of a "hedging" strategy: the Pakistani military sees little reason to antagonize the Afghan Taliban conglomerate that represents essentially the only political force across the Durand Line that is not entirely antagonistic to Pakistani interests (Yusuf 2011b). Facing a worsening security situation in Afghanistan, Pakistan's planners will become more certain that they have no option but to be in "self-help" mode to safeguard their interests and will likely continue hedging.

Moreover, within the broader South Asian regional context, Pakistan resents the United States for having tilted its policy in India's favor without requiring New Delhi to address Pakistan's concerns and outstanding disputes such as Kashmir. Pakistan sees the post-9/11 US engagement in South Asia to have upset the regional balance it had worked so hard to maintain; the Indo-US nuclear deal was perhaps the single most consequential development as far as eroding Pakistan's trust where US neutrality was concerned.[33] Normative debates on the fairness and legitimacy of Pakistan's concerns aside, the fact is that Pakistan remains obsessed with India. Unless the United States helps reconcile India–Pakistan differences, there is little chance of Pakistan giving up its hedging strategy. This is a reality from which Washington has continued to shy away.[34]

It is also true that while Pakistan has persistently criticized US policy toward Afghanistan, it has failed to come up with an alternate vision of its own. For over a decade, Pakistan's stance has been reactive; it does not like the course the other major players are pursuing as it sees these as favoring non-Pashtun Afghan factions who are hostile to Pakistan and as allowing countries like India and Iran greater ingress on Pakistan's western border, but its own remedies are unimaginative and clichéd. Islamabad has stressed the need for an "inclusive peace process," but even here it has been accused of holding back in terms of facilitating dialogue with the Afghan Taliban conglomerate present on its soil (Borger 2012; Yusuf 2013a). Ultimately, Pakistan's behavior may be a function of the troubling reality that it has few friends in Afghanistan beyond the radical Pashtuns and that it cannot compete in terms of soft power with rivals like India. It is therefore forced to employ its spoiling power to avoid being left out of the post-2014 calculus, even at a tremendous cost to its reputation. Some would argue that Pakistan's strategy boils down to encouraging managed chaos in Afghanistan—just enough to keep the US presence troubled so that it is forced to reconcile with the Afghan Taliban but not so high that the United States either contemplates direct action against Pakistan or gives up completely on Afghanistan, thereby plunging it into total chaos (Yusuf 2013a).

On internal militancy, the Pakistani narrative comes across as too convenient. While Islamabad's plea to appreciate its constraints—discussed earlier—must be heeded, it cannot realistically expect the world to be convinced of its sincerity when militant organizations like LeT, despite being formally banned, continue to exist without much pushback from the state. In fact, right-wing forces are often seen uniting under umbrella organizations that are allowed to hold massive rallies in major cities under state protection, a recent example being the Defense of Pakistan Council set up to oppose the US–Pakistan relationship.[35] Hafiz Saeed, the founder of LeT, continues to make hateful public speeches, only to see the Pakistani state turn a blind eye, if not facilitate him. Pakistan has also dragged its feet on prosecuting those involved in the Mumbai terrorist attacks of 2008 (Quinn 2012). Privately, Pakistan's own liberal elite scoff at the military's explanations and continue to believe that the promilitancy policy remains intact. Furthermore, even civilian law enforcement and intelligence institutions remain unconvinced of the military's sincerity as they often find themselves under pressure from their military counterparts to release certain arrested militants or not to act against specific individuals or groups.[36] The military argues that this is not a sign of lack of resolve but that these incidents are only aimed at securing the institution's assets and plants, a normal part of the intelligence business.

The political parties also cannot be fully absolved. Let alone religious parties, even mainstream political outfits like the Punjab-based Pakistan Muslim League-Nawaz (PML-N) have been under scrutiny for their reluctance to allow action against Islamist organizations based in the province. In 2010, the province's chief minister and PML-N's former president, Shahbaz Sharif, drew attention by urging the Taliban to "spare" Punjab and stating that he and the Taliban were "fighting for the same cause."[37] His close aide and the provincial law minister, Rana Sanaullah, was seen currying favor with the banned SSP for political gains (K. Ahmed 2011).

It is hardly surprising, then, that policy confusion prevails among Pakistani minds on how the state intends to put an end to militancy in the country. The country's leadership is yet to present a coherent long-term plan to address both the supply- and demand-side factors discussed earlier. The absence of such a vision raises serious doubts on the will of the state to tackle the problem sincerely.

Western commentators are also not prepared to take the Pakistani military's concern about negative public opinion at face value. The Pakistan military is an extremely image-conscious institution and has continued to stress that it cannot sustain its efforts against the TTP, let alone other militant outfits, without public support. Outsiders, however, are quick to note that the military still maintains significant clout in terms of shaping public option. They often point to the military's public relations campaign that subtly manipulates public opinion to its liking—often to keep the United States and US dictates unpopular—and then uses this as an excuse for inaction against militants. For skeptics of the military's line, the abrupt promilitary swing in public opinion just before the decisive Swat operation in 2009 and the operations in FATA immediately following that was more than a coincidence; they would argue that the military actively helped create that through a deliberate media campaign.

Finally, there is evidence to confirm the Western world's view that ultimately all militants are a threat and must not be seen as policy tools. The Pakistani contention that Pakistan would not have faced a retaliatory response had it not been for Musharraf's decision to send troops into FATA in 2002–3 is somewhat simplistic. The fact is that the anti-India groups trained by the ISI were already beginning to challenge some of the state's policies; the pot had begun to simmer much before 9/11. As far back as the mid-1990s, some military officers going through their Staff College and National Defense College courses were writing internal papers arguing that the "Frankenstein" the ISI had created would turn against it sooner or later. True, that this may not have happened without a trigger, and that trigger came from Pakistan's forced policy U-turn post-9/11, but this was certainly not where the roots of the problem lay. More recently, there have also been a number of verified incidents where members of groups like LeT, JeM, and even Haqqani network have defied the state and have even indirectly aided terrorist attacks within Pakistan.[38] How these occurrences are interpreted as far as countering militancy is concerned will be disconcerting to a Western reader. Some military officials when interviewed argued that this is evidence of how easily these groups, if antagonized, can join other anti-Pakistan outfits and force the situation completely out of the state's control. They therefore see even less reason to go after groups that are not actively targeting the state at the moment even if they are fighting regional forces.

Conclusion

Pakistan is engulfed by a violent Islamist threat that has grown exponentially over the last ten years. The Pakistan military has managed intermittent tactical victories, and urban terrorism incidents have decreased in the recent past. However, the protracted history of state sponsorship to militancy, Pakistan's regional strategic paradigm, the spillover of the instability in Afghanistan, the many institutional weaknesses constraining a coherent CT policy, the Western world's insensitivity to the acuteness of the challenge, and the blowback Pakistan has had to face since 9/11, encompassed within the "capacity versus will" debate, combine to make Pakistan's CT problem virtually unsolvable in the short run. For the foreseeable future, Pakistan will not only be under threat itself, but its territory will continue to be used against regional and global targets, something that will keep Pakistan's international perception squarely in the negative. Pakistan needs to demonstrate greater resolve, whereas the world must be more understanding and must resist the temptation of walking away from Pakistan. Only then can we hope for the world's fifth largest nuclear power (Williams 2011) to overcome Islamist militancy on its soil.

Notes

1. Balochistan has been experiencing a subnationalist insurgency since 2006 that has led to a large number of casualties on all sides. Even more deadly in terms of the number of deaths has been the targeted killing of Shia Hazaras by Sunni extremist sectarian groups, most prominently the Lashkar-e-Jhangvi, in and around the province's capital of Quetta. For a background on the killings and a timeline of incidents, see Al Jazeera TV's coverage of the issue at http://stream.aljazeera.com/story/pakistans-hazara-under-attack-0022197.

2. For some time the Pakistani embassy in Washington, DC, issued the "Pakistani Casualty Scorecard," which updated casualty figures on a weekly basis. According to these estimates, the figure had crossed forty-four thousand by the spring of 2012. The South Asia Terrorism Portal's figures put the fatalities count until early 2013 at more than forty-seven thousand. South Asia Terrorism Portal, "Fatalities in Terrorist Violence in Pakistan 2003–2013," www.satp.org/satporgtp/countries/pakistan/database/casualties.htm.

3. In December 2001, terrorists associated with JeM attacked the Indian Parliament building in New Delhi. The attacks resulted in the deaths of a dozen people, including the terrorists, and precipitated a ten-month-long India–Pakistan military standoff. The 2008 terrorist attack on Mumbai was a coordinated bombing and shooting campaign that resulted in the deaths of 166 people. The terrorists' association with LeT, a Pakistan-based militant group, led to the collapse of dialogues between India and Pakistan that had been ongoing since 2004.

4. For a discussion on what the next India–Pakistan crisis may look like should India not show restraint, see Yusuf 2011b, 20–27.

5. Subsequent to British withdrawal from South Asia in 1947, the central government in Islamabad established seven autonomous "agencies" in Pakistan's northwestern border region of FATA. This region remains a distinctly different legal entity from the other provinces of Pakistan and has traditionally retained a high degree of autonomy in its functioning.

6. For data on drone strikes since 2004, see New America Foundation's Counterterrorism Strategy Initiative website at http://natsec.newamerica.net/drones/pakistan/analysis.

7. In May 2010, Faisal Shahzad, a Pakistan-born US citizen, attempted to detonate a bomb in New York's Time Square. The bomb was disarmed by authorities before it was able to cause any damage. Shahzad confessed to having visited Pakistani tribal regions and having received training from the TTP.

8. In reality, even as the state has attempted to impose a Muslim identity on its citizens, Pakistan's ethnic plurality has led to persistent tensions between the religious and ethnic identities of Pakistan. Ultimately, ethnic identities have remained strong and competitive even as the state has continued to impose Islam for politically motivated reasons. See Wilder 2005. For a discussion of the origins and persistence of the tension between Pakistan's various identities, see Jaffrelot 2002a.

9. United Kingdom Home Office, "Country of Origin Information Report—Pakistan," January 17, 2011, www.unhcr.org/refworld/docid/4d37e8622.html.

10. For a detailed account of the TTP, see Qazi 2011, 574–602.

11. For a detailed account of the role of the Central Intelligence Agency (CIA) and the Inter-Services Intelligence Agency (ISI) in the anti-Soviet campaign during the 1980s, see Coll 2004, 21–170.

12. The Jamaat-e-Islami, perhaps the best organized and largest religious political outfit, benefited the most from Zia's pro-Deobandi Sunni policies. The party even managed to gain access to domestic and foreign policies even as it failed to generate a popular vote bank. See Nasr 1994, 192–93, 195.

13. UN Security Council Resolution 1386 authorized the deployment of an International Security Force for Afghanistan (ISAF) for six months. In 2003 the UN Security Council approved Resolution 1510 to extend the authorization and mandate of the ISAF.

14. The Pakistani leadership at the time was well aware of the potential backlash of this move but felt that it had no option given the pressure it was facing from the United States. Prior to ordering the military into Khyber Agency in FATA in April 2002, then chief executive of the country General Musharraf was candid in admitting to a group of journalists he had invited for a press briefing that he was sending in troops under duress.

15. Many of these tribesmen had earlier fought in Afghanistan in the 1980s, where they had already been trained and radicalized. Nek Mohammed was one of these fighters who, immediately after the army's incursions in 2002, mobilized a movement against the Pakistani state (Qazi 2011, 577–79).

16. The term "Afghan Taliban" is often used to refer either to Mullah Omar's group or for all the major factions that fall under the network of Taliban belonging to Afghanistan. To avoid this confusion, we use "Afghan Taliban conglomerate" to refer to the predominant Afghan factions operating from Pakistani soil. These include Mullah Omar's group, the Haqqani network, and the Hizb-e-Islami.

17. In January 2002, at the peak of a military standoff with India, General Musharraf announced a reversal of any support to militant groups and banned the prominent anti-India outfits. The authors' discussions with decision makers at the time suggest that the decision to roll back the anti-India promilitancy policy was in fact genuine. Once India and Pakistan initiated a peace process in 2004, infiltration levels decreased substantially. The Indian government has acknowledged this on a number of occasions since.

18. The Red Mosque incident not only precipitated a rise in militant violence across Pakistan but is also the event that triggered the emergence of the militant umbrella organization in the form of the TTP. United by their intensified interest to resist the Pakistani state, the TTP declared the state illegitimate following the Red Mosque incident, due to its cooperation with the United States in Afghanistan and its military actions against Pakistanis.

19. The Swat Valley is a tourist hub in KPK. It had experienced agitation in favor of introducing Sharia even in the 1990s, which the government partially agreed to at the time. From 2007 onward, however, Maulana Fazlullah, a firebrand cleric operating as the de facto head of TTP's Swat chapter, began challenging the writ of the state violently and ultimately almost completely eroded the state's presence.

20. While the Haqqani network and Hizb-e-Islami are based in FATA, Mullah Omar's Taliban mainly operate out of Quetta and, increasingly, Karachi. Their sizable presence in Quetta has earned them the title "Quetta Shura Taliban."

21. UK Home Office, "Country of Origin Information Report—Pakistan," 30.

22. For a timeline of the turbulence in Swat, see IRIN 2009.

23. SATP, "Fatalities in Terrorist Violence in Pakistan 2003–2012."

24. Drones remain one of the most contentious issues between Pakistan and the United States, but even as Pakistan objects to their use publicly, leaked diplomatic cables suggest that the Pakistani military had agreed to the use of drones. The Pakistani government, however, claims that this permission was only with regard to surveillance through drones, not armed strikes (Yousaf 2011).

25. The author received this figure from official military sources. As many as 140 operations are classified as "major" while 263 were "minor" operations.

26. This is based on a number of informal discussions with military officers and with journalists who have embedded with the Pakistan Army in the northwest over the past three years.

27. The US officially adopted "clear, hold, and build" as the core of its counterinsurgency doctrine in the Iraqi context. See Secretary of State Condoleezza Rice's statement to the Senate Foreign Relations Committee in 2005 where she endorsed this as official strategy (Rice 2005).

28. UK Home Office, "Country of Origin Information Report—Pakistan," 31.

29. Critics not only blame MMA for not allowing the military to operate in a concerted fashion but they also saw the MMA as being sympathetic to the Taliban and ignoring their expansion in Swat and adjacent areas. See, for example, Abbas 2010.

30. Anti-American sentiment in Pakistan has been rising steadily. A Pew survey in June 2012 found that as many as 74 percent of Pakistanis consider the US an "enemy" (Pew Research Center 2012).

31. Just before the 2009 Swat operation that ultimately cleared the area of the TTP, support for using the Pakistan Army to fight terrorism had risen above 50 percent. This support has waned again since and was down to 35 percent in June 2012 (Pew Research Center 2012).

32. For a detailed discussion of the "pull" and "push" factors for the youth to become radicalized, see Yusuf 2011a.

33. For a summary of Pakistan's concerns with the growing India–US relationship, see M. Hussain 2011.

34. For a critical view of the US inability to grasp this reality, see Yusuf 2009a.

35. "Rightwing Alliance Is Revived," *Dawn*, February 16, 2012, http://dawn.com/2012/02/16/rightwing-alliance-is-revived/.

36. This is based on off-the-record conversations with police officials from Punjab and KPK provinces.

37. "Sharif and the Taliban," *Dawn*, March 16, 2010, http://archives.dawn.com/archives/32514.

38. This is based on multiple conversations in 2009 with a senior police official serving in the Special Investigative Group, the Federal Investigation Agency's counterterrorism unit.

CHAPTER 2

Militancy and Extremism in Pakistan

A US Perspective

MARVIN G. WEINBAUM

PAKISTAN and the Western world do not see eye to eye on the causes of Islamist militancy in Pakistan and the means to tackle it. As seen from the United States' perspective, Pakistan is the epicenter of international terrorism. It hosts organizations that challenge the political stability of Pakistan and its region and that also directly threaten Western security interests. From safe havens in Pakistan, al-Qaeda, along with Mullah Omar's Quetta Shura Taliban and other Afghan insurgent groups, has planned and carried out attacks against American and North Atlantic Treaty Organization (NATO) forces in Afghanistan. Pakistan has also given wide berth to domestic extremist organizations intent on bringing harm to Western interests. Several jihadi groups directly linked to terrorist attacks in India and Afghanistan threaten to metastasize into global threats. To varying degrees, all these organizations influence Pakistan's willingness or capacity to be an active ally in counterterrorism (CT) efforts.

Despite often distinctive priorities and agendas, Pakistan-based militant groups are much alike in their shared opposition to Western, and especially, US policies in South Asia. Ideologically, most adhere to socially conservative beliefs strongly at odds with core Western values, and most accuse Americans and Europeans of waging war against Islam. While claiming to reject the modernity of the West, all are increasingly adept at using the technology it affords. Militant extremist groups cooperate tactically and strategically, have overlapping sources of funding, and increasingly share membership. None shun the use of terrorism in pursuing their objectives. Whether against Pakistani or Western targets, they have learned of the gains to be made from causing disruption as well as bringing destruction. All are highly adaptable, able to adjust their strategies, and assume various guises in order to survive.

Depending on the size of their Pakistani diasporas and their legal systems, Western countries have reacted differently to Pakistan-based terrorism. Domestic politics and political culture also separately frame their responses. Diaspora-rich countries are perhaps unable to criticize and question the Pakistani state as openly as they would otherwise like to. Nonetheless, bombings in London and Madrid and threats made elsewhere in Europe together with the plots against the United States have highlighted their common vulnerability. To a Western observer, the anti-Western rhetoric of these groups seems of one piece, as is their determination that ties to the West should be severed. On the other hand, Pakistan views its radical Islamic groups more selectively. Its policies distinguish between those militant organizations that pose a menace to the state and others considered to serve the national interest.

The purpose of this chapter is twofold: to provide an understanding of how Western views of Pakistan's extremist groups are distinguishable from those held within the country, and to highlight the reasons why there is so often a clash of policies. The chapter identifies and describes those militant organizations that have taken aim at Western interests. It also points out how groups with more parochial agendas ordinarily have fallen under the influence of anti-Western groups and become increasingly threatening to the Pakistani state. The chapter then explains why Pakistan and the West, most specifically the United States, have nevertheless often persisted in their diverging perspectives on the extremist threat. One group, Lashkar-e-Taiba (LeT), is singled out for discussion to illustrate the conflicting concerns of Pakistan and the West. The chapter concludes with observations on how these differences can possibly be bridged.

The analysis in this chapter is crucial because the disparity with the West has not only led to disagreement over the identity and severity of terrorist threats, it has also carried obvious consequences for the ability of the US-led presence to confront the insurgency in Afghanistan. Pakistan has been held complicit by providing sanctuary for insurgent groups in direct combat with Western coalition forces. It is also criticized for failure to crack down on those domestic jihadi organizations abetting the Afghan insurgency. Pakistan's patronage of certain jihadi groups has shaded attitudes in Western countries toward disputes between Pakistan and its neighbors, notably with India over Kashmir. Most significantly, Pakistan's toleration of certain Islamist extremist groups casts doubt on whether Pakistan can be counted on as a reliable ally in thwarting international terrorism or has instead to be considered as part of the problem. The question is fundamental and underpins the ability of the

Western world to work with Pakistan in the future—with its attendant implications for Pakistan's outlook and capacity to tackle terrorism.

The Sources of Threat

Of the nearly fifty domestic and transnational groups that are officially banned in Pakistan, most are inactive and many merely spinoffs from parent organizations. Probably no more than a dozen are effectively operational and actively engaged in militant activities. For all that these extremist groups have in common, many differ in their primary areas of operation, preferred tactics, and avowed goals. Several are especially noteworthy for targeting both the Pakistan state and the West. A few are singled out by Western countries as warranting special concern—of course, none more so than al-Qaeda.

With its believed sanctuary in Pakistan's North Waziristan, al-Qaeda takes aim at Western interests in Afghanistan and beyond while also publicly declaring its intent to destroy a Pakistani establishment that it considers as being in the clutches of the United States. Rather than a significant fighting force, al-Qaeda, with perhaps no more than a few hundred hardcore members in Pakistan, is instead thought to act as a force multiplier in channeling funds, notably from private sources in Persian Gulf countries, and providing logistical advice and inspiration to other militant organizations. Drone strikes in the Federally Administered Tribal Areas (FATA), the Pakistani tribal belt bordering Afghanistan, have taken a heavy toll on al-Qaeda's core leadership, and the US raid that killed Osama bin Laden in the Pakistani garrison town of Abbottabad on May 2, 2011, may have served as a blow to morale among the rank and file. Even so, al-Qaeda's continued presence in Pakistan and its far-flung franchises abroad leave the West still fearful of the organization's capacity to mastermind global attacks and regenerate at its base.

Also finding safe haven in Pakistan are the Afghan Taliban, both the fighters loyal to Mullah Omar, believed to be commanded from Quetta in Balochistan province south of FATA, and those linked to a disaffected offshoot group located in Peshawar in Pakistan's settled Khyber Pakthunkhwa (KPK) province adjacent to FATA (Giustozzi 2013). Together with members of the Haqqani network centered in the North Waziristan agency of FATA, and a smaller group belonging to the Hizb-e-Islami of Gulbudin Hekmatyar, Afghan insurgents are estimated to number about eleven thousand active fighters in Pakistan (Mullick 2010a). These Afghan groups funnel recruits, funds, and arms to the Afghan insurgency but plan and execute their operations independently. All enjoy, to varying degrees, the protection of the Pakistan military's spy agency, the Inter-Services Intelligence (ISI), which is alleged to facilitate their cross-border activities (Yusuf 2013a, 14–16). In return, Afghan insurgents have refrained from participating with Pakistan's own Taliban insurgents in terrorist attacks against the Pakistan state. At least for the time being, Afghan insurgents have not set their sights beyond pushing foreign troops out of Afghanistan and displacing the Kabul government along with its political system.

Another foreign group, the Islamic Movement of Uzbekistan (IMU), was routed from Uzbekistan after trying to bring down its secular regime. The IMU fled to Afghanistan in the late 1990s and took refuge in Pakistan's mountainous tribal areas when the United States attacked in Afghanistan in 2001. An IMU force of two thousand to three thousand, spread among several factions, is usually described as well trained and brutal. They have worked in concert with Afghan insurgents and maintained a particularly close alliance with al-Qaeda. The IMU is believed to provide explosive training and on occasion suicide bombers; with Waziri tribal militants, the IMU has joined armed Afghan groups in attacks in northern Afghanistan. The organization is also increasingly active throughout Central Asia and has been linked to terrorist plots in Europe (Siddique 2010; Shahzad 2010).

The tribally based Tehrik-e-Taliban Pakistan (TTP) serves as an umbrella organization for a number of tribal militias (Siddiqa 2011).[1] Although it cooperates closely with the Haqqani network leadership and acknowledges the spiritual leadership of Afghan Taliban leader Mullah Omar, the TTP is operationally distinct. Notwithstanding a weak central command, it seeks to extend its political and military control over the tribal areas and impose its version of Sharia law throughout Pakistan. As discussed in detail in the preceding chapter, in recent years, the TTP has been behind attacks across Pakistan against the army and civilian population. But the group's leaders have also attracted the West's attention for their stated intention to carry out attacks in Europe and the United States. On the second anniversary of bin Laden's death, the TTP vowed that the organization would follow in his footsteps.[2] Evidence that the TTP, along with other groups, had a hand in the training of the would-be New York Times Square bomber, Faisal Shahzad, in May 2010 suggests that such statements may be more than mere rhetoric (Ghosh 2010).[3]

Sectarian attacks within the country are most often associated with the anti-Shia Sipah-e-Sahaba Pakistan (SSP) and Lashkar-e-Jhangvi (LeJ). Officially listed as terrorist organizations by Pakistan, these organizations have overcome their rivalries and increasingly melded their operations with the TTP and other militant groups in taking on the Pakistani establishment and its pro-Western policies (Lester 2010). The LeJ in particular has drawn the attention of American and European governments because of its having become a staunch ally of al-Qaeda. Split into small cells to better ensure its survival, the group is believed to have executed many of the attacks in Pakistan attributed to al-Qaeda (Z. Khan 2010). The organization is also held responsible for the July 2002 killing of American journalist Daniel Pearl in Karachi (Perlez 2011).

Several Pakistani jihadi groups that aid the Afghan insurgency are associated with domestic violence, including attacks against American assets in Pakistan. Principal among these are Jaish-e-Mohammed (JeM) and the Karachi-based Harakat-ul-Mujahideen Al-alami (HuMA). JeM is known to sponsor training facilities for Afghan and Pakistani militants. HuMA is suspected of involvement in a 2002 bombing of the US consulate in Karachi and an assassination attempt on President Pervez Musharraf in the same year (Abbas 2009a).[4] Another militant group, Harakat-ul-Jihad-al-Islami (HuJI) has received more recent attention because its leader, Ilyas Kashmiri—killed in a 2011 drone strike—was a senior member of al-Qaeda. Kashmiri is alleged to have been involved in the planning for the November 2008 Mumbai attacks that killed more than 160 people in the Indian metropolis, as well as a plot against the offices of the Copenhagen newspaper that in 2005 published cartoons of Prophet Muhammad (Yousafzai, Moreau, and Dickey 2010).[5]

But the most prominent of these groups is the Punjab-based LeT, which is generally believed to have carried out the Mumbai massacre. LeT stands apart from most other jihadi groups for its declared disassociation from domestic violence and closeness to the ISI. The organization owes its existence to the Pakistan Army's recruitment of surrogate forces to aid the insurgency in Indian Kashmir since 1989. When in 2003 the Musharraf government forced the LeT along with other jihadi groups to curtail their cross-border activities in India, most of their fighters shifted to the Afghan front. Among these jihadi groups, LeT is increasingly viewed in Western capitals as the most ambitious and potentially dangerous, having acquired the capacity to mount operations internationally.

The notoriety of several extremist groups in Pakistan is especially of concern to Western countries for their attraction to prospective terrorists. Individuals from Europe and the United States are most likely to train in TTP, JeM, and LeT camps along the Afghan frontier and return home either to act on orders received in Pakistan or to independently hatch terrorist attacks. The West also worries about the impact of groups in Pakistan in fomenting problems regionally. It is well known that tribal militants have given protection to and trained not only Uzbeks but also individuals from Chechnya and several Arab countries.

The boundaries delineating Pakistan's extremist organizations are not always clear. Moreover, banned organizations find it possible to continue to function by changing their names or by merging with seemingly benign organizations. Leaders frequently insist on their affiliation with a political wing that claims to have no connection with militancy. Increasingly over the past several years, Pakistan-based Islamic radical groups have blended into what often appears to be a virtually seamless network of extremists and terrorists.

Threat Perceptions

Important areas of convergence exist between the West and Pakistan in their perceptions of the dangers presented by several extremist groups. Together their governments acknowledge the increasing radicalization of militant organizations and the growing popularity of global jihad among their followers. There is agreement that many of the same domestic groups against which the Pakistan Army has been waging war also aim at Western interests and are active in the Afghan insurgency. Pakistani officials have become acutely conscious that any successful attack on Western soil traceable to Pakistan could present a security threat for the country as Pakistan may face possible retaliation from targeted states. Formally at least, there is agreement on labeling certain groups as terrorist. The LeT appears on the US State Department's Foreign Terrorist Organization List and was officially banned by Pakistan in 2002. Cooperation between American and Pakistani intelligence over the years has contributed to the degrading of al-Qaeda and the disruption of TTP operations. One of the worst-kept secrets was the tacit approval from Pakistani officials for the launching of American drone missiles against these groups. Official denials of cooperation by Pakistan's civilian and military leadership turned into genuine opposition only when the frequency of drone attacks sharply increased after 2010 and the American program became a convenient whipping boy following a series of perceived national humiliations by the United States in 2011.

Plainly, Pakistan and the West are not always on the same page in identifying or prioritizing the agents of terrorism. Even while in agreement that al-Qaeda constitutes a shared danger, it elicits little of the apprehension for Pakistanis that it does for Americans. Western and Pakistani governments have long differed over whether jihadi groups infiltrating Indian Kashmir should be considered terrorists or freedom fighters. Conversely, the West views as an essentially Pakistani domestic problem the terrorism associated with its decades-long ethnic conflict with the Balochistan Liberation Army. Pakistan complains that while it has been accused of supporting violence in Kashmir and elsewhere in India, its protests alleging Indian backing for the Baloch insurgency do not receive the same scrutiny. Nor are accusations that

India funds the Pakistan's Taliban insurgency taken seriously in Western capitals. In addition, while Pakistan grapples with religious and sectarian terrorism directed against the Shia sect, minority Ahmadis, and Christians, it attracts little sympathy in the West, where Islamabad's human rights policies are regularly criticized.

Pakistan's often contradictory policies toward its indigenous extremists also frustrate the West. Musharraf officially banned JeM in 2002, after which the group changed its name and was permitted to continue to operate. A creation of the ISI, JeM remains protected despite some of its members having been involved in a planned 2009 attack on Pakistan's Army headquarters in Rawalpindi (Abbas 2009b). Although outlawed, LeT found cover as Jamaat-ud-Dawa (JuD), its social welfare and charity arm. The organization's broad popularity and the Pakistan government's fear of reprisals if it were suppressed have allowed LeT to raise funds openly and have allowed its leader, Hafiz Saeed, to address public meetings and move about freely in the country. In general, the West views Pakistan's leaders as playing a double game; they officially proscribe some groups while in reality tolerating, facilitating, and possibly even orchestrating their operations. Western officials are often perplexed that while most Pakistanis have come to accept that Islamist-linked extremists pose a grave threat, the country seemingly lacks the resolve to crush them. The West wonders when Pakistan will realize that protected groups like the LeT may eventually turn against the state. Similarly, rather than a concerted effort to destroy the TTP with which the government is at war, Pakistan's current strategy seems better designed for political accommodation, using only enough force to enable the army to negotiate from strength rather than weakness, as in the recent past. Periodically revived negotiations with the TTP reflect the military's oft-exercised tactic of trying to divide the organization's more pliable leaders from its more intractable ones.

Western observers have difficulty understanding how it is that after thousands of Pakistani soldiers and civilians are reported as having been killed, Pakistan has resisted seeing the fight against Islamist militants as its war. There is similar difficulty in understanding the reluctance to conclude that Pakistan's extremists rather than India stands as the country's major national security threat (Walsh 2011; Livingston et al. 2011). Yet on both accounts, a shift in perspective may be occurring. In an August 2012 Independence Day speech, army chief Gen. Ashfaq Parvez Kayani criticized those who cast the battle against extremism and terrorism as American's war by stating that it is "our war" (*Express Tribune* 2012).[6] And in January 2013, an army spokesman confirmed a report that the army's doctrine now acknowledges that the gravest threat to the country comes from homegrown militants. He insisted, however, that it does not mean that the "conventional threat"—read: India—has receded.[7]

The United States and its allies have aimed some of their sharpest criticism against Pakistan's sheltering of Afghan insurgents, notably those linked to Mullah Omar's "Quetta Shura" and the Haqqani network. While for NATO these organizations represent the face of the enemy in Afghanistan, they have served Pakistan as strategic assets, held in reserve for a time when international forces will have quit Afghanistan without leaving behind a stable government. In the event that Pakistan cannot have a pliant regime in Kabul, the intention is to have one that will not be unfriendly or close to India. At a minimum, were Afghanistan to fracture and a civil war to ensue, an obliging Taliban force occupying its southern and eastern provinces could provide Pakistan a security belt across the border.[8]

While the opposed strategic approaches of Pakistan and Western countries have long been taken for granted, there is now a seeming agreement on an "end game" in Afghanistan marked by the drawdown of international troops from Afghanistan by December 2014. Both prefer a political solution to the conflict. The decision in Washington and European capitals to draw down nearly all NATO military personnel by the end of 2014 gave a timeline to the goals of counterinsurgency (COIN). As it became clear that the surge of troops that began in 2010 would fall short of extinguishing the insurgency and that the survival of the Kabul regime post-2014 was by no means certain, diplomatic efforts to explore the possibilities of concluding a negotiated end to the conflict expanded. Meanwhile, many in Pakistan's military, fearing the consequences of a civil war, have come to have doubts about the desirability of having Taliban control of Kabul. Their experiences with the Taliban leadership both during the 1990s and since have indicated the difficulty Pakistan would have trying to influence, much less dictate, to the Taliban leadership, once it returned to power. Like the United States and its NATO-led allies, getting the Taliban to agree to a power-sharing arrangement with the Kabul government has seemed the best possible outcome. The West could take some comfort that the constitutional system and social and economic gains in Afghanistan since 2001 could be largely preserved. For Pakistan, a stable, inclusive coalition government would be more likely to limit Indian influence (Yusuf 2013a). The Taliban's governing partners might foreclose any plans to eventually align with extremist Islamic forces in Pakistan.

Converging policies on Afghanistan's future notwithstanding, the United States continues to be accused of being responsible for Pakistan's radicalization and violence.[9] The popular view among Pakistanis is that the threat from domestic militants will dramatically decline once the United States and its NATO partners end military operations in Afghanistan. Western observers argue that militant extremism, especially in Pakistan's tribal areas, owes much to the Afghan jihad waged in the 1980s and the Afghan civil war of the

1990s. They concede that American policies in the so-called war on terror in Afghanistan and elsewhere have bolstered radical groups but that Pakistan's promotion of jihadi groups in Kashmir and Afghanistan is a principle contributor along with its neglectful domestic policies, especially in the tribal areas. The West is exasperated by widely shared conspiracy theories in Pakistan that claim that the United States and its allies give sustenance to insurgent groups in a deliberate attempt to destabilize the country. As told, the United States is set on seizing Pakistan's nuclear arsenal—a view held even by some senior army officers.[10]

The West and Pakistan often work from different timetables. Because the United States and NATO countries feel domestic pressures for successes in Afghanistan, they are anxious to see progress in getting Pakistan fully on board against insurgent Afghan groups and those Pakistan-based organizations that support them. But Pakistani authorities take a longer view. Against domestic extremist groups, a gradual approach is seen as the safer course of action, either because those groups are difficult to uproot militarily, as in North Waziristan agency of FATA, or because their broad grassroots support stands in the way. Many in the Pakistani establishment recognize that over the long run the LeT and other favored jihadi organizations could challenge the Pakistani establishment, and they will have to be dealt with aggressively. But for the time being, at least while they have utility as proxies, priority will be given to confronting extremist groups that have taken up arms against the state. For the West, however, any of these terrorist groups represent a genuine threat, especially those enjoying state sanction.

The Case of Lashkar-e-Taiba

No domestic extremist group serves better than LeT to portray the contrasting threat perceptions of the West and Pakistan. LeT has evolved from being a government-sponsored Pakistani jihadi group dedicated to an insurgency in Indian Kashmir into a terrorist organization with regional and global aims and reach. The United States, in its preoccupation with the perils of al-Qaeda, was slow to focus on LeT and the extent of its aspirations to target Western interests (Rotella 2010). Only very recently have American officials become alarmed by LeT's potential to rival al-Qaeda as a terrorist threat worldwide. With the largest militant network in Pakistan, LeT has the capacity to recruit and fundraise across much of the Islamic world.[11]

Before 9/11, LeT operated several camps in eastern Afghanistan where it gave training to thousands of Pakistanis and militants from other countries, and also provided its own fighters. The organization's members are also known to have fought during the 1990s in Tajikistan's civil war and in the conflicts in Bosnia and Chechnya. But LeT operations during these years were largely devoted to Kashmir, where it was one of the Pakistan military's most reliable proxy forces against India. Following an American-brokered stand-down with India in 2002, the Musharraf government pressured the group to move many of its camps in the Pakistani-controlled portion of Kashmir to the Afghan border. Musharraf also acceded to the West's demands by officially banning the organization. However, not only did the military not cut its ties with LeT, it has allowed the organization to maintain a steady flow of logistical and technical know-how to Afghan insurgents (Tankel 2010). Successful terrorist attacks against Indian interests in Kabul appear to have a LeT imprint.

The LeT's domestic infrastructure and access to funds, and its network in the Islamic world, make it an attractive partner for terrorist groups operating both in Pakistan and internationally. Members of the LeT are reported to have begun to team up on certain operations with TTP—despite one being a Punjabi organization and the other Pashtun, and despite their different postures toward Pakistan's security forces. They share highly compatible ideologies and are both critical of the Pakistani establishment's cooperation with the United States. The LeT is also believed to have established ties to militant religious groups worldwide, including in the United States. These may amount to cells of just a few people who come together for a specific operation, but by joining with al-Qaeda, they are capable of Mumbai-style attacks on London, Paris, Berlin, and other European cities.[12] Abu Zubadah, the senior al-Qaeda leader implicated in the 9/11 attacks, was captured in 2002 at a LeT safe house in Faisalabad, Pakistan. Because LeT has operated more freely than other militant groups in Pakistan, it serves as an appealing destination for would-be militants from the West (Tankel 2010, 4). Western intelligence believes that LeT recruits and trains foreigners, such as Pakistani-American David Hedley, who conspired with LeT to launch the 2008 Mumbai terrorist attacks. LeT's chief, Hafiz Saeed, spent two decades indoctrinating Pakistani students while a professor in one of the country's top engineering universities. Concerns raised that he has sympathizers within Pakistan's scientific community, especially in the nuclear and missile fields, may not be misplaced (Imran 2010b).

Within the LeT there is reported tension between those who believe that the organization should remain focused on India and Kashmir and those who welcome its expanded role in the Afghan insurgency. LeT fighters have been reportedly crossing into Afghanistan's Kunar and Nuristan Provinces to attack US, NATO, and Afghan forces (Gannon 2008).[13] Members also differ on whether the LeT should look inward by aligning more closely with those groups in Pakistan that have challenged the government or envision for itself a larger Islamic global role. Even if more cohesive than most jihadi groups, these divisions within LeT have accelerated the fracturing of the organization, leading some members to fall more deeply into the orbit of al-Qaeda and its affiliates (MacDonald 2010).

While LeT currently eschews attacks on the Pakistan state, its pooling of resources with the TTP in the tribal areas and other groups leads many Western observers to expect that elements of LeT will eventually be drawn into confrontation with the Pakistan government. For several years, LeT leaders have been frustrated with the government's restraint on their activities in Kashmir, and with Pakistan's broader India policies. There is increased indication that some LeT cadres are unwilling to toe the line of their long-time ISI overlords (MacDonald 2010). One fear is that LeT could join forces with other extremist groups in the Punjab in mobilizing widespread popular resentment in the country over rampant corruption and economic hardships. However improbable for the time being, LeT's reputation for charity, piety, and patriotism, together with its allegedly close ties to some senior officers of the Pakistani military and intelligence services, make it a potential leader in a radical transformation of the Pakistani state. Because LeT's ultimate goals seem incompatible with those of a liberal constitutional state, a break is probably inevitable, but its delay will likely make the government efforts to uproot the organization more difficult.

Bridging the Perceptual Gap

A stable, terrorist-free Afghanistan is impossible without a cooperative Pakistan, and aligning views on the dangers of militant Islamists is also essential to lessening the chances of nuclear proliferation and avoiding armed conflict between Pakistan and India. The strategic interests of Western countries are not expected to always overlap with those of Pakistan. But getting Pakistan to accept the idea that no group that uses terrorism as a weapon can be tolerated as a national asset remains indispensable to the West's confidence in Pakistan as a strategic partner in the region. To succeed, Pakistan needs to accept the idea that resolute actions have to be taken for the country's sake and not just to satisfy its Western allies and benefactors.

Because Western governments wish to continue being seen as committed to supporting democratic institutions in Pakistan, they prefer that extremist groups be confronted politically as well as militarily. A convergence of views with the West cannot begin without Pakistan's leaders making an effort to capture a popular narrative. This requires countering the influence of extremist groups by exposing them as cultural and national threats. It also calls for credible political reforms and development policies, especially in the grossly underdeveloped FATA. The popular hold of groups like LeT is unlikely to be broken without the Pakistani state being able to furnish competing and sustained social programs. Even while public attitudes may have turned against those extremist groups taking responsibility for violent attacks in Pakistani cities and against security forces, print and electronic media continue to impugn the West's motives in fighting terrorism in the region. Thus far, very few among the country's elected leadership or opinion makers have been willing to take the increasingly steep political risks needed to publicly defend cooperation with the West and contest the widely shared view that the Pakistani COIN and CT efforts against militants serve only American interests. None of the major candidates directly challenged Imran Khan, the latest serious contender for political power in Pakistan, during the 2013 national elections campaign when he rejected confrontation with the Pakistan's Taliban in favor of dialogue and earlier called the insurgency in Afghanistan a "holy war" (Boone 2012). It is the same reticence that keeps leaders from speaking out against right-wing extremism that was manifest following the January 2011 religiously motivated murder of Punjab Governor Salmaan Taseer and the killing of Federal Minorities Minister Shahbaz Bhatti two months later.[14] All this is adding to Pakistan's CT challenge and making the task to fight back against this menace even tougher.

For its part, the West needs to figure out how best to craft its aid policies and public diplomacy to help undercut the influence of militant groups and their supporters—to make it easier for the Pakistani state to succeed in countering terrorism and extremism. The willingness of American envoys to engage in dialogue with diverse publics has shown some promise as a means to reshape public attitudes. Well-designed aid programs may over time break down negative impressions of Western intentions and motives. Meanwhile, despite the serious strains that developed in US-Pakistani relations during 2011, Washington may have no alternative to continuing military assistance that improves the army's capacity to train and equip its forces to confront the militants. But money alone cannot compensate the Pakistani military enough to turn on extremist groups that are still perceived as having significant strategic value. Any hope of altering Pakistan's strategic calculations over its security needs may hinge on being able to do more to address Pakistan's concerns about India's intentions in Afghanistan.

Many in the West see improvement in relations between Pakistan and India as a necessary condition for gaining greater cooperation from the Pakistan military on Afghanistan and for Pakistan to find the space to tackle its internal militancy problem wholeheartedly. Only then is the army believed likely to feel secure enough to deploy greater numbers of troops to the northwest frontier and remove support from jihadi groups. The West has a limited role in encouraging the composite dialogue between Pakistan and India, and trying to convince New Delhi to pursue policies in Afghanistan that will help to relieve Pakistan's anxieties. A more immediate fear is that if extremist organizations again mount terrorist attacks deep within India, the Indian government will feel obliged to retaliate militarily and Pakistan will redeploy most of its forces from the Afghan border. Armed conflict is also likely to elevate the standing of jihadi organizations as a frontline force for the defense of the Pakistani nation against India.

The strongest possibility that Pakistan will cool on its Afghan proxies and favored Islamist groups may rest with the ability of a post-2014 Afghan government to demonstrate its staying power. This would require in the wake of sharply diminished international military presence and reduced assistance programs that the Kabul government successfully navigate a difficult security, economic, and political transition. An Afghan government strengthened by holding a credible presidential election in 2014 and parliamentary elections the following year would be a critical contributor to a desired political outcome. An expected residual force of troops from the United States and other countries left behind to help train Afghan security forces and deal with certain terrorist threats would demonstrate the international community's continued commitment to the country.

These developments would force Pakistan to reassess whether it made sense any longer to bank so heavily on a militant Pashtun force to secure Pakistan's future with its neighbor. Even if a broad coalition government is unlikely any time soon, the doubts already visible among Pakistan's strategists about the trustworthiness of the Afghan Taliban could lead to its marginalization in favor of a more politically oriented approach aimed at building ties with all ethnic groups. A stable, peaceful, and prospering Afghanistan could be a boon to Pakistan economically as a trade and energy corridor. Normalizing relations between Pakistan and Afghanistan would turn those extremist groups dedicated to jihad in Afghanistan into liabilities.

Unless the West and Pakistan bridge their differences over the nature and severity of the threats posed by Pakistan-based militant extremist groups, important building blocks in their security architecture will be put at risk. Progress in overcoming the perceptual gap about these groups may decide whether the West can salvage any semblance of success in Afghanistan and lower the vulnerability of Western societies to terrorist attack. Without a narrowing of differences, an increased future reliance on US predator drone strikes against militants inside Pakistan cannot be ruled out. Alienation of its

Western allies could also cut Pakistan's military off from equipment deemed vital to the country's defense as well as jeopardize its standing with its international creditors.

Above all, fuller cooperation with the West in dealing with its extremist groups requires Pakistan to reassess its security requirements, and especially what it needs to do for itself. A different sense of urgency often makes the West impatient with Pakistan. Yet even while many Western officials are convinced that Pakistan's top generals have come closer to their views about militant extremists, for the time being the Pakistan Army remains doubtful that its forces have the capability and popular support needed to act decisively. There are red lines for Pakistan's military and civilian leaders beyond which cooperation with the United States and others cannot be bought with any level of aid (Walsh 2011). In making demands on Pakistan, Western countries have also often underestimated the role of national pride and the Pakistani yearning for respect. American policymakers certainly failed to grasp how the use of armed drones and the issue of sovereignty would stir popular emotions. Pakistan's fear of Indian aggressive intentions embedded in its national psyche and the West's high anxiety over Pakistan and Afghanistan hosting terrorists with weapons of mass destruction also help to explain their often divergent strategic priorities. Yet, from a Western perspective, the most immediate contributor to a wide trust deficit is Pakistan's continuing policies toward its extremist groups that only poorly recognize the enemies that it shares with the West.

Notes

1. The TTP was estimated to have about twenty-five thousand fighters in 2010 (Mullick 2010b, 7).
2. "Taliban Vow to Follow in Bin Laden's Footsteps," *Dawn*, May 5, 2013, http://dawn.com/2013/05/02/pakistani-taliban-vow-to-follow-in-bin-ladens-footsteps/.
3. Also see Brulliard and Constable 2010.
4. See also "Factbox: Assassination Attempts against Pakistan's Musharraf," *Reuters*, July 6, 2007, www.reuters.com/article/2007/07/06/us-pakistan-musharraf-factbox-idUSL0649978720070706.
5. In both cases, the advance man for the plots was the Pakistani-American David Hedley, who was later picked up in Chicago in October 2009 and pleaded guilty to his role (Yousafzai, Moreau, and Dickey 2010).
6. "Militancy Poses Risk of Civil War, Warns Gen Kayani," *Express Tribune*, August 14, 2012, http://tribune.com.pk/story/421855/militancy-poses-risk-of-civil-war-warns-gen-kayani/. Just two years earlier in an interview General Kayani had declared that the Pakistan Army remains "India-centric" (Almeida 2010).

7. "Fighting Words: Army Chief Fires a Salvo for Democracy," *Express Tribune*, January 3, 2013, http://tribune.com.pk/story/542879/fighting-words-army-chief-fires-a-salvo-for-democracy/.

8. For an exposition of Pakistani goals in Afghanistan, see Yusuf, Yusuf, and Zaidi 2011.

9. According to a Pew Global Attitudes Survey published in June 2012, 74 percent of Pakistanis see the United States as an "enemy." For the survey's complete results, see Pew Research Center 2012.

10. "Pakistan: A Great Deal of Ruin in a Nation," *Economist*, March 31, www.economist.com/node/18488344.

11. For a fuller argument of this, see Weinbaum 2010.

12. A US investigation uncovered evidence that the LeT has identified 320 targets for terrorist attacks, only 20 of them in India (Ghosh 2010, 26; Rotella 2010).

13. Also see Fair 2009.

14. Salmaan Taseer was killed by his security guard, Mumtaz Qadri, for criticizing Pakistan's blasphemy law; allegedly his statements on this issue constituted blasphemy for some. Shockingly, his assassin received accolades from sections of Pakistani society. See "Lawyers Shower Roses for Governor's Killer," *Dawn*, January 5, 2011, http://beta.dawn.com/news/596300/lawyers-shower-roses-for-governors-killer.

CHAPTER 3

Counterinsurgency

The Myth of Sisyphus?

EJAZ HAIDER

THIS CHAPTER gives an overview of the major military operations conducted by the Pakistani state over the past decade in the country's insurgency-hit northwest. The focus is on military campaigns that could be best described as counterterrorism military operations (CMO), but there are references to issues broader than just the operational headaches that military commanders faced in conducting a war against elusive adversaries in one of the most difficult operational terrains in the world, Pakistan's Federally Administered Tribal Areas (FATA) bordering Afghanistan.

In early April 2002, two brigades from the Pakistan Army's XI Corps were first deployed to the Tirah Valley in Khyber Agency and later to the Shawal Valley in North Waziristan Agency, both located in FATA. The induction, in addition to the standard deployment in the tribal areas of the paramilitary Frontier Corps (FC) wings, was meant to check the movement of al-Qaeda militants slipping into FATA following the American assault in Tora Bora in Afghanistan and, where and when necessary, to conduct selective operations against them. The military units were meant to boost the FC and generally wave the flag of Pakistan. The military deployed its troops in the area without any battle inoculation or training for conducting operations in such a difficult terrain against an adversary that was merged with the population. After starting poorly from this point, the military has learned on the job and done well in capturing physical space in the FATA; it did not do nearly as well in incorporating a broader counterinsurgency (COIN) agenda. Moreover, there is much greater need to improve counterterrorism (CT) efforts dealing with operations conducted by the police forces, especially in the urban centers. Such operations require a different set of priorities and measures that Pakistan has largely failed to take over the last decade. This reinforces the importance of coordination between various aspects of CT, lest even the gains made in one sector are reversed due to tardy performance in another.

The Pakistan Military's Many Challenges

Given that the Pakistani military's traditional threat lies on the eastern border with India, there was very little logistics infrastructure on the western front to support large-scale operational deployments of the kind Pakistan has had to undertake since 2004 and the kind of war it has fought since then. The only other time Pakistan had established active forward-defended localities in the tribal agencies through formal deployment was after the December 1979 Soviet occupation of Afghanistan. But at the time there were no additional elements added to army's XI Corps, which operated with its own two divisions.[1] During the 1980s, army troops were based in all the tribal agencies, so it is a popular misconception that Pakistan deployed its regular troops in FATA only in 2002. That said, this deployment was a conventional one and the army had no internal threat in FATA and did not conduct any operations in its own territory. Its posts along the border with Afghanistan were defensive in nature, and the control of the area was also meant to launch into Afghanistan the mujahideen, who were trained in FATA. Pakistan, the mujahideen, and the "free world" were on the same side against the Soviets.

At the time of the initial deployments in 2002, no one seemed to have realized that the al-Qaeda elements with the support of indigenous groups would come to dominate FATA or that, consequently, Pakistan was on its way to becoming a victim of a full-fledged insurgency that has since also resulted in hundreds of terrorist attacks across the country, targeting both civilians and security personnel. Since then, however, the XI Corps has become the largest formation of the Pakistan Army, subsuming under its operational command elements from other corps. Currently it has some eight-division strength beefed up by enhanced numbers of paramilitary FC whose total strength now exceeds fifty thousand troops is under the total control of the XI Corps.[2] While the exact order of battle and number of lower formations and the actual fighting elements are not a matter of public record, according to one available estimate, 140,000 army regulars and 30,000 FC personnel were deployed in FATA and its adjacent Khyber Pakhtunkhwa (KPK) province in 2010 (Mullick 2010b, 7).

As events unfolded, the military saw itself facing rising numbers of battle-hardened insurgents whose knowledge of the terrain, interior lines of communication, kinship and religious bonds, and ability to tightly couple itself with the population would make the army lose large swaths of territory in the tribal areas that run along the Durand Line, the Pakistan-Afghanistan border. Since hostilities broke out in 2002, every military operation in the tribal areas, minor or major, has resulted in a wave of attacks in Pakistan's urban centers, mostly suicide bombings, but also armed raids, and sometimes a combination of both. The frequency and deadliness of these attacks has increased since the military action against the Red Mosque in the capital city of Islamabad in July 2007, after which the militants vowed revenge.[3]

A decade after the US campaign in Afghanistan began, Pakistani civilian casualties stood at 37,000 while the military had lost over 2,795 personnel and had taken in more than 8,500 injured, some 25 percent of them maimed and disabled for life.[4] Multiple CMOs have also resulted in the killing and capture of approximately 18,000 militants. Additionally, according to various official estimates and statements, Pakistan has lost about $70 billion in direct and presumptive costs due to direct fighting and broader national economic losses.

The war has also deepened the fractures in Pakistani society, with people increasingly asking why Pakistan is fighting this war. The question reflects a deep irony inherent in Pakistan's "war on terror": the more aggressively that Pakistan targets militants, the more frequently they retaliate. It also does not help that terrorist groups attack key targets in central areas, and the presence of instant media coverage only adds to the spectacle. Not only does this further dent Pakistan's international image, but it also displays the frailty of the state's writ. These fractures are becoming more and more obvious, and the world now considers Pakistan-based militant groups to be an international threat and worries whether Pakistan has the capacity to handle the rising tide of militancy.

The war has also encouraged preexisting but perhaps previously latent sentiments of anti-Americanism. Many Pakistanis now view the United States as an adversary that has placed a terrible burden on Pakistan for trying to prop up and sustain a failed Afghan regime on the one hand and allowing Pakistan's traditional adversary India to play an increasing role in Afghanistan on the other. This resentment is given a fillip by unilateral US actions. Sentiments like these make the conduct of the current war even more controversial.[5] Thus, for the last decade Pakistan has oscillated between taking military action against multiple militant groups and talking to them in order to wean them from mounting insurgent and terrorist attacks inside Pakistan.

Pakistani military and intelligence agencies also claim with increased frequency that the groups attacking Pakistani civilians and military are funded and supported by hostile agencies from Afghanistan.[6] The perceptions are as follows: the groups attacking Pakistan are funded and supported by a combination of Afghan, Indian, and US intelligence agencies; the United States is planning to retain bases and some military presence in Afghanistan beyond 2014, the date of its drawdown from the conflict;[7] the United States wants India to play a more active role in Afghanistan as a counterweight to both Pakistan and China; and the war that Pakistan is currently fighting has been imposed on it to pressure it to succumb to the US and Indian plan to defang its military and render it subservient to India within the region. The corollary belief: Pakistan should not fight this war.

It should be obvious that this view is somewhat contradictory. If we can acknowledge that the groups fighting Pakistan are supported by hostile agencies, then there is no way Pakistan can talk itself out of the situation. It will have to fight, though it is a different argument how that fight must be conducted and whether Pakistan has so far been able to do that effectively. Groups garnering support from hostile agencies will most likely not be amenable to talking and ceasing fire, especially if they retain space for their activities. In any case, it does not make sense to call for a dialogue with militant groups and simultaneously brand them as foreign sponsored. Also, most of these groups exploit religious and sectarian fault lines within Pakistani society, attacks against the Shia community being a case in point. This is a proactive agenda that dates back to the early 1980s, much before the US invasion of Afghanistan. These groups cannot be disarmed merely through talking since their use of violence as a tool in practicing and promoting their exclusionary ideologies is deeply rooted.

In Western literature, Pakistan's military efforts are often compared to US efforts in Afghanistan and, to a lesser extent, in Iraq. These contexts are not entirely comparable. One crucial factor that complicates the military's efforts as compared to US campaigns in Afghanistan and Iraq is that the Pakistani military is fighting its own people, not just in some areas in the northwest—which shares a long, porous border with Afghanistan where a coalition of forty-three states is fighting another insurgency and failing[8]—and it is also facing a terror campaign in its major urban centers. This is no trivial distinction.

The three environments are similar in that the respective militaries are fighting an irregular conflict in which the zones of war and peace are enmeshed (Smith 2007). There is no defined battle space in such wars, and the adversary can strike anywhere, anytime. The difference is born out of the centrality of the local populations and their outlook in any such operations. Most literature on the subject is written in COIN environments, although the term is often fungible and fully applicable to the context in the Pakistani northwest. In such irregular warfare, strength of the COIN force must be assessed by the extent of support from the population (Nagl 2002;

Galula 2006; Kilcullen 2006b; Van Creveld 2008). The greater the use of force, the higher the potential for collateral damage and alienation of the people and their possible support to the insurgent. While foreign militaries operating on invaded lands cannot dismiss the importance of gaining support from the local population, an army fighting its own citizens in its own territory has to be far more mindful of dislocations and collateral damage. This was clearly the case with the Pakistan Army's operations in the initial years where it did not go beyond targeted operations even when the military logic demanded otherwise precisely because it did not want large-scale upheavals in the tribal agencies. That its targeted policy was still seen as excessive and ultimately led to an insurrection, justified by the fact that the state was killing its own citizens, only helps underscore the difficulties any military faces in such a situation. This is by no means to trivialize the very serious challenges foreign militaries face in terms of being seen as occupiers, as less attuned to the local cultures, and perhaps as less sensitive to collateral losses. Ultimately, though, foreign militaries have an exit option with few lasting repercussions in case of failure; a state fighting on its own soil does not have this luxury. This fundamentally changes a counterinsurgent's outlook to the battle at hand. Moreover, as has been done in Afghanistan and Iraq, the US-led campaigns used their handpicked national governments, beholden to their interests, as buffers against local dissent. Again, a state fighting domestic insurgencies and terrorism is unable to hide behind a potentially more amenable face.

Three other factors make the Pakistani situation different from that in Afghanistan and Iraq; these ought to be kept in mind when looking at the "success" graph. First, when the military deployed to FATA in early-2002, it was ill-equipped and ill-prepared to fight the kind of war it has since had to fight. Its resource base has not really expanded since then, even though its ability to fight has definitely improved.[9] Not only did it lack the resources for a costly CMO effort, at least in the initial years, but the objectives and timelines were not of its choosing. The second factor deals with the question of the extent to which a state like Pakistan can—given its many constraints—address an internal threat, despite notching partial operational successes, when that threat is also determined by exogenous factors, in this case the insurgency in Afghanistan that shows no signs of abating. Third, how effectively can a state put down an insurgency when the insurgent groups, in order to relieve pressure on themselves, can mount terrorist attacks across the country and do so effectively because their ability to recruit people to their cause is greater than the capacity of the state to preempt and respond to such a threat?

In many ways the last factor is the most important because it points to the manner in which Pakistan has developed as a state and society and how that evolution has dovetailed with the security policies pursued by the state. There is a vast and growing corpus of literature on this evolution within Pakistan and, generally, in the Islamic world (Roy 1994; Kepel 1986, 2000; Sivan 1990; Nasr 1994, 2001; Alavi and Halliday 1988; Lieven 2011; Lodhi 2011). In Pakistan, Islamization begun by Prime Minister Zulfikar Ali Bhutto during the 1970s was later intensified under the military dictator General Zia ul-Haq in the following decade. It served much to change the direction of state and society. While the relationship between state and society has always been tenuous, worsened not only by the state's inability to tackle ethnic, religious, and sectarian diversities but also by the civil–military imbalance, the introduction of religion into constitutional legal space has created a mindset that allows large sections of society to think and act in ways that are suprastate and therefore inimical to state interests and its ability to establish its writ. Sections of the population, which also include active militant groups, refuse to accept the state's writ where they feel the state is impinging on their religious obligations. Jihad against the "infidels" is one such area.

While the Pakistani state is part of the international coalition to fight al-Qaeda and its affiliates, these groups continue to fight on behalf of such entities and to attack the Pakistani state itself for being part of a coalition that directly attacks the Muslims and must therefore be branded as infidel itself. Sunni-Deobandi groups have routinely attacked and killed Shia Muslims because they refuse to accept the operation of state laws that considers such acts to be murderous. A police guard entrusted to protect the governor of Punjab, Pakistan's most populous province, unloaded twenty-seven bullets into the governor's body because he considered him to be blasphemous. The governor's murderer was hailed by sections of people as a hero. Within two months of this gruesome murder, another federal minister, a Christian, was also killed for opposing the blasphemy law. There are innumerable examples of this kind. This has resulted in the state being "hard" rather than "strong," to use Nazih Ayubi's definition in his remarkable study of the Arab states (Ayubi 1996).[10]

Pakistan Military's Experience in the Northwest: How Has It Fared?

Any study of Pakistan's CT efforts must bear in mind the multiple constraints of the state. It is not enough to identify what Pakistan has been unable to do. More important is the effort to identify what it has been able to do and why it has not been able to do what it is still required to attain. Given the constraints, the operational part of Pakistan's military campaign has, mostly, proved more successful than US-led efforts in Afghanistan. The question is whether operational successes and the capturing of physical space can be translated into sustainable success. This section will look at the Pakistan military's efforts so far, dividing it into three distinct phases.

Phase I: Operations al-Meezan, Kalosha I, and Kalosha II

Operation al-Meezan is the overhang under which hundreds of other large- and small-scale operations have been conducted, each code-named separately. The first phase of these operations, from early 2002 to 2005, was sporadic and focused on targeted operations. These included ground and airborne operations, often with support from helicopter gunships and later the Pakistan Air Force. The activity ranged from snap actions to raids and extraction operations. Some were focused on smaller areas while others involved larger bodies of troops and support elements. But all of them depended on intelligence, generally provided by technical means from the United States and sometimes corroborated by human intelligence. Pakistani troops also conducted operations when they came under fire or were attacked in a particular area.

While the deployment of troops in and around FATA gradually increased, the fighting elements were unprepared for the fight that awaited them. The government of Gen. Pervez Musharraf, who was both the army chief and the president, made no attempt to develop a comprehensive COIN policy. There was also no policy to hold territory and exploit or conduct sustained operations; nor was any attempt made to train troops in irregular warfare. This is why even when operations were successful, as some were, they failed to win over the population or effectively curb the spread of the militant groups in FATA and its adjoining areas. Their nature remained tactical. Given the classical definition of COIN operations, this phase can be better termed as purely military-led CT because it did not involve any effort to control the area fully or to pull it into the political and socioeconomic mainstream. There was no attempt to apply the municipal law to the border agencies of FATA or to change any of its traditional structures.

Operations were conducted in spurts, with objectives determined by American advisors attached to the Pakistan Army's military operations directorate. Musharraf had also made secret deals with the United States and allowed the CIA to place drones on bases inside Pakistan (Haider 2011).[11] The American objectives were to take out al-Qaeda and Afghan Taliban leadership hiding in FATA and moving along the Durand Line, and to degrade the leadership and, where possible, kill the Afghan Taliban fighters to reduce their ability to cross over into Afghanistan and conduct operations there. Musharraf went along with this strategy without much regard to the consequences or the fact that without plugging the operational side into a more comprehensive strategy to bring the tribal areas under effective control, al-Qaeda and its affiliates would be successful in using the vast ungoverned stretches of FATA to strengthen themselves and capture socioeconomic space in the region.

The army deployment was initially thin, and most targeted operations relied on the use of the Special Services Group (SSG) ferried by an aging fleet of army aviation helicopters. These were primarily raids and extraction operations, though some of them managed to kill and net high-value al-Qaeda targets. Overall, tactical CT efforts were prized over a holistic COIN strategy. This allowed al-Qaeda and its foreign affiliates like the Islamic Movement of Uzbekistan (IMU) and Eastern Turkestan Islamic Movement (ETIM) to entrench themselves in the area and also link up with indigenous extremist groups like the Jaish-e Mohammed (JeM), Lashkar-e Jhangvi (LeJ), and Harakat-ul-Jihad-al-Islami (HuJI), who were traditionally focused on Indian Kashmir or on promoting sectarian agendas. The primary deployments in the area were the paramilitary FC, Levies, and the local police, called Khasadars. This force had no expertise to deal with the highly trained and motivated extremist militants. In addition to these groups, al-Qaeda also managed to finance and influence many local tribes like the Mehsud, Dawar, Wazirs, and others.[12]

The first major retaliation from the militants in phase I came in June 2002 when al-Qaeda fighters attacked a security post in the Azam Warsak area of South Waziristan Agency near agency headquarters in Wana and killed nearly a dozen soldiers. The war had begun. From that point onward, it has been a contest not just for space but for winning over the local tribes. In the early days of the contest, the Ahmadzai Wazirs, the dominant tribe in South Waziristan Agency, sided with the al-Qaeda militants. The tribes, enraged by the US invasion of Afghanistan, considered fighting the United States a duty perceived for reasons of both religious and Pashtun affinity with the Afghan Taliban. This was not altogether surprising since tribes have helped each other in situations of adversity. This came to pass during the anti-Soviet jihad in Afghanistan during the 1980s. This time, because the Pakistani state actively sought to prevent the tribes from joining the war in Afghanistan, not only did these tribes support the Afghan insurgency but they also turned FATA into a hotbed of insurgency against the state itself.[13]

Washington was increasing pressure on Pakistan to conduct operations against al-Qaeda leaders and fighters hiding in and moving along the Durand

Line on the eastern side. The al-Qaeda attack in Azam Warsak precipitated the fight. On June 22, 2002, shortly after the al-Qaeda attack, Pakistan launched its first major operation in the Azam Warsak area. The bulk of the fighting force was composed of FC supported by elements from the army. The operation left eleven FC personnel and six foreigners, believed to be Chechen and Uzbek, dead. The bulk of the foreign militants escaped. The operation was largely a failure because the troops had no support to speak of from the local tribes.

Following the operation, the army changed its tactic. In a meeting on June 27, officers met with the tribal *jirga* and assured them that the security forces will not take unilateral action against al-Qaeda militants without taking the tribes into confidence. The army also told the tribes that it wanted them to ensure that no support was extended to these fighters. The tribes, according to this plan, were to take action against foreign fighters and anyone harboring them. The army would act only if the tribes failed to keep their end of the deal (Shahzad 2011).

Washington, however, kept up the pressure. Despite the deal, according to local sources, the army continued with small-scale operations that attempted to kill or capture al-Qaeda fighters. The army, for its part, blames the tribes for continuing to harbor these militants. The truth, say some old FATA hands, lies somewhere between these two narratives.[14] Given the presence of militants in the area, the army also began dealing with the tribes directly instead of using the old system of the political administration—whereby the political agent acted as the state's formal representative to each FATA agency and dealt with such matters—that had held the balance in the region. A separate attempt in 2002 to reform FATA through a committee report that suggested a number of measures was allowed to gather dust because the Musharraf government argued that the time was not propitious for those reforms, given the situation in the region. Whether those reforms would have allowed the government to tackle the growing militancy better is a hotly debated topic between the pro-reform lobby and those advocating for continuation of the status quo.

The situation continued to deteriorate throughout 2002 and 2003 with the army deployments steadily increasing. By 2004, the army had deployed some eighty thousand regular army troops to the South and North Waziristan agencies and their adjacent Frontier Regions. There were two divisional headquarters, eight brigade headquarters, twenty infantry battalions, one SSG battalion, six engineers, and two signals battalions. The total deployment strength included thirty-nine FC wings in addition.[15] The bulk of these troops manned checkpoints and posts on strategic locations. They were also available for raids, extraction operations, and snap actions. This deployment was complete by mid-2003.[16] Earlier, SSG personnel were ferried to the operational area aboard MI-17 helicopters from Dhamiyal air base near Rawalpindi. The forward refueling and rearming point was in Mianwali in Punjab province. Later, for some time the forward operating base was shifted to Bannu, the last settled town east of FATA's North Waziristan agency.

By this time al-Qaeda had begun to bankroll the local Ahmadzai Yargulkhel Wazirs, and while there were many local commanders, Nek Mohammad, a former Wazir-Taliban commander, emerged as the main leader of the local Taliban.[17] The army launched many small operations against him and his al-Qaeda backers but failed to capture him or any other high-value al-Qaeda target, one of whom, the leader of the IMU, Tahir Yuldashev, was operating in the area rather audaciously.

During this time there were also many attempts to hold *jirgas* to get Nek Mohammad's group to withdraw support from al-Qaeda fighters. Intelligence was also coming in that dozens of Ahmadzai tribesmen might be sheltering al-Qaeda fighters (one report put the number at over seventy). In October 2003, the army launched a commando assault supported by helicopter gunships in Baghar, near Angoor Adda. The operation netted many al-Qaeda fighters, including Abdur Rehman Kennedy, and it was conducted under the command of Maj. Gen. Faisal Alvi (retired) who was later killed in retaliation in Islamabad by al-Qaeda (Shahzad 2011, 3, 93, 99; Z. Hussain 2010). The operation sent al-Qaeda into disarray, but the army could not take advantage of the situation because al-Qaeda, in a very clever move, got the Lal Masjid (Red Mosque) in Islamabad, a mosque with some religious and political clout in the middle of Pakistan's capital, to issue a fatwa signed by five hundred clerics across Pakistan denouncing army operations against the "mujahideen" and apostatizing the soldiers taking part in these operations. In many cases, parents of soldiers refused to accept the bodies of their sons, and clerics would not lead the funeral prayers of killed soldiers and officers (Shahzad 2011, 41–43).

This caused many desertions and court martial proceedings in the army (Shahzad 2011, 42–43). While the army's morale plummeted, the militants managed to regroup. Another operation in January 2004 in the Azam Warsak area did not manage to achieve its objectives, and the militants eventually surrounded the raiding force. Subsequently after the army–FC units had broken through the cordon, they were ambushed. That same night, the militants attacked the army camp in Wana with rockets and mortars. Throughout this period, the security forces were alternating between trying to talk to the militants and operating against them when army units were either attacked or when the state forces received information on militant activity and concentrations. This policy has been much criticized by Western analysts but the criticism fails to capture the central dilemma: Pakistan was operating against al-Qaeda and foreign elements while trying to avoid, as much as it could, armed action against its own people. But the state had underestimated two factors: the ability of al-Qaeda at that point to ideologically motivate sections of Pakistani society, and the resentment among Pakistanis in general to the US war in Afghanistan, the latter not helped by the fact that the Pakistani leadership at the time continued to portray it as America's war. Al-Qaeda capitalized on this resentment and presented the initiative as jihad; by that logic, the Pakistani military—trying to keep the area clear of al-Qaeda and other militants—was looked upon as a mercenary force in the pay of the infidel US government. In this phase of the war, the Pakistani state and the military lost out badly to the extremist narrative.

The 2004 Operation Kalosha (I and II) in South Waziristan, in an area comprising more than nineteen square miles, is a good example of Pakistan's strategy at the time. Intelligence reports indicated heightened al-Qaeda activity in the Wana Valley, the area from Wana to Kalosha in the west and Karikot in the north and Shin Warsak in the south.[18] Local administration also confirmed these reports through its own network of informants. The army and FC launched an operation against al-Qaeda and its harborers, like Nek Mohammad, Noor-ul-Islam, Haji Mohammad Sharif, and some other local leaders. The situation soon escalated after the army lost sixteen personnel in initial fighting and fourteen others were captured by the militants. The militants destroyed army trucks, some armored personnel carriers, and mortars. After the initial reversals, the army brought in reinforcements and Cobra gunships, and in subsequent raids and sectoral battles it killed a number of local and foreign fighters. The operation also disrupted a major al-Qaeda command and control center. The troops also found a network of tunnels that had earlier been used by the militants to attack the army and captured electronic equipment, ammunition, and other supplies.

Lt. Gen Mohammad Safdar, then commander of the XI Corps in Peshawar, declared victory only to see army–FC bases come under attack in Shah Alam, Barmal, Sarwekai, Angoor Adda, Laddha, Tiarza, and Wana. This was the manifestation of the "balloon effect": put them down here and they will pop up somewhere else. The balloon effect has been a recurring theme in this war. After the operation, the army made a deal with Nek Mohammad at Shakai, an agreement that broke down before the ink on it had dried. The government's demands in the agreement highlighted both the dilemma and its strategy: get rid of foreign fighters and prevent them from infecting the region by making local alliances, and avoid—as much as possible—fighting the local tribes (Khattak 2012). The pattern remained unchanged throughout 2004 and 2005, with the army conducting multiple targeted operations in South and North Waziristan. Most of these operations were tactically successful in that they managed to kill and net al-Qaeda fighters and their supporters in a local area. But none of these operations had any significant strategic impact on the growing strength of the militant groups. In some ways these operations can be likened to the joint special operations command night raids in Afghanistan that, despite tactical successes, have had little effect on the overall situation in Afghanistan.[19]

Phase II: Operations Sherdil, Rah-e-Rast, Rah-e-Nijat

In the following years, militant groups kept expanding their hold on FATA and in Swat (Malakand), much deeper into Pakistan and fairly close to the main highways, both the National Highway and Motorway I, which connect the province of KPK to the capital territory of Islamabad, the seat of the federal government, and Rawalpindi, which houses the army's general headquarters, and further south to the rest of the country. The situation reached a point where, after the militants controlled Malakand and Lower Dir in KPK, they began to descend into Buner, about sixty miles from Islamabad (Constable 2009). There was much debate about what to do. An earlier half-hearted operation in Malakand, Rah-e-Haq I, followed by smaller actions code-named Rah-e-Haq II and III, did little to break the momentum of the militants except for a brief period between November 2007 and April 2008.

In February 2008, Pakistan conducted general elections and a new civilian government took office with the Pakistan People's Party (PPP) at the helm and its coalition partner, the Awami National Party (ANP), in government in KPK.[20] The ANP wanted to make a deal with the militants in Malakand. The idea was to concede to their demand of implementing the Sharia and get them to disarm as a quid pro quo (Haider 2009). That did not happen. Additionally, a video emerged showing the Taliban flogging a young girl (Walsh 2009). While this video was circulating and shown on national television, Sufi Muhammed, the head of Tehreek-e-Nafaz-e-Shariat-e-Mohammadi (TNSM), the cleric with whom the government was dealing and who was supposed to get the Malakand-based Taliban to disarm, made a speech in Mingora, the main city of Malakand, and rejected the central foundations of the Pakistani state, including its constitution (Roggio 2009a). In tandem, these developments created a public uproar in Pakistan and, with it, the space in which the military found support for a sweeping operation in the area. By April 2009, Operation Rah-e-Rast, targeted at the Taliban presence in Swat and adjoining areas, had begun. Some 3.5 million people were internally displaced by the operation (the United Nations estimated 2.4 million), making it one of the biggest internal displacements ever (IPRI 2009). It is a measure of the relative efficiency with which the operation was launched that the army not only cleared the area in about six weeks of an operation that was three-pronged and consisted of multiple smaller operations, including sectoral battles, snap actions, raids, and so on, but also managed to get the internally displaced persons, uprooted because of the operations, back home in about three months.

The operation also established for the first time the army's reputation as a force concerned with the growing internal security threat and prepared to commit resources to addressing and eliminating it. Prior to this, owing largely to the long history of the army's use of militancy as a strategic asset and its failure to quash the Pakistani Taliban's rise post-9/11, the local population was suspicious of how sincerely the army was approaching the CMOs. The population also remained ambivalent about the Taliban's threat, given that they had successfully conflated their designs with the anti-American sentiments prevailing in the country. The flogging video, however, transformed this sentiment overnight, and the popular support for concerted action against the militants stuck throughout phase II. A key role in achieving this was played by the media. Reflective of the ambivalence about the militant threat for reasons to do with the religiously inclined popular narrative in Pakistan (see chapter 8 in this volume for a discussion on the issue), the media personalities abruptly switched to promoting the state's perspective and actively exposed the brutality of the Taliban. The lesson the military took away from this period was that its operations could only succeed when fully backed by public opinion.

Interestingly enough, unlike Operation Rah-e-Rast, which unfolded in the full public glare, the phase of sustained operations that aimed to clear and hold the territory had actually begun earlier in September 2008 when the FC and army troops launched Operation Sherdil in the Bajaur Agency in FATA and cleared much of the area, establishing proper posts to ensure the militant groups could not regain physical possession of the area. The gains in Bajaur were partially lost when the provincial government forced the federal government into making a deal with the TNSM, allowing the militants to relocate and create trouble in some parts of Bajaur. But after the main operations in Malakand, Lower Dir, and Buner, the army and FC troops launched two more operations in the Damadola area of Bajaur Agency and the territory was cleared by March 2010.

The most important operation against the center of gravity of the TTP, however, was launched in South Waziristan in the Mehsud tribe's triangle.

Elements from three divisions (7th, 9th, and 14th) participated in Operation Rah-e-Nijat and advanced on three axes beginning October 17, 2009. By mid-November the army–FC troops had secured the area and had established their own posts. The operation was a major blow to the TTP and its al-Qaeda affiliates, both Punjabi groups, LeJ and JeM, as well as foreign fighters like Uzbeks, Chechens, Uighurs, and Arabs. The army had learned from its operations in other areas while the TTP had failed to adapt to the army's new tactics. The army also managed to counter the TTP propaganda and retained public support for its operations.

The most important aspect of the second phase of operations was the army's clear conception of what it had to do, which it postulates as "clear, hold, build, and transfer." In Malakand, it has succeeded in its first two phases and partially succeeded in the last two. In other areas abutting Afghanistan, which are all tribal agencies of FATA, it has managed well the first two phases of clear and hold but has had partial success in the build phase and has yet to transfer the administration of the area fully to the civilian authorities. Even so, in most cases it has done fairly well to rehabilitate displaced persons. It is also running centers in Malakand, in collaboration with nongovernmental agencies and civil society groups that seek to reform and reintegrate captured Taliban fighters, especially those that were coercively recruited by the TTP and its affiliates (Temple-Raston 2013).

One factor that has directly helped the army gain the upper hand in the tribal areas is the late-2008 decision to establish three battle inoculation training centers, which it calls CTCs (counterterrorism centers). As opposed to the first phase in which the army was conducting targeted operations and inducting troops without training them to fight the new irregular war, the army took the crucial decision under the current army chief, Gen. Ashfaq Parvez Kayani, to train the troops before putting them into battle. The CTCs have greatly helped in inoculating and acclimatizing troops in the conduct of these operations. The army has also learned on the job and through several reverses, including humiliating experiences where the Pakistani Taliban managed to capture large bodies of troops. The FC was trained and equipped better, and Maj. Gen. Tariq Khan, as inspector general of the FC, did much to instill confidence in his troops. The FC, which had earlier been succumbing to the Taliban, has since emerged as an impressive fighting force, though much needs to be done to improve its equipment, standard operating procedures, and battle drills to bring down the number of casualties.

Phase III: Preventing Militant Resurgence

The military operations being carried out have now entered the third phase. This phase is essentially about conducting targeted operations while continuing to hold ground and build and rehabilitate. In many areas, the Taliban still retains the ability to mount suicide attacks and occasional surprise raids on isolated posts. The army and the FC have been conducting several small-scale operations in Khyber, Kurram, and Orakzai agencies. But the main difference now is that the army and FC troops hold the ground rather than going in for a particular target and then leaving the area unattended. That strategy failed badly, and this lesson was learned through terrible losses. However, as argued earlier, the overall strategy of military operations has done what it could. There is not much more that can be done in that area except to retain ground and keep acting as and when required. Militant groups, having been squeezed in FATA, now rely on urban terrorism. That is the phase of this war that has to be dealt with differently, and it involves a sound urban-based CT strategy involving a capable police force and effective intelligence. It also requires a sound legal regime to prosecute terrorists that are captured. The terrorist groups have used urban terrorism effectively; one reason the army has not conducted an operation in the North Waziristan Agency, the last TTP stronghold in FATA, is because it knows the reprisals will come in the urban centers, and that is where the state lacks capacity badly. The next phase of this war, therefore, has to involve reformed police and intelligence agencies, a process that has yet to start in earnest.

Briefly, three important areas, each discussed in greater detail elsewhere in this book, have gone largely unattended. First, despite a feeble attempt in 2002 to reform the police, not much has happened on the ground either in terms of rethinking recruitment and training or in obtaining the equipment required to create an efficient force. The police's stock among the people continues to be low, and the force, broadly speaking, remains ill-trained and poorly equipped to deal with internal security threats. Debating what needs to be done requires a sizeable study in itself. Second, no attempt has been made to review the laws related to acts of terrorism, and as yet there is no viable national level legal framework either to cover the military operations that have been conducted so far or to deal with alleged insurgents and terrorists captured during various operations and raids.[21] Third, there is no comprehensive national security strategy that identifies the various threats and devises policies to deal with them.

The one serious attempt to have an authority that would serve as the nerve center of CT efforts both in terms of conceptualizing and formulating a broad policy, and operationally as a national intelligence-sharing commission to coordinate the efforts of all civil and military intelligence agencies, was the creation of the National Counter Terrorism Authority (NACTA). NACTA was well conceived. It had a broad mandate as an umbrella organization to coordinate the activities of the three main intelligence agencies, the Intelligence Bureau, the Federal Investigation Agency (FIA), and the Inter-Services Intelligence (ISI). It was also tasked with conceiving a strategy beyond the strictly operational. NACTA officials began by holding meetings across Pakistan to consult public intellectuals and professionals on how to successfully create a counternarrative. But the initiative never really took off for three main reasons: there were never enough funds for the authority to be viable, it got entangled in petty bureaucratic turf wars with the Interior Ministry wanting NACTA to be placed under the ministry as opposed to directly reporting to the prime minister, and the all-powerful ISI continued to operate on its own. The latest suggestion seems to be to reduce its mandate and have it as an appendage to the prime minister's secretariat. That would defeat the entire purpose of the exercise (Bukhari 2011a).

The strategy of the groups attacking Pakistani interests has been to exact reprisals in the urban centers. The more the military squeezes them in the tribal areas, the more intense the attacks become in the cities and towns of Pakistan. NACTA was vital as an overall coordinating body, in addition to reorganizing the police. An additional problem in this regard is the approach of the military. Whereas army officers under General President Musharraf would lament the lack of capacity of the police, the army continues to be averse to doing anything to enhance the real capacity of the police beyond training some units of the elite force. There is also reluctance on the part of different intelligence outfits to share information.

Another hurdle in enhancing the capacity of the police or even letting it do its work is the role of Pakistan's premier intelligence agency, the ISI. The ISI is far more advanced than all other intelligence agencies combined. It also guards its turf fiercely and acts as the master of all other outfits. Its interference in police investigations and interrogation has often led to legal problems for the police, who under law are required to take the lead on registering the first information report of any criminal or unlawful activity. Very often culprits have managed to walk off because the courts found that there was no legal framework under which the suspects were apprehended or even interrogated.

CT Dilemmas and the Way Forward

Having examined the Pakistan military's performance, we can conclude that it has learned on the job after making a terrible start and has done fairly well in terms of conducting military operations since 2009. The CT aspect of the military's role, then, has produced satisfactory results, although of late the TTP has shown its resilience by striking the state where it remains weak—the cities, where army cannot be used. The broader COIN strategy that includes addressing the ideological, socioeconomic, and political root causes of the rise of Islamist militancy, however, is a whole different matter where the state has done far less. Even though these broader issues remain outside the scope of this chapter, it is important to note that a permanent solution will remain elusive unless CT is complemented by a holistic COIN effort.

If Pakistan has to make use of its relative successes through military operations, it has to establish an overarching body to coordinate CT efforts. The failed NACTA has to become a success but that would require giving it real authority. This body must then formulate an overall strategy, identifying key areas where CT efforts are to be strengthened. A reorganization of the police is also necessary. The military operations have achieved what they possibly could—that is, capturing physical space. Now the effort must move from the tribal areas to the urban centers because the real contest is unfolding all across Pakistan. This change of direction is also important because the terrorist groups are in no position to actually hold territory as they did, and could, until 2009. But they still retain the ability to strike back, even if sporadically. Until this ability is diminished, the military will not be able to turn physical dominance of terrain into psychological and socioeconomic dominance. Troops for the battle in the towns and cities will have to be drawn from the police and civilian intelligence agencies. This is the only way to expand the military's CT success into broader CT gains, and eventually into a comprehensive COIN victory.

Notes

1. The actual operational role of XI Corps is that of a strike corps in case of hostilities with India. XI Corps is one of the four strike corps in a war against India, a concept that was developed by former army chief Gen. Mirza Aslam Beg and exercised in 1990 under code name Exercise Zarb-e Momin.

2. These numbers are based on the author's interviews with senior officers who were either part of the corps' operations or commanded the corps at some point.

3. The Lal Masjid (Red Mosque) siege led to the killing of more than one hundred people inside the mosque compound, many of whom were seminary students hailing from Swat. The militants, led by al-Qaeda, took advantage of this episode by painting the state as committing atrocities. Authorities found letters written by Ayman al-Zawahiri to Maulana Aziz and Rashid Ghazi, the chief of Lal Masjid and his brother, respectively, urging them to lead a full-scale revolt against the government. After the mosque was secured, al-Zawahiri quickly condemned the action, and in a four-minute videotape titled "The Aggression against Lal Masjid" urged Pakistanis to rise up against the government and avenge the atrocity. "Al Qaeda Issues Pakistan Threat," *BBC*, July 11, 2007, http://news.bbc.co.uk/2/hi/south_asia/6293914.stm.

4. "Forgotten Victims of Pakistan's Taliban War," *Express Tribune*, April 25, 2011, http://tribune.com.pk/story/156227/forgotten-victims-of-pakistans-taliban-war/. By mid-2013, the total casualty count had reached more than forty-seven thousand.

5. The majority of political parties in Pakistan are opposed to operations in FATA and press for negotiating with the Pakistani Taliban. They have held all-party conferences to promote the notion of talks but remain unclear on the grounds for negotiations, given that the Taliban rejects the very concept and institutions on which the state is currently based. Even so, one of the most pressing themes for the 2013 national election campaigns was the question of how to eliminate terrorist attacks. There is little appetite for more war, and the military is unlikely to get a free hand to conduct operations, a problem toward which the army chief Gen. Ashfaq Parvez Kayani pointed to in his speech on Martyrs' Day, April 30, 2013. The text of the speech is available on the Inter-Services Public Relations website at www.ispr.gov.pk/front/main.asp?o = t-week_view&id = 1692.

6. This belief comes across clearly in conversations with military officials. They also produce evidence of cross-border support to anti-Pakistan militants. The author gathered this information through off-the-record briefings to which he was party.

7. This has been confirmed by the United States although the exact number of residual forces has not been determined yet (Zengerle 2013).

8. While voluminous literature produced in the West and elsewhere argues that America's Afghanistan venture has failed, nothing illustrates the failure and the resultant frustration better than this *New York Times* editorial, "Time to Pack Up," published in the newspaper's Sunday edition, October 13, 2012, www.nytimes.com/2012/10/14/opinion/sunday/time-to-pack-up.html?pagewanted = all.

9. The army has put in place three battle inoculation training centers, and all troops inducted in the operational area have to undergo four to six weeks of training; officers and men are made aware of the importance of deradicalization strategies; the battle tactics have improved as has the optimal use of equipment. These facts have been gleaned from various briefings under Chatham House Rules; the author's interviews with former inspector general of the Frontier Corps, Lt. Gen. Tariq Khan, and former director general of Inter Services Public Relations, Maj. Gen. Athar Abbas; the author's travels to FATA; and talks with various officers and other ranks.

10. Also see Alavi 1972.

11. Musharraf, in a recent interview with CNN, accepted that he had cut a secret deal with the United States on the use of drones. The deal has been a widely known fact, but no other official has conceded this publicly. Earlier, cables from the US embassy in Islamabad released by WikiLeaks mentioned a discussion between former US ambassador to Pakistan Anne Patterson and former prime minister Yousaf Raza Gillani and interior minister Rehman Malik that revealed that even the PPP-led government carried on with this policy. See Robertson and Botelho 2013 and Lister 2010.

12. Arguably the best description of the local tribes and cultures is in Sir Olaf Caroe's *The Pathans* (1958). Caroe served as governor of India's Northwest Frontier Province in the last two years leading to Indian independence in 1947.

13. The jihad against the Soviets and the communist regime backed by them brought Islamist fighters to this region from around the world. The induction of these jihadis into this region gradually changed the socioeconomic and power structures of FATA. A new element, the militant commander charged with Islamist zeal, had crept into the equation. He was part of the larger "Islamist International" that the jihad had created and was averse to the statist framework. He was sans boundaries (Coll 2004; Hussain 2007; Abbas 2005).

14. Saleem Safi, Rahimullah Yusufzai, and Ambassador Rustam Shah, interviewed by the author, 2011.

15. This information was gathered through a number of interviews with senior military officials who either commanded in FATA or were in positions that allowed them access to this information.

16. Most divisions and brigade headquarters come under the operational command of XI Corps on rotation. They are drawn from other formations. Initially, only infantry battalions were inducted into battle but that policy has been changed because units were being rotated very fast. Now even other arms and support elements are being inducted in an infantry role to the operational areas.

17. For Nek's profile, see Khan 2004.

18. The author verified this through local briefings and the military operations directorate.

19. For details on night raids which the US military claims have been a success, see Open Society Foundation and Liaison Office (2011). http://www.opensocietyfoundations.org/sites/default/files/Night-Raids-Report-FINAL-092011.pdf.

20. The previous government had an elected prime minister but was headed by the president-cum-army chief, Pervez Musharraf. This phase also saw two separate developments that had a major impact on the state's ability to tackle extremist violence. In March 2007, General Musharraf sacked the chief justice of Pakistan, unleashing a nonviolent but countrywide civil society protest. The media coverage of the movement weakened the government tremendously. A court case restored the chief justice of Pakistan and made the court more active against the Musharraf government. This forced Musharraf, on November 3, to sack sixty-four judges of high courts and the Supreme Court and declare an emergency. Simultaneously, Musharraf ordered a military operation in Malakand that began within days of his declaration of emergency. Rising levels of terrorist violence following the raid on the Red Mosque in July 2007 necessitated this. With the government having been badly bruised because of political pressure and its legitimacy under question, Musharraf was forced into announcing elections, which were held in February 2008. The operation in Malakand was called off just when it was time to pack the punch and deal the final blow to the militants in the area.

21. The military operations are given cover under Article 245 of the constitution, which deals with the military's deployment and functions in aid of civil power. However, many legal experts challenge the employment of this article for CT operations. The parliament also passed the 2012 Fair Trial Bill, which was signed into law by the president in February 2013. The law allows intelligence agencies to monitor electronic communication and to surveil suspects. The law has come under fire from human rights groups.

CHAPTER 4

Political Instability and Its Implications for an Effective National Counterterrorism Policy in Pakistan

SAVAIL MEEKAL HUSSAIN and MEHREEN ZAHRA-MALIK

ON MAY 25, 2011, the Defense Committee of the Cabinet, Pakistan's highest forum for defense policymaking, met under Prime Minister Yousaf Raza Gillani and decided to take "pre-emptive measures to eliminate terrorist hideouts across Pakistan through a coordinated effort involving all state institutions" (Ghauri 2011a). The emphasis was to be on diversifying the national approach to terrorism by adopting new anti-terrorist strategies. Faced with an intensified wave of terrorist attacks, the prime minister and his team sat down to chalk out a "new" policy. But, as analysts pointed out, nothing fresh and tangibly different could be conceived without first defining what was being abandoned as ineffective policy or "nonpolicy."

This chapter explains the absence of a comprehensive national counterterrorism (CT) policy in Pakistan. It provides an explanation for political instability and outlines its implications for framing and implementing an effective CT policy. We define political instability in terms of both frequent regime changes and formal rule changes, including repeated amendments to the constitution and other national laws and policies. By an effective national CT policy, we mean a set of laws and implementation mechanisms that not only address the problem of terrorism explicitly but are enduring and underpinned by a broad political consensus. Legitimacy and durability of policy are vitally important if the Pakistani state and society are to successfully address the existential challenge posed by Islamist terrorism.

The chapter's approach draws on the neo-institutionalist theory of institutions and institutional change, and on recent literature on the political economy of factionalism. The central argument is that political instability in Pakistan is rooted in the highly factionalized nature of its society and polity and the absence of organized, cohesive, and strong political parties. Parties with these attributes can integrate preferences, provide a framework for resolving factional disputes at low cost, and contribute to the formation of a political consensus. Consensus regarding the legitimacy of formal rules is essential for political stability and for effective policymaking. The primary conclusion we draw is that in a factionalized, fractured polity, the transactional costs of building a national consensus around a core policy on terrorism are likely to be prohibitively high for any individual faction. Furthermore, a weak factionalized polity perversely distorts societal incentives to yield to state authority and cooperate with its attempts to build and implement CT measures. Only a strong central government with a medium- to long-term time horizon and comprising a robust factional coalition can push through a national agenda against terror.

Institutions Matter

Institutions are humanly devised constraints on behavior that structure human interaction in a world of uncertainty (North 1990a, 2005).[1] Institutions include formal rules such as a constitution, informal constraints such as norms and conventions, and the enforcement characteristics of those rules and constraints. In short they are the "rules of the game" that govern our interaction with others to the extent that they are "enforced" and thus provide the framework within which economic and political activity takes place (North 1990a, 2005).

For our purposes, it is useful to draw North's analytic distinction between institutions, which guide behavior, and organizations through which behavior manifests itself. Organizations are consciously derived human associations that operate within a given institutional framework. They include a diverse set of entities such as corporations, political parties, bureaucracy and the military, educational establishments, and religious bodies. In game theoretic terms, organizations are the "players" while institutions are the "rules" (North 1990a).

Institutions, especially formal rules, are generally derived by self-interested political entrepreneurs in a position to make policy. As North (1990b) has shown, political markets, when they exist at all, are notoriously imperfect.[2] Time preferences of political entrepreneurs are also important. If the time horizon of those in power is short and they discount the future heavily, we could have the state functioning as what Olson (2000) terms the "roving bandit" who loots only for today. It follows, then, that the efficiency implications of formal institutions for the economy and polity are ambiguous.[3] Institutional change is rooted in changing relative prices in economic and political markets and evolving perceptions of political and economic agents through learning and knowledge accumulation. An example of how a change in relative prices in political markets impacts institutional change is provided by the changed international environment following the events of 9/11. These events raised the political price for Pakistan's military and political regime of remaining ambivalent to all the terrorist groups operating within Pakistan and the Taliban in Afghanistan. The Bush administration's ultimatum of "you are either with us or against us" illustrates vividly how relative prices changed for Pakistan's political entrepreneurs.

As economic and political entrepreneurs function within a given institutional framework, they learn about its incentive structure, which can lead them to push for incremental change. Changing perceptions and new situations that provide incentives for incremental changes to the institutional structure also follow from the investment that individuals and their organizations make in knowledge. The investments made in particular types of knowledge streams depend on the incentives implied by the original institutional structure. In Pakistan's case, if the state nurtures militant proxies such as the Lashkar-e-Taiba (LeT), then offshoots such as the multiple militant factions that have emerged post-9/11 and a madrassa system that imparts a militant ideology are logical outcomes. Also, institutional change is generally incremental and is likely to be heavily path dependent. Path dependencies perpetuate when individuals and organizations that benefit from the existing institutional framework are likely to form interest groups that resist an abrupt change.[4]

Political Factionalism in Pakistan

An important but under-researched aspect of the political process in Pakistan is the ubiquity of power-sharing arrangements between dominant political factions such as the military and various civilian groupings. Existing historical and political science literature focuses mostly on explaining authoritarianism in Pakistan through an emphasis on the military's dominance of the political process (Sayeed 1980; Weiner 1989; Jalal 1990, 1995). Such accounts ignore a critical aspect of the problem: successive regimes, both military and civilian, have always had to share power and resources with other influential factions. Any productive account of the political process in Pakistan then has to explicitly engage with the creation and persistence of power and resource-sharing arrangements between various political entrepreneurs and their associated factions.

Similarly, much of the literature on political instability in Pakistan has ignored the politics of factionalism that drives the political process. Pakistan, much like the rest of the Indian subcontinent, has multiple and decentralized organizational centers of power, the roots of which lie deep in India's long social and political history. Common features of factional politics include the personalization of politics by faction leaders and the organization of politics as a competition between multiple factions. Faction leaders make payoffs to those who support them, and they capture the resources for making these payoffs by organizing their supporters into factions. The existence of multiple centers of power in Pakistan has meant that political entrepreneurs have been able to mobilize large numbers and form political factions to lobby the state for power and resources (Khan 1999; Khan and Jomo 2000). Consequently, Pakistani politics has been the politics of factionalism, with multiple factions competing for the reins of government as well as the resources commanded by the state. More recently, ideologies associated with a militant form of Islam have provided space for the development of militant factions such as the Pakistani Taliban (Tehrik-e-Taliban Pakistan, or TTP) and the Lashkar-e-Jhangvi (LeJ), among others.

The exclusive focus on the dominance of the military ignores the complex dynamics of factional competition and, hence, obscures the underlying determinants of political instability and the challenges involved in crafting national policies, including those relating to CT. There are at least four common explanations for the extent of political factionalism in Pakistan, which in turn elucidates how incentives established by larger institutional structures impact the outcomes of its CT policy. Each of these has significant implications for the formation for an effective, coherent, and holistic vision on CT.

The Dispersion of Political and Organizational Power

As Khan and Jomo (2000) note, "while capitalists and landlords may, as individuals, control significant resources, they are too few in number to control the political process by themselves. In contrast, the middle and lower middle classes have the organizational power to dominate politics" (91). These middle- and lower-middle-class groups, or what Khan and Jomo term the "intermediate classes," form an important group of political entrepreneurs.[5] Given that they can mobilize significant chunks of the populace in the absence of overarching political organizations such as political parties, they tend to stimulate political fragmentation.

While Pakistan has flirted with party politics throughout its history, political parties have often been patchwork coalitions of various competing interests. They have generally lacked what Huntington (1968) calls "autonomy," "stability," and "cohesion,'" even if Pakistan has managed to maintain some semblance of a political process.[6]

The Scarcity of Public Resources

Given that Pakistan is a developing country with a turbulent political history, public resources have always been limited. This provides an incentive for small factions to spring up and grab whatever resources they can and pass them down the line via patron–client relations. The political entrepreneurs in various factions are the patrons who pass along a chunk of acquired resources to their clients, who in return mobilize support that makes up factions (Lieven 2011, 204–8).

The Lack of Incentives to Form Broad-Based Interest Groups

Pakistan also lacks the political structure that collates the preferences of various groups in a political organization to represent broad interests. In such an environment, parties and political candidates are incentivized to campaign along the lines of parochial interests. The economic system in Pakistan can best be described as a hybrid, feudal–capitalist one. There is also the conspicuous absence of a dominant ideology that can serve as the basis of nationalism in a society fragmented along the lines of class, ethnicity, culture, and language instead of issue-based platforms. Therefore, there are few incentives for broad-based interest-group formation that would enlarge the size of factions and limit the number of political factions. The smaller the number of factions, the easier it can be to build and maintain political consensus around core policy such as on CT.

The Absence of Grassroots Political Parties

A relatively stable set of formal institutions, where change is incremental and gradual, requires a corresponding set of complementary informal constraints that underpin them (Weingast 1993; Alston, Eggertsson, and North 1996). This informal set of constraints is crucial for the stability of formal rules because it provides the latter with legitimacy. For the development and maintenance of these informal constraints, political parties representing broad interests are key. By integrating preferences, resolving internal disputes, disciplining dissenters, and framing political and economic programs, political parties can make for consensus that legitimizes and strengthens formal rules and effective policymaking. Following partition of British India, the Congress Party in India did precisely this, thereby playing an important role in containing political instability (Kohli 2001; Dasgupta 2001; Manor 2001). This starkly contrasts with the political experience of Pakistani provinces, which had no history of national grassroots political parties (Weiner 1989; Talbot 1991).

In Pakistan's case, the development of cohesive, strong political parties that can limit political factionalism has also been retarded by the military, which has continuously involved itself in the political process by picking and choosing selective civilian factions and making and breaking political parties while seeking to control the political system. Consequently, an essential mechanism of institutionalizing consensus that could have helped the cause of counterterror policymaking has been absent. In the absence of national grassroots political parties, framing CT policy has become an exceptionally daunting task.

How Praetorian Factionalism Undermines Policy Framing in Pakistan

Institutional change in the context of "praetorian" factionalism—where there are a large number of competing political factions, and where coordination within and across factions is limited—is likely to be rapid as competing political entrepreneurs, backed by their factions, strive to alter rules to their advantage. This is evident in the nature of factionalism within Pakistan, which contributes directly to frequent changes in formal rules and hence undermines the framing of national policies such as those on CT.

The intensity of competition between factions is likely to be high and factional coalitions unstable in such environments. This type of factional competition is described as "chaotic" by Huntington (1968), and it is reminiscent of the factional squabbles between Pakistani politicians in the early 1950s and the 1990s (Ziring 1980, 1997; Rizvi 1998). Unsurprisingly, this period in Pakistan's political history was one of rapid institutional change as constitutional rules were enacted and discarded, multiple and varying drafts of the future constitution were drawn up and shot down, and contention between the legislature and the executive leadership worsened and ultimately degenerated into martial law. It also follows that factional coalitions in factionalized polities are likely to have short time horizons, and the dominant coalition at any point in time is likely to look to grab as many resources as it can and thus end up behaving like Olson's "roving bandit." This has two consequences vis-à-vis institutional change. First, institutional and policy changes are likely to be frequent as various roving bandits alter rules in the context of short time horizons. Second, given the opportunistic nature of resource capturing, social welfare considerations are likely to diverge from the private interests of the dominant factional coalitions.[7] Rampant factionalism in Pakistan, then, prevents consensus building along national lines, and it makes medium- to long-term policymaking transient and ineffective, and regime and rule changes frequent. This pattern is evident in the CT regime in Pakistan today.

Political Factionalism: Implications for Counterterrorism in Pakistan

In a factionalized, fractured polity, we have argued, the transaction costs of building a national consensus around a core policy are likely to be prohibitively high for any individual faction. Only a strong central government with a medium- to long-term time horizon and composed of a factional coalition led by a dominant faction can push through a national agenda against terror. Consider the row between Punjab chief minister Shahbaz Sharif and federal interior minister Rehman Malik over the latter's use of the term "Punjabi Taliban"—a loose network of members of banned militant groups based in the southern part of Punjab province—with Sharif insisting that terms like "Punjabi terrorism" create interprovincial disharmony. This instance portrayed the personalization of politics by faction leaders and the organization of politics as a competition between factions in Pakistan.

Political Parties and Factionalism

Parties exist to integrate preferences and establish coordination across factions via party discipline. Yet the Pakistan Muslim League-Nawaz's (PML-N) vehement display of irritation and anger over the use of the term "Punjabi Taliban" shows the extent of political factionalism and populism in Pakistan. The PML-N, it is clear, would much rather protect the name of the province it rules and shirk responsibility for acts of terror in Punjab than acknowledge and work to counter operatives from LeJ, Sipah-e-Sahaba Pakistan (SSP), and Jaish-e-Mohammed (JeM)—all banned extremist groups of Punjabi origin—who increasingly support Taliban elements from Pakistan's tribal regions to conduct attacks in sensitive cities such as Lahore, Rawalpindi, Islamabad, and Faisalabad (Abbas 2009b, 1–2). Imagine the implications of this, given that

Punjab is the most densely populated and prosperous province in Pakistan and home to the army's headquarters and sensitive nuclear installations.

The provincial PML-N government that has been in power in Punjab since 2008 has publicly tried to appease the militants by offering them a quid pro quo: allowing them space in return for not attacking the Punjab. In March 2010, Punjab Chief Minister Shahbaz Sharif said he did not understand why the Taliban were targeting Punjab when his party, the PML-N, and militants alike opposed the policies of former military ruler Gen. Pervez Musharraf, who allied with the United States after the 9/11 attacks: "Gen. Musharraf planned a bloodbath of innocent Muslims at the behest of others only to prolong his rule, but we in the PML-N opposed his policies and rejected dictation from abroad," Shahbaz said while visiting an Islamic seminary. "If the Taliban are also fighting for the same cause then they should not carry out acts of terror in Punjab."[8]

Shahbaz's comments laid bare the ethnic and provincial tensions that have been inflamed by violence by the mainly Pashtun TTP, the group responsible for more Islamist violence in Pakistan than any other. Although most of the Taliban violence has been focused in the mainly ethnically Pashtun Khyber Pakhtunkhwa Province (KPK) and Federally Administered Tribal Areas (FATA) on the Afghan border, the militants have carried out several high-profile attacks in Punjab in recent years. Some Punjabis consider the Taliban a Pashtun problem and not a problem for all of Pakistan, or for them. Indeed, political opponents accused Shahbaz of promoting parochial politics. Newspapers also published pictures of the Punjab law minister loyal to Sharif campaigning in a by-election with leaders of an outlawed Islamist group. The PML-N has continued to flirt with political fronts of militant outfits even at the cost of heavy criticism (Abbasi 2013); the pattern was repeated in the 2013 general elections. These are all illustrative examples of how factional competition, in this case along provincial lines, has produced negative national outcomes, especially in terms of the framing of a provincial CT policy that is clearly at odds with the larger goal of eradicating terrorism nationally.

If and when the government decides to fully embrace the problem of Punjabi militants, the provincial and federal tiers will have to come together to devise an extensive program for deweaponization and deradicalization in order to remove weaponry from the area, with incentives of cash and jobs training (Nawaz 2011). Ideally, then, the federal and provincial governments must unite to ensure that the Punjabi Taliban network is not able to transform itself into a much more organized group in the future. However, as indicated all along, rampant factionalism in and between the Pakistan People's Party (PPP) and PML-N governments at the center and provincial level between

2008 and 2013 prevented consensus building on CT along national lines and made policy thinking transient and myopic. Parties that should ideally be involved in integrating preferences are instead focused on their selfish, personalized, parochial, and short-sighted political gains. In these circumstances, the durability of a national CT strategy will only meet with limited success, if any. While the results of the May 2013 elections have brought PML-N to power both at the center and in Punjab, thereby removing the problem of factionalism in this case momentarily, it remains to be seen whether this will translate into more effective and concerted policy and action given the various other levels of factionalism at play (PML-N versus political fronts of Punjabi militants, Punjab versus KPK governments, etc.).

The Civil–Military Disconnect

There is also an obvious lack of coordination between the civil government and the military on CT issues, which have become unmanageable because civilian authorities have been historically unable to raise their game to meet and support the armed forces while the army has been mostly unwilling to integrate its civilian counterparts in CT matters. The prevalence of factional politics in Pakistan also helps explain why the military, in the absence of cohesive political organizations that represent broad interests, has been able to sideline civilian governments, especially in the realm of national security decision making.

Our interviews with various parliamentarians from Pakistan reveal that while they have received briefings on the terrorist threat and CT challenges from the military leadership, they are not in contact with the Inter-Services Intelligence (ISI). This is unfortunate, as briefings by the intelligence community to members of the National Assembly are essential because many in the assembly do not fully understand the magnitude of the challenge posed to the militant forces. In that regard, the dissolving of the National Security Council (NSC) in 2008 by Prime Minister Gillani's government was a blow to the CT challenge. A mechanism such as the NSC, where the military can sit down on a regular basis with civilian leadership and intelligence officials and talk about a national strategy, would go a long way to ensure that all stakeholders are on the same page. The dissolution of the NSC is an excellent example of Pakistan's framework whereby factional competition closed the door on an organization that could have coordinated various civilian and military factions in the articulation and implementation of a national CT policy.

Moreover, in early 2008, soon after the PPP-led civilian government took over at the center, the army chief and the director general of the ISI briefed political leaders of all parties about the insurgency, asking them to come up with directions for the military, to which there was no response. After much cajoling by the military, the new civilian government managed to get all parties in the parliament together to unanimously support a resolution passed on October 23, 2008, which spelled out a policy against insurgency and terrorism inside Pakistan. Having passed the resolution, however, the various parties withdrew from public view, and little was done to support the government's efforts in this direction. "Party politics took over and the effort fizzled, leaving it to the military to bear the brunt of the COIN effort" (Nawaz 2011, 24). Until a joint system of policy deliberations and actions emerges, CT efforts will remain constrained and limited to military action. Additionally, because there is no consensus on the CT approach, it ends up being counterproductive and one-dimensional.

In sum, even as Pakistan has been under democracy since 2008, civilian politicians have not been able to wrest total policy control from the army. They have almost entirely surrendered security and strategic policy to the generals, who have handpicked politicians of choice to work on such issues based on convergence of views and willingness to tow the army line. The army has actively manipulated the political process in Pakistan in the past and continues to do so, even if to a lesser extent. Political factionalism has not come about with the military standing by and watching helplessly. It has actually ensured this outcome by directly intervening in the political process. As Akbar Zaidi writes in *Dawn*,

> It has ruled, governed, manipulated, deformed and interfered in the political process in the country, as if it had a right to do so. . . . The military has acted with a mind of its own, and made judgments which benefited itself as an institution, and which it believed were in its vision of the "national interest," often under what it felt was a moral obligation to save the country under different meanings of the doctrines of necessity. Importantly, the military has always been anti-politician—but never anti-politics—singularly going after elected representatives individually, and against political institutions elected outside the ambit of the rules created by the military. It has not had a problem dealing with some elected politicians, as long as these elected politicians have accepted the hegemony of the military and played according to its rules (Zaidi 2012).

Thus, overall, political parties in Pakistan have lacked "autonomy," "stability," and "cohesion" for all the reasons stated earlier, including the active manipulation of, and interference in, the political process by the army. The factious relationship between Pakistan's elected political leaders and the military undermines the ability of the civilians to formulate policies to address the country's pressing domestic challenges, including terrorism. This is partly why absence of unanimity on a CT vision underpins much of the problem Pakistan faces in devising concrete policies.

The problem has been compounded further by two factors: (a) the carefully cultivated ethos of the Pakistan Army, which emphasizes the defense of the state in religious terms (for instance, the centrality of the concept of "jihad" in the Pakistan Army, imbued at the level of the foot soldiers and in the battle cry of Allah-Hu-Akbar [God Is Great]); and (b) the use of militant proxies in the furtherance of political and military objectives. These two factors complicate and cloud the identification of the enemy, especially when the Pakistan Army faces off with former militant allies who use the same religious symbols and battle cries. It is only recently, in the face of significant military casualties and barbaric tactics employed by the militants, that the categorization of these militant forces as enemies of Pakistan has been cemented in the minds of junior officers and at the level of the foot soldier. Even now, the military continues to pick and choose groups to target, leaving anti-India militant outfits largely untouched.

Unanimity was achieved in the past, but whenever this happened, it was more an outcome of a series of fortunate—largely unexpected—events, and courtesy of mistakes made by the militant enclave rather than a result of any thought out policy by the state. The most obvious example of the abrupt shift in public opinion in support of a military was the operation in Swat in KPK in 2009. When speaking before an audience of tens of thousands in April 2009, Sufi Mohammed, the founder of Tehreek-e-Nafaz-e-Shariat-e-Mohammadi (Movement for the Enforcement of Sharia Law, or TNSM), declared democracy and Pakistan's judicial system "un-Islamic." He also rejected all political and religiopolitical parties that embodied Western-style democracy. He famously said: "There is no room for the vote in Islam and the concept of democracy which some religious political parties are demanding is wrong" (Mir 2009). This image remained in the minds of the Pakistani public, led to the "convergence of broad public opposition to the Taliban" (Lodhi 2009), and created the extraordinary enabling conditions to deliver a decisive blow to militancy in Swat.

Consensus on the eve of the military action, Operation Rah-e-Rast, emerged not through a systematic effort by either the military or the civilian enclave but through a series of incidents such as the ones highlighted earlier that made it clear to the masses that things were moving to a point of no return. People across the country were alarmed, especially in Swat. In fact, it was only after it was clear that there was overwhelming public opposition to the militants that leaders of forty-three parties and religious organizations from across the political spectrum assembled in Islamabad at a meeting convened by Prime Minister Yousaf Raza Gillani on May 18, 2009, to endorse the security operation. This was a rare show of unanimity: "The clear stance taken by the head of the Pakistan Muslim League (N), Mian Nawaz Sharif, swung the balance of opinion in the meeting and ensured the unanimous adoption of the fifteen-point resolution. Certain opposition parties which took a dissenting view were isolated by the support voiced by Mr. Sharif" (Lodhi 2009). Here, political and public consensus gave the military action the necessary support that past operations lacked.

Besides demonstrating that consensus is possible when things appear to be heading to a point of no return, this episode also illustrates how a coordinated CT strategy enhances the possibility of success. It also points to an urgent need to address the civil–military imbalance in Pakistan, without which a coordinated CT strategy is impossible to draft and implement.

Ultimately, the institutionalization of an effective CT strategy in Pakistan requires balancing both the civilian and military sides of the equation. It is important to build civilian capacity. While exerting sustained civilian control over the military poses a formidable challenge for any transitional democracy, Pakistani governments also face the additional burden of resolving a complex array of economic, political, and security crises. In this scenario, "wherein the civilian government is responsible for and under pressure to squarely tackle broad governance issues (especially the potentially destabilizing economic and energy crises)—the military will continue to operate in the shadows and rattle its sabers at will to prevent undesirable outcomes in domestic politics and foreign policy" (Cohen 2011, 29). This latent military power will likely act as an additional source of political instability and civilian institutional erosion in the next decade and prevent the emergence of a comprehensive, widely accepted CT policy.

It is also important to remember that while the Pakistani military has, since the departure of President General Musharraf in 2008, generally withdrawn from government, this shift was not the result of a change in its core praetorian ethos. Hence, there is an urgent need for reform within the Pakistani army that would lead to its firm commitment, behaviorally and attitudinally, to a subordinate role in a democratic framework, and would lead it to realize, as the Rah-e-Rast example illustrated, that—contrary to what it likes to project—its policies will have little support without civilian and popular backing. Scholarly literature on civil–military relations can provide several insights into achieving civilian control of the military.[9] Most important in this transition is the development of strong institutional rules and channels (legislative oversight, civilian-controlled ministry of defense, and the like) to induce military subordination by enforcing sanctions for irregular behavior backed by an entrenched norm of civilian supremacy. To be sure, institutions do need time and space to develop. Changes in the military belief system may require internally driven reform or a sustained process of democratization that facilitates positive "unlearning" within the institution (Shah 2011, 207). This is a long-term task, but one that the civilians, along with the army, need to take up together.

Factionalism at Play: The Failure of the National Counter Terrorism Authority

The case of the National Counter Terrorism Authority (NACTA) provides a vivid example of how factionalism can undermine positive ideas and efforts to bring coherence in national policies—in this instance, CT policy. Both the failure of political parties to integrate preferences and the failure of the civilian and military enclaves to rise above personal and institutional interests were on display in this instance.

NACTA was set up by the PPP government in January 2009 to draft the National Counter Terrorism and Extremism Strategy. NACTA was to be a "homeland security coordination body, the primary public organ entrusted with counterterrorism, counter-extremism, and de-radicalization efforts of the state" (Zaidi 2010, 1). It was to follow to some extent the model of the Department of Homeland Security in the United States since 9/11, which emphasizes the centrality of intelligence sharing to the war on terror.

NACTA was formed as an acknowledgment of the lack of a national intelligence-sharing body, and it was created to coordinate the activities of various intelligence and investigation agencies, including the Intelligence Bureau (IB), the Federal Investigation Agency (FIA), and the ISI. In essence, NACTA was created as an umbrella organization to coordinate efforts in countering the threat posed by terrorism that had spread across Pakistan. According to the NACTA Ordinance of 2010, NACTA's functions were to include: (a) to receive and pool together information and intelligence, and to coordinate between all relevant stakeholders to formulate threat assessments with periodic reviews to be presented to the federal government to facilitate adequate and timely efforts at countering terrorism and extremism; (b) to coordinate and prepare comprehensive national CT and national counterinsurgency (COIN) strategies and review them on a periodic basis; (c) to develop action plans against terrorism and extremism and report to the government about their implementation on a periodic basis; (d) to carry out research on topics relevant to terrorism and extremism, and to prepare and circulate documents; and (e) to maintain liaisons with international entities for facilitating cooperation in areas relating to terrorism and extremism.

To head NACTA, a highly trained and well-regarded police officer, Tariq Pervez, who had developed an extensive informal system of tracking persons with contacts with terrorist or banned outfits based on informers during his tenure as director general of the FIA, was brought in. But Pervez was denied access to resources, largely due to professional rivalries and alleged differences with the minister of interior: Pervez favored direct reporting to the prime minister, whereas the interior minister preferred a role for his ministry in managing NACTA's operations.[10] Due to their inability to reach a consensus on the organizational and reporting structure of NACTA, Pervez resigned from the position in the summer of 2010 (Nawaz 2011).

The Interior Ministry in April 2010 drafted a new version of NACTA legislation, and the new head amended it to make the prime minister the chair of the governing body, with the minister of interior serving as vice chair. However, only in March 2013 did the Pakistani Senate pass the NACTA ordinance that was to provide the body its much-needed legal cover (Hussain 2013). Without the status of a lawful, constitutional body with legal reach and constitutionally mandated powers, NACTA could not have been expected to fulfill its mandate. Even with the ordinance in place, however, the fundamental challenges emanating from political factionalism and perverse incentives for political entrepreneurs remain intact. Indeed, even senior officials at NACTA themselves admitted to the authors that NACTA had "gone from being the umbrella coordination body it was conceived as to being a mere government think tank."[11] The reason: factionalized competition between stakeholders, all of whom neither have the will nor the political capacity to put aside their differences to develop a national CT policy.

The persistent delay in providing NACTA with a clear mandate and effective machinery was also partly a result of the political tussle over who was to oversee the body. The Punjab government, led by the PML-N, the main opposition party at the center, had serious reservations about placing NACTA under the control of the federal (PPP-led) Interior Ministry.

Other obstacles in the way of NACTA include the absence of a culture of institutionalized control of intelligence agencies, as well as the inability of different arms of the state to coordinate with each other and check their internal discord. In theory, NACTA was created to oversee the workings of other intelligence agencies including IB, FIA, and ISI. The FIA is the bailiwick of police officers that also normally dominate the IB. Unlike the ISI, which formally reports to the prime minister but in reality is under the control of the army chief, the FIA and the IB work under the Interior Ministry. If NACTA is also overseen by the Interior Ministry, it would work as a mechanism to indirectly bring all intelligence functions under the tutelage of this ministry. This could work in theory, but in practice we remember that in July 2008

Prime Minister Gillani's attempt to subject the ISI to the authority of the Interior Ministry was unsuccessful (Niaz 2008). The Press Information Department issued a memorandum late on the night of July 26, 2008, stating that the country's two premier intelligence agencies—the ISI and the IB—had been placed under the administrative, financial, and operational control of the Interior Division. Just the next morning, the PPP government reversed its decision and "clarified" the earlier notification, saying that the ISI would continue to operate at the prime minister's discretion. Sources say the reversal happened because the top military brass had not been consulted on the issue and essentially thwarted the government's move, leveraging its privileged position within Pakistan's institutional makeup. On the matter of NACTA, Nawaz had rightly observed in 2011: "The effort to enact a law in support of the National Counter Terrorism Authority continues to be delayed as a result of bureaucratic inertia, infighting, and a lack of coordination with the military" (1). The sentiment was confirmed by one observer who spoke to the authors on condition of anonymity: "the army would have been prepared to work with it [NACTA] on specific programs and projects, provided it was not located inside the Ministry of Interior."

Given how jealously the ISI guards its terrain and given the absence of institutionalized control of intelligence agencies, it is highly unlikely that NACTA would be allowed to perform one of the key functions of oversight mentioned in the ordinance. Hence, after more than three years of being instituted, NACTA functions as a mere government research institute and does not enjoy any of the important powers originally envisioned, partly because the interior ministry has never extended NACTA the much-needed cooperation and, most importantly, because political parties have not been able to reach any consensus on the fate of NACTA. The one body conceived and created to formulate a national CT policy for Pakistan and to provide decision makers with a carefully analyzed and comprehensive view of threats to national security by the entire intelligence community, including civilian, military, and crime intelligence structures, has fallen victim to a bureaucratic and institutional cesspool.

Again, at the heart of the problem lies the inability of those in power to be able to channel their differences through institutionalized means and achieve a consensus on important goals. Specifically, "institutional intelligence reform is difficult because it involves the coordination of multiple intelligence agencies" as well as between the military and the executive, legislative, and judicial branches (Grare 2009, 6). But institutional intelligence reform and coordination are particularly important because the agencies, especially the ISI, are known to create political factions and play them off each other to influence domestic politics to their advantage; they maneuver behind the scenes to prevent the election of governments that seek to reduce their role, and they have an interest in perpetuating the conditions that justify their existence (Grare 2009). Regaining legitimacy by reforming intelligence agencies and developing institutionalized political parties is thus crucial in creating consensus on issues of national security.

Pakistan's Future Challenge

To be sure, dealing with the CT challenge in Pakistan requires commitment and changes at the broadest structural level. The highly factionalized nature of Pakistani politics and society as well as the absence of viable and stable institutions will continue to stand in the way of making effective policies to curb terrorism and deal with other pressing problems that the country faces.

If Pakistan is to remain within a democratic political structure, then building strong national political parties that can forge unity among disparate social forces is key to facing the CT challenge. Parties are tools of social organization that help manage differences and institutionalize uncertainty; in Pakistan, however, where major political parties emerge suddenly in response to political exigencies and are not organically linked to any particular organized social group, parties have often mobilized people along the lines of identity and parochial issues such as ethnicity, religion, and opposition to structural reforms without regard for long-term consequences. Most political parties have tended to manipulate rather than aggregate interests. The civil–military disconnect adds another major complication. This makes consensus building on issues of national concern highly difficult and victim to political warmongering. Until this tendency changes, building a comprehensive policy to meet the CT challenge will continue to prove elusive.

There are plenty of parallels between Pakistan's situation and those faced by other South Asian states challenged by terrorism and organized insurgency over the years to substantiate the argument presented in this chapter. From India to Sri Lanka to Nepal, South Asian states have fared with varying degrees of success in formulating coherent policy and undertaking concrete steps to tackle terrorism. The results are often linked to how well they have managed to rise above political factionalism and aggregate interests. In a forthcoming volume that examines armed insurgencies in South Asia, the case studies provide unflinching evidence that the armed insurrections were in no small part caused by, and managed to persist due to, political factionalism and the inability of political actors to form a grand consensus on the state's responses (Yusuf 2014).

Sri Lanka and Nepal perhaps provide the clearest contrasting examples of this. For years, political and electoral priorities trumped consensus building for Sinhalese-dominated political parties in power in Sri Lanka. This was ultimately directly responsible for alienating moderate Tamil politicians and allowing radicals to take center stage and fuel a full-fledged insurgency. For a quarter of a century after the active insurgency took off in 1983, the Sri Lankan state tried various policies and strategies, including a mix of peace talks and military assaults, but remained unable to pacify the Liberation Tigers of Tamil Eelam (LTTE) threat. Underlying this failure was inconsistency in policy across governments; frequent and abrupt changes in the thinking of successive Sri Lankan governments about the use of foreign patrons like India, whose peacekeeping forces were brought in to tackle the LTTE in 1987, and then thrown out in 1990 after the state backed the LTTE to challenge the force's presence; and tensions between the executive and legislative heads, such as the one between President Chandrika Kumaratunga and her rival party's prime minister, Ranil Wickramasinghe, between 2002–5 when the Sri Lankan state was attempting a crucial peace bid with the LTTE through Norwegian brokering, among many other examples of factionalism. One major difference marked the final phase of the Sri Lankan war, the Ealam War 4, which eventually terminated the insurgency in favor of the state. In 2005, a right-wing, nationalist coalition led by Mahinda Rajapaksa took over. The very cohesion of the coalition was based on a promise by Rajapaksa to pursue an unwavering policy toward the LTTE. What was to end up being a highly controversial military campaign, nonetheless, was made possible by a political consensus on a particular strategy that had total buy-in from the military and backing of the majority Sinhalese nationalist sentiment, whipped up constantly by the Rajapaksa-led coalition. The point here is not to back a military-dominated outlook but to highlight that rising above political factionalism can provide states with the political will and wherewithal to make concerted progress toward a specific goal, no matter how intractable the problem appears.[12]

In Nepal, the state could never overcome factionalism. In fact, in 2005 the monarchy—first by seeking to prolong an unrepresentative system that was widely unpopular and then by overplaying its hand in usurping total control of all state powers at a crucial time in the armed insurrection—managed to alienate not only the Maoist insurgents but also all political parties who otherwise were amenable to keeping constitutional monarchy intact. The monarchy, operating with the support of the military, made the cardinal mistake of converting a tripartite tussle between itself, the mainstream political parties, and the armed Maoist opposition that had allowed the status quo to hold into a bilateral one by squeezing the space of the political parties and forcing them to join hands with the insurgents. It was the political consensus on forming a new constituent assembly and ousting the monarch on the part of the political parties and Maoist militants—and the failure of the monarchy, military, and mainstream political parties to overcome factionalism—that led to the "defeat" of the state in 2006. The army also backed down in the face of the political consensus against the monarchy.[13]

The polar opposite outcomes in the two cases and the role of political factionalism and institutional consensus (or lack thereof) are clear in these two examples. The good news for Pakistan, as born out by the Sri Lankan case, is that states can overcome long-standing structural anomalies to forge consensus positions. The Nepalese case, however, is a clear reminder that a persistent failure to do so can lead to the surrender of states. In Nepal, this only meant a change in government; in Pakistan, such an outcome would mean handing over the reins of a densely populated nuclear power to Islamists of various varieties who harbor national, regional, and global agendas.

As we have argued, it will be no mean feat for the Pakistani state to craft an enduring and effective national CT policy in a context riven by a highly factionalized polity, rapid institutional change, and rampant political instability. At the moment, the transaction costs of building a consensus that can be translated into a national policy are prohibitively high. This is especially so, given the presence of competing factions such as the TTP and their sympathizers actively opposing (with or without the use of force) any effort that aims to address the absence of an effective CT policy. The antiterrorism courts are a good example of how even existing laws are not enforced due to a lack of evidence, coercion of witnesses and law enforcement personnel, and lack of political will to get tough on violence in the name of religion. The January 2011 assassination of Salmaan Taseer, the governor of Punjab province who sought a revision of the country's controversial blasphemy laws, by an assassin who was supported by cheering crowds and showered with petals is a brutal illustration of this.[14] Incidentally, this kind of ideological ambivalence was also witnessed in Nepal as the Maoists began to gain popularity among the masses, and these supporters increasingly approved of violence as a legitimate tool to achieve desired ends.

Even if a national policy is successfully crafted and implemented, the state has to ensure that it is not ephemeral. This challenge emanates from the dynamics of factional competition where, in the absence of an overarching set of organizations that can regulate competition and resolve factional disputes at a low cost, sustaining a consensus around a set of core policies is going to be short lived. As coalitions are made and broken, the policy structure will remain in flux, even more so when some civilian and military factions use religious ideology as a basis of political power.

Looking ahead, given the sociopolitical context of present-day Pakistan, the minimum conditions and basic political structure under which an enduring, effective CT policy can be brought to fruition likely need a coalition that is led by a dominant faction; this will help maintain factional stability from within and without. The Sri Lankan political coalition in the post-2005 period is a case in point. The longevity of the factional coalition is in turn directly related to the stability of national policies, especially those that hinge on building and maintaining a national consensus in times of conflict. Further, economic performance that is broad-based and inclusive is essential both for building a durable coalition and for ensuring that the consensus is sustained. This can only be achieved if there is political stability and a focus on the economy with at least a medium-term time horizon.

In terms of forging a consensus, although we do not pursue this argument in detail, there is a need to examine the link between institutions and social attitudes toward CT measures. Terrorism also requires an ideological response. Since most terrorist activity in Pakistan is legitimized in the name of religion, lending support to moderate clerics and developing a counternarrative—but one that does not pit religion against security—can help raise awareness and tolerance of different views (Gunaratna 2007). Once again, however, in a highly factionalized polity, building the kind of consensus that culturally sensitive CT policymaking would require is a daunting task. Indeed, this is one aspect that none of the other South Asian states faced to the extent Pakistan has over the years and continues to do so today. It only makes the task of the Pakistani state that much harder.

Notes

1. The uncertainty arises from imperfect information as well as our limited cognitive abilities to compute and comprehend the information available.

2. An illustration can help clarify this point. Consider the average voter in a democracy. She is unlikely to be well informed about the range of issues affecting her and has little incentive to acquire all relevant information. This follows from the fact that the marginal benefit of doing so is likely to be small relative to the cost. Similarly, the legislator's ability to integrate oft-competing preferences of his electors is limited.

3. We use the term "efficiency" in the sense of promoting growth in the context of the economy and enhancing political stability with respect to the polity. We recognize that static political systems need not imply economic efficiency or provide for welfare enhancing political and social development. For our purposes, however, where the concern is to understand political instability, this definition suffices.

4. Furthermore, the existing set of institutions, and in particular informal institutions, are rooted in our mental models, our everyday actions, and the belief system that underpins the institutional structure. The result is that since the existing institutional structure

provides the guide for subsequent institutional developments, even a completely altered structure is likely to embody significant remnants of its predecessor—that is, path dependence. The Pakistani military is a case in point. It has jealously guarded its role in politics and has always resisted substantive rule changes that would deprive it of political power (see, for example, Rizvi 1998, 2000).

5. Interestingly enough, in the case of Pakistan, the importance of the intermediate classes is not limited to the civilian sphere. While little formal data exists on the socioeconomic origins of the officer corps of the military, indications are that it too is dominated by members of the "intermediate classes" (educated professionals, sons of rich peasants, etc.). See Cohen 1983; Rizvi 2000; Fair and Nawaz 2011.

6. For instance, the absence of an organized political party that enjoyed grassroots support is an oft-cited reason for Pakistan's early descent into authoritarianism. See Huntington 1968; Ziring 1980; Weiner 1989.

7. For example, while indices on corruption are largely subjective, the general consensus that emerges in the literature is that corruption as measured in terms of the number of bribes that need to be paid per transaction with the state was particularly high in the 1990s. This was precisely a period when political instability was rife and institutional change was rapid. It was in 1996, for instance, that Pakistan achieved the dubious honor of standing second in Transparency International's most corrupt nations list—its highest position since the index was launched (see Burki 1999). Corruption, an oft-cited malady that has afflicted Pakistan, is just one consequence of this divergence, and it undermines economic efficiency (Mauro 1995; Burki 1999, ch. 5; Khan and Jomo 2000, chs. 1 and 2).

8. "CM Shahbaz Wants Taliban to Spare Punjab," *Dawn*, March 15, 2010. http://archives.dawn.com/archives/43949.

9. For a concise discussion of main approaches, see Pion-Berlin 2001, 1–35. Samuel Huntington (1958) produced the seminal work focusing on distinct institutions to enforce civilian control of the military. See also Finer (1962), which emphasizes the military's internalization of the norm of civilian control as a check on its intervention in politics.

10. Authors' interview with Tariq Parvez, Islamabad, 2012.

11. Interview with senior NACTA official, Islamabad, 2012.

12. For a discussion of the Sri Lankan case, both the role of political factionalism in the onset of the insurgency and its persistence, see Weerasinghe's and Rupesinghe's chapters in Moeed Yusuf's forthcoming book, *Insurgency and Counterinsurgency in South Asia.*

13. For a discussion of the Nepalese case, both the role of political factionalism in the onset of the insurgency and its persistence, see Muni's and Upreti's chapters in Yusuf's forthcoming book, *Insurgency and Counterinsurgency in South Asia.*

14. Salmaan Taseer, a member of the PPP, served as the twenty-sixth governor of Punjab Province from 2008 until his assassination on January 4, 2011, in Islamabad by his own security guard, Mumtaz Qadri, who disagreed with Taseer's opposition to Pakistan's blasphemy law.

CHAPTER 5

Counterterrorism Efforts of Law Enforcement Agencies in Pakistan

SUHAIL HABIB TAJIK

ZAKI YAMANI, the famous oil minister of Saudi Arabia, once said that the Stone Age did not come to an end because it ran out of stones.[1] In a similar sense, the "traditional policing era" has come to an end not because the police have stopped patrolling the streets or sacrificing in the line of duty; rather, it has ended because the nature of the threat has changed. This new threat is an overlapping trio of "insurgency-terrorism-radicalization."[2] While the first line of defense against an insurgency is generally the army supported by other institutions, the first line of defense against terrorism is the police force reinforced by other institutions.

What internal security apparatus exists to tackle terrorism in Pakistan? How have the police fared in tackling terrorism? What are the reasons behind the police-related failures in the counterterrorism (CT) domain in Pakistan today? What structural and police-specific issues have incapacitated the law enforcement infrastructure in the fight against terrorists? What is required to rectify the system? These are some of the issues this chapter addresses.

The Ladder of Statistics

Pakistan, the second-most-populous Muslim state (Pew Research Center 2009), has the seventh-largest military establishment in the world, and is one of the eight states possessing nuclear weapons (Negroponte 2008). Concomitantly, it has become the thirteenth-most-violent nation and is ranked the thirteenth-most-fragile country on the globe (Carment and Samy 2012).[3] Moreover, based on the frequency of recent "terrorist incidents and intensity of attacks," Pakistan faces the highest risk of extreme terrorist attacks after Somalia.[4] Statistics from the past five years reflect the frequency and intensity of this violence (see table 5.1).

The bright side of these dark statistics is the slight "dip" observed in 2010 and 2011. Without doubt, the double-punch of the military operations in Swat in Khyber Pakhtunkhwa (KPK) province and in South Waziristan in the Federally Administered Tribal Areas (FATA) in 2009–10 has softened the militant infrastructure and is responsible for deceleration of the Tehrik-e-Taliban Pakistan (TTP, or Pakistani Taliban) rollercoaster. Prior to military operations in Swat in 2009, the writ of the state shrank from Swat's more than two thousand square miles to the limits of its regional headquarters of Mingora—a city of approximately fourteen square miles. Mingora's central square, the Green Chowk, came to be known as "*Chowk zeba khana*"—or the slaughterhouse—as the Pakistani Taliban killed scores of civilians and often hanged them in the square (Khan 2009). At that time, militants were busy nominating their "governor" for Peshawar, the capital of KPK. Simultaneously, the provincial government was mulling whether to move its capital from Peshawar to Abbottabad. However, these territories were "reclaimed" from the expanding wave of insurgency, with the blood of soldiers, policemen, politicians, and civilians. Successes like this can only become sustainable when the state structurally reforms the institutions that directly fight terrorists, expands the legal-constitutional framework into areas where the writ of the state is weak or absent, synchronizes diverse CT efforts, and improves the quantitative and qualitative deficit of law enforcing agencies. The following sections explore these issues in more detail.

The Scattered Solar System of Pakistan's Internal Security

The law enforcement apparatus of Pakistan is a jigsaw puzzle that mirrors the complexities of the Federation of Pakistan. Pakistan comprises five unequal provinces: Punjab, with more than 50 percent of the population; Balochistan,

TABLE 5.1
Terrorism in Pakistan

	2006	*2007*	*2008*	*2009*	*2010*	*2011*
Number of Attacks	907	3,448	7,997	12,632	10,003	7,107
Persons Killed	675	1,503	3,816	3,816	3,393	2,985

Source: PIPS 2012.

with 43 percent of the total area but a miniscule percentage of the population; Sindh, KPK, and Gilgit-Baltistan; the Islamabad Capital Territory (ICT); and the largely autonomous FATA. The geographical entity of Azad Jammu Kashmir (AJK) is adjusted under "such state and territories as are or may be included in Pakistan, whether by accession or otherwise" of Article 1 of Pakistan's 1973 constitution; it is officially recognized as a disputed territory with India. The law enforcement infrastructure owes itself to this complex federal structure, and it is multinodal with crosscutting functions; it also has to deal with blurred lines of authority. All law enforcement organizations (LEO) inevitably end up having complex recruitment, planning, administrative, and leadership structures. For the sake of clarity, these LEOs are grouped into federal and provincial functionaries (Abbas 2011).

Federal LEOs are more task-specific; hence, they can be grouped into those organizations attached to the Ministry of Interior (MOI) and those independent of it. Those attached to MOI include paramilitary organizations (Pakistan Rangers, Pakistan Coast Guards, Frontier Constabulary, and Northern Areas Scouts), nonparamilitary organizations (the Federal Investigation Agency [FIA], Islamabad Capital Territory Police, and the National Counter Terrorism Authority [NACTA]), and police planning and management organizations (National Police Academy, National Police Management Board, and National Public Safety Commission). The federal organizations not attached to the MOI include the Anti-Narcotics Force (ANF), Pakistan Railways Police, National Highways and Motorway Police, Airport Security Force (ASF), National Accountability Bureau (NAB), Levies, and Khasadars. The total strength of these diverse federal organizations is more than 225,000 (see table 5.2).

Since law and order is a provincial subject under the country's constitution, the five provinces have accommodated this by establishing their own police forces. The five provincial police organizations as well as the AJK police and the ICT police apply the same procedural and substantive criminal laws (Pakistan Penal Code, Criminal Procedure Code, and Qanun-e-Shahadat) to their respective areas (Abbas 2011). Including the ICT police, the total number of police stations in Pakistan is 1,479, and the total strength of police forces is around 410,000 (see table 5.3).

Failing Hydraulics?

Traditionally, the main functions of the police were watch and ward and investigations along with secondary functions of traffic management, security duties, and so on (Jamal and Patel 2010). However, the threat that the police

TABLE 5.2

Federal Law Enforcement Agencies in Pakistan

Federal Law Enforcing Organizations Attached with Ministry of Interior				
Organization	*Type*	*Founded*	*Strength*	*Function*
Pakistan Rangers	Paramilitary	1958	43,246	Border Security along Pak-Indian border; security reinforcement in Karachi
Pakistan Coast Guards	Paramilitary	1973	3,832	Security of coastal areas of Sindh and Balochistan
Frontier Constabulary	Paramilitary	1958	19,387	Security interface between FATA and settled areas; assists police in law and order
Frontier Corps	Paramilitary	1959	90,318	Border security along Pak-Afghan, Pak-Iran borders; counterinsurgency in FATA
Gilgit-Baltistan Scouts	Paramilitary	2004	2,477	Security of Gilgit-Baltistan borders; assists police in law and order
Federal Investigation Agency	Immigration	1975	3,500	Enforces immigration laws; investigates organized crimes
Islamabad Capital Territory Police	Police	1981	10,995	Policing the federal capital territory of Islamabad
National Police Bureau	Planning	2002	50	Focal point for police-related research and development
National Counter-terrorism Authority	CT analysis, strategy	2009	203	Threat assessment on extremism, terrorism, and insurgency

TABLE 5.2 (continued)

Federal Law Enforcing Organizations not Attached with Ministry of Interior				
Organization	*Ministry*	*Founded*	*Strength*	*Function*
Anti-Narcotics Force	Narcotics Control Ministry	1995	3,100	Narcotics control in the country
Pakistan Railways Police	Ministry of Railways		7,074	Security of trains, train stations, and railway lines
National Highways and Motorway Police	Ministry of Communications	1997	5,000	Traffic control and policing of motorways
Airport Security Force	Ministry of Defense		4,500	Protection of airports
National Accountability Bureau	Ministry of Law	1999	800	Investigates corruption cases
Khasadar Force	States and Frontier Regions	1921	16,242	Supports political administration in FATA
Levies	States and Frontier Regions	1889	16,562	Supports administration in FATA and Provincially Administered Tribal Areas (PATA)

Source: Author's compilation. Data sources: Abbas 2011. Interviews with officials from the Ministry of Interior (2010); Ministry of States and Frontier Regions (2010); Ministry of Defense (2010); Pakistan Railways (2010); ASF (2010); and NAB (2010). Author also interviewed former chairman NACTA, Tariq Parvez in 2012. Information also used from Perlez 2010.

TABLE 5.3
Provincial Police Strength in Pakistan

Province/Territory	*Population (millions)*	*Police Strength*	*Police Stations*
Punjab	93	177,492	637
Sindh	36	107,445	440
Khyber Pakhtunkhwa	21	78,300	250
Balochistan	8	33,481	84
Gilgit-Baltistan	2	4,662	26
AJK	5	8,373	42

Sources: Data collected from Ellahi 2010; Government of KPK 2010; Balochistan Police 2007; and interviews with officials of the Sindh government (2010), and with officials of the Ministry of Kashmir Affairs and Northern Areas (2010).

are facing today has changed from the conventional criminal motivated by personal or financial goals to the ideologically motivated terrorist who is ready to fight the state. Despite their various shortcomings, members of the police are often at the forefront of fighting terror, sacrificing their lives along the way. Fayaz Toru, ex-chief of the KPK police, told the media after a bomb blast at the police colony in the city of Kohat in 2007, "Frontier Police are writing history in blood."[5] The police continue to literally embrace suicide bombers to save people and property; more than two thousand police officers have lost their lives fighting terrorism in Pakistan.

Militants have adopted extremely lethal techniques of violence, such as the use of improvised explosive devices, rocket launchers, and suicide bombings. An analysis of terrorist incidents shows that suicide bombings are only 4 percent of total terrorist incidents, yet they are responsible for more than 45 percent of all casualties.[6] Members of the police are targets of more than a quarter of all suicide attacks.[7]

Despite the amount of sacrifice on behalf of police officers, the law of diminishing returns is evident in the CT efforts, from the rank of the police constable to the highest rank of chief constable. One CT official aptly commented on Pakistan's response to the scourge of terrorism: "Pakistan is ruined by ordnance (arms and ammunition) and ordinances (ad hoc political measures)."[8] The factors responsible for this state of affairs are grouped into structural problems and police-specific problems, each of which is deliberated upon in the following paragraphs. Together these explain the woes of the Pakistani police, and law enforcement more broadly, when it comes to countering the kind of terrorism Pakistan is facing today.

TABLE 5.4
Number of Suicide Attacks

	2006	*2007*	*2008*	*2009*	*2010*
Suicide attacks on police	2	14	16	33	14
Suicide attacks in Pakistan	9	55	67	87	52

Source: Author's compilation, with data collected from South Asia Terrorism Portal, "Fatalities in Terrorist Violence in Pakistan 2003–2012," www.satp.org/satporgtp/countries/pakistan/database/casualt ies.htm; SIG, "FIA (Federal Investigation Agency) Analysis of Terrorist Attacks in Balochistan" (2010); and FATA Secretariat.

Structural Problems

In the context of the police and CT in Pakistan, structural problems are not "police-specific" issues, but they directly or indirectly contribute to violence and extremism and, given their nature, do not allow the police to exercise authority or control. All of these are linked to geographical considerations and the weak writ of the state across particular areas. There are two fault lines (the line of control [LoC], and the Durand Line) and three blind spots (FATA, the Provincially Administered Tribal Areas [PATA], and the "B areas" of Balochistan). These underpin Pakistan's external and internal security paradigms as well as the crises that emanate from them.

FAULT LINES

The LoC, the status-quo boundary between India and Pakistan in Jammu and Kashmir, signifies the struggle for Kashmir, over which these two countries have fought three wars in 1948, 1965, and 1999, and have been embroiled in numerous crises. The nonresolution of the Kashmir issue encouraged militancy—backed as it was by Pakistani intelligence agencies—which eventually increased in its scope and fervor, spreading into both India and Pakistan. In India, major terrorist attacks such as the Indian Parliament attack of 2001 and the Mumbai attacks of 2008 were traced back to Pakistan-based Kashmiri groups (Sweeny 2011). A number of these groups, such as Lashkar-e-Taiba (LeT), Harkat-ul-Mujahideen (HuM), and Jaish-e-Mohammed (JeM), once active across the border in Indian Kashmir, are now destabilizing Pakistan.

Ilyas Kashmiri, originally the leader of the Kashmir-focused Harakat-ul-Jihad-al-Islami (HuJI), formed the dreaded 313 Brigade, which is affiliated with al-Qaeda. Likewise, the splinter groups of HuM morphed into the Abdullah Azzam Brigade of al-Qaeda, headed by HuM militant Badar Mansoor

(Roggio 2009b). The Abdullah Azzam Brigade was involved in the Pearl Continental hotel attack in Peshawar in 2009; the killing of Dr. Mohammad Farooq Khan, the vice chancellor of Swat University (Mayar 2010); and the 2010 attack on the Ahmadiyya mosques in Lahore (Cole 2010). As long as the Kashmir issue remains unresolved, militants as "freedom fighters" or "terrorists" (depending on which side of the fence you are on) will continue to go back and forth across the LoC and perpetrate violence on both sides of the line.

The other fault line is the Durand Line. This is the 1,529-mile-long border between Afghanistan and Pakistan that meanders across the region known for the "Great Game"—the political rivalry of the great powers competing for influence in the region.[9] In the nineteenth century, Britain and Tsarist Russia competed for influence, while for a century the United States and the Soviet Union fought a proxy war in the region (Hopkirk 1992; Rashid 2001). Now in the twenty-first century, the lone superpower, the United States., is battling al-Qaeda on both sides of the Durand Line. Pakistan remained an integral part of the second and third Great Games (Rubin and Rashid 2008). Pakistan's continuation of Britain's "Forward Policy" diluted the sanctity of the Durand Line, which made it difficult to control the osmosis of men, money, and materiel across the border.[10] According to Khalid Qureshi, the director of the Counter Terrorism Wing of the FIA, nations that cannot control the movement of these "3 M's" across their borders also struggle to control transnational crimes including terrorism.[11]

Not surprisingly, when the notorious sectarian militant Riaz Basra, the founder of the anti-Shia Lashkar-e-Jhangvi (LeJ), was targeted by the Pakistani authorities in the mid-1990s, he would cross this porous border to hide in Afghanistan (Roul 2005). Today, when Pakistan chases militants, they often find sanctuaries in Afghanistan, including figures such as Maulana Fazlullah of the Swat chapter of the Pakistani Taliban, who escapes to Nuristan in Afghanistan; Khyber Agency (FATA)-based Mangal Bagh of Lashkar-e-Islam, who finds safe haven in Nangarhar; the TTP commander Hakimullah Mehsud, who hides in Paktika; al-Qaeda-affiliated TTP commander Qari Ziaur Rahman, who disappears in Kunar (there are conflicting reports about his death in August 2013); and Brahamdagh Bugti and other separatist leaders from Balochistan, who have settled in Kabul by crossing the "soft border." Moreover, the United States and NATO allies present in Afghanistan have constantly criticized Pakistan for not controlling movement of Afghan Taliban and the Haqqani network who use sanctuary in Pakistan's tribal areas and move across to attack foreign troops in Afghanistan with relative ease. This has been the single most crucial sticking point in the Pakistan–US relationship in recent years.

BLIND SPOTS

In one of the most extensive studies on civil wars, counterinsurgency (COIN), and terrorism using data from 1945 to 1999 in 161 countries, James Fearon and David Laitin (2003) find that a significant factor contributing to the likelihood of violence (insurgency, civil wars, and terrorism) is a weak central government reinforced by ineffective local policing and a corrupt COIN apparatus. The three blind spots where the central authority of Pakistan has been diminished due to a weak policing structure have become hotspots of militancy: FATA, the Malakand Division in PATA where Swat is located, and the "B areas" of Balochistan province.

The first blind spot is the geostrategically located FATA. FATA is the point of entry and exit for most people crossing over from or to northeastern Afghanistan. It has made the headlines as the "global hub" of Islamist terrorists in the past decade. FATA is approximately the size of Albania in area and of New Zealand in population, and is wedged between two weakly administered countries, which provide space for criminal networks of all sorts (ICG 2009). This is coupled with the fact that Pakistan's legal-constitutional framework freezes at the boundary of FATA. The Criminal Procedure Code (CrPC), Pakistan Penal Code (PPC), income tax and customs laws, and Anti-Terrorism Act (ATA), among others, are not applicable to this conservative, largely autonomous tribal belt of Pakistan. There are no police and no police stations; there is no judge and no writ of the Supreme Court. The tribal areas are administered under the draconian Frontier Crimes Regulation (FCR), an administrative system devised by the British after occupying FATA in the middle of the nineteenth century. Initially, ordinary criminal law that was enforced in British India was extended to these areas, but in order to more specifically control the ethnically Pashtun population in the tribal areas, British colonialists devised special laws that were first promulgated in 1871 and then reenacted in 1873 and 1876 with minor modifications. This archaic law has significantly contributed to an inherently unrepresentative and unresponsive system of authority, and it has created a legal-constitutional and administrative vacuum in the tribal areas.

This vacuum in law enforcement, coupled with a fervor for jihad that lingered from the anti-Soviet war in Afghanistan during the 1980s (FATA was in part the staging ground for Afghan fighters at the time), attracted al-Qaeda and Taliban fighters who were dislodged from Afghanistan after the US invasion in 2001. A number of these transnational fighters were killed in FATA, including heavyweights Mustafa Abu al-Yazid (chief of al-Qaeda finances), Abu Khabab al-Masri (al-Qaeda's expert on weapons of mass destruction),

Qari Tahir Yuldashev (the commander of Uzbek fighters), Abdul Haq Turkestani (the commander of Chinese Uighur fighters), Atiyah Abdul Rahman (al-Qaeda chief of staff), Osama al-Kini (wanted in the US embassy bombings in Kenya and Tanzania in 1998), and Eric Breininger, a member of the German Taliban (Gardner 2010; Roggio 2009c, 2010; Crilly 2012).

These perennial fighters systematically annihilated the three weak pillars of FATA governance—the tribal elders or *maliks*, the political administration, and the Scouts—and started a parallel system of criminal justice administration and taxation for their own purposes. Radicalized youth, like fish swimming upstream, travel north from mainland Pakistan to engage in "capacity building" for carrying out terrorist attacks. For transnational warriors, also known as "Speen Taliban" (white Taliban), the area has become a universal congregating spot; they come to FATA for skill sharing and for plotting against their respective governments, and are finally certified by al-Qaeda as global fighters. Most of the Punjabi Taliban, locally also known as the "Tor Taliban" (black Taliban), were either trained in the tribal belt or used these regions as a base to plot attacks in mainland Pakistan, such as the attack on the Sri Lankan cricket team in Lahore in 2009, the attack on Ahmadiyya mosques in Lahore in 2010, the military headquarters raid in Rawalpindi in 2009, the Marriott Hotel attack in Islamabad in 2008, and the attack on the Inter-Services Intelligence (ISI) offices in Multan in 2009. Noting these diverse elements in the region, a police officer aptly deemed FATA the "Serengeti Park of terrorists."[12]

PATA, mainly Malakand Division, is the second blind spot. Malakand Division is equivalent to Belgium in area (11,780 square miles) and was carved out of the princely states of Swat, Dir, and Chitral in 1969. The areas were administered under PATA regulations, according to which civil cases were decided by the Qazi (local judge) and criminal cases by a *jirga* (tribal assembly of elders) headed by the revenue official. In 1989, a local uprising started in Malakand with the slogan of "Shariat ya Shahadat"—that is, the demand for the complete implementation of Sharia (Islamic law) or else martyrdom. They demanded the enforcement of Sharia not only in the criminal justice system (*adalat*) but also in the political (*siyasat*), economic (*mayeeshat*), and social (*maashirat*) realms. While the uprising fizzled out, the underlying tensions remained, and the TTP finally took advantage of this to galvanize locals against the state and ultimately brought the area under its total control in 2008–9. This uprising became progressively more violent and turned Swat Valley, the heart of Malakand Division, into a hub for suicide attacks. Almost one-third of all the suicide attacks in KPK took place in Malakand Division during this period.[13] The Pakistan military eventually had to launch a full-scale operation to dislodge the TTP.

Malakand Division became a hub of extremism due to the weak administrative writ of the state. The region was exempted from various legal-constitutional provisions that were otherwise implemented in mainland Pakistan. As an example, the income tax and customs laws were not implemented in Malakand Division, and as a result, cheap vehicles in large numbers make their way there without incurring any customs expenses. A large number of suicide attacks in Malakand Division, especially Swat Valley, were carried out using these cheap non–custom paid vehicles. Compared to the entire country, where approximately 40 percent of all suicide attacks were carried out in vehicles packed with explosives, two-thirds of all suicide missions in Malakand were conducted in this fashion. In 2007 and 2008, attackers used car bombs in 85 percent and 75 percent of all suicide attacks in Malakand Division, respectively (CID Punjab 2008).[14]

The "B areas" of Balochistan province are another grey area for criminal justice administration. Balochistan has been in the headlines recently due to the raging insurgency in the province where separatists have gained momentum and are challenging the state's authority. Unlike other provinces, the British Raj evolved a cheap, decentralized administrative system when Balochistan province was captured in 1876. It was bifurcated into "A areas" and "B areas." In the A areas, mainly urban centers, the watch and ward as well as the investigative functions are carried out by police. In the B areas, which form 95 percent of Balochistan, watch and ward is carried out by Levies, but investigation is carried out by revenue officials (the *tehsildar* and his staff).[15] On the role of revenue officers in criminal justice administration, the Balochistan High Court commented: "In B areas investigation is conducted by Naib Tehsildars (assistant revenue officials), who are neither trained nor well conversant with the investigation, because they lack legal knowledge and expertise in this respect."

This failure to integrate the B areas into mainland Pakistan has not only made these "undergoverned" areas safe havens for militants and insurgents in Balochistan, but they also have a domino effect on the adjoining stable districts of Punjab and Sindh provinces.[16] In the areas where there is a stronger *sardari* system (a decentralized system of governance whereby tribes hold their principal loyalties to a tribal or clan chief, especially the predominantly ethnically Baloch areas), there is more violence. These areas include Khuzdar, Kalat, Mastung, Lasbella, and Panjgur. On the other hand, regions where local governance is more egalitarian in nature, for example, the Pashtun areas, violence levels are lower. These areas include Zhob, Qilla Saifullah, and Pishin.[17]

There is another area where police exist and the constitutional laws apply but the area is especially problematic due to the high numerical presence of

TABLE 5.5
Balochistan: "A" versus "B" Areas

	A Areas	*B Areas*
Area covered	5 percent of land	95 percent of land
Population	43 percent population (3 million)	57 percent population (4 million)
Geography	Urban centers	Rural areas
Criminal Justice	Police and judiciary	Revenue officials, Levies, and judiciary
Policing	Regular police	Balochistan Levies
Investigations	Police	Revenue officials
Recruitment	State	Tribal and clan chiefs, revenue officials

Source: Author's compilation.

militants and potential militants: Southern Punjab. Southern Punjab's principal terrorism-related concerns are the men from mainly rural backgrounds who act as foot soldiers for terror plots. According to the Crime Investigation Department of Punjab, 1,496 Afghan-trained boys (ATB) and returnees from Afghan prisons (RAP) are present in Southern Punjab (the Multan, Bahawalpur, and Dera Ghazi Khan regions) as compared to only 1,225 ATBs and RAPs in the rest of Punjab. Likewise, despite being a relatively small proportion of the area of Punjab province, there is a high concentration of sectarian militants (545) who are under surveillance as compared to the 971 in the rest of the province. Similarly, 188 clusters of seminaries, or madrassas, are present in South Punjab as compared to the 216 in the rest of Punjab.[18]

Police-Specific Problems

Apart from the earlier-mentioned structural problems, the following "police-specific" factors are responsible for the weakness of CT efforts by the Pakistani law enforcement apparatus.

DISUNITY IN DIVERSITY

The law enforcement infrastructure of Pakistan is a solar system without a sun. There is neither unity of command nor unity of effort among various

Map 3. Balochistan Province

LEOs. Moreover, the military carries out a number of policing functions. The Border Police in 1947 became the Pakistan Rangers and then gravitated toward military command.[19] Today a serving two-star general commands the Rangers. Of the five paramilitary outfits, serving armed forces officers head four of them. Likewise the ASF, ANF, and NAB are often headed by serving or retired military officers. Moreover, almost 60 percent of the paramilitary group the Sindh Rangers is regularly involved in fighting urban crimes in Karachi, even though their primary function is supposed to be policing the international border.[20] In all, approximately 64 percent of the federal policing structure is directly or indirectly under the military's command and control.[21] The complexities and confusion increase when one examines the deployment, recruitment, and financing of these organizations. Although Balochistan is a provincial territory, federal levies are deployed there. Khasadars operate as law enforcers in FATA, but the Home Department in KPK pays their salaries while the Federal Ministry of States and Frontier Regions (SAFRON) carries out their recruitment.[22] The Frontier Constabulary is recruited from tribes for Frontier Regions, but it performs watch and ward duties in urban areas such as Karachi and Islamabad (Babar 2009). The Chitral Border Police, the Malakand Levies, and the Dir Levies operate in KPK province with a police mandate, but they are controlled by a revenue officer and managed from the federal ministry of SAFRON.

The CT functions are even more compartmentalized. There are CT units in each provincial police department in the form of the criminal investigation departments (CID) (Rodriguez 2010). However, there is also a CT unit in the FIA, the ISI, military intelligence (MI), the Pakistan Rangers, the Frontier Corps (FC), and the Intelligence Bureau (IB). The ISI, FC, MI, and IB arrest terrorists, but they cannot prosecute them, whereas the provincial CIDs and the FIA continue to prosecute terrorists but cannot arrest them in the FATA, the escape for virtually all Pakistan-based militants because police have no jurisdiction there. The overlapping of jurisdictions of various LEOs, instead of unifying efforts against the terrorists, acts as a thorn in the side of CT actions and any attempts to be more holistic. It leads to key gaps or duplication, which is a drag on resources and the attrition of organizations, and it has a tremendous stove-piping effect on fighting terrorism. Often enough, each organization, while defending its own "island," watches benignly as other islands succumb to extremism. Additionally, the militarization of Pakistan's internal security apparatus leads to the inculcation of a military ethos of "engaging the target and eliminating it" instead of a policing ethos of "detaining the target and prosecuting it," a norm that is prevalent in successful policing experiences elsewhere.

QUALITY AND QUANTITY DEFICITS

The police face both qualitative and quantitative deficits while fighting terrorism. A police officer candidly summarized this by likening the police's efforts to "fighting war in the air with a Cessna."[23] The KPK has faced the brunt of most terrorist attacks. It has suffered almost half (135) of the total 272 suicide attacks occurring in Pakistan over the past five years.[24] During the peak of the insurgency, the KPK police operated with only 66 percent of its sanctioned strength, and 47 percent of authorized transport; eleven of the twenty-five districts lacked police lines and eighty-six police stations lacked proper buildings; 70 percent of senior police officials and 55 percent of lower police ranks performed their duties without arms.[25] Even today, the highest-ranking officers of ICT are accommodated in a local market that is highly vulnerable to terrorist attacks.[26] In the high-profile case of former prime minister Benazir Bhutto's assassination in December 2007, the investigating team was not provided a single penny to probe the incident.

A senior journalist identifies the qualitative deficit well, stating: "they [the Taliban] have been fighting the war in the name of religion while the police officials are fighting because they get salaries" (Sahi 2009). The dipping morale of the police force was visible at the peak of the insurgency in Swat in 2008–9, where nearly eight hundred policemen, half of the total sanctioned strength of police in Swat, deserted the force out of fear of being killed by the Taliban (Khan 2009). Pakistan also lacks the technical capacities, including the ability to retrieve DNA from items used by the accused. Hence, the clothes of the suicide bomber in Benazir Bhutto's case were sent to the Federal Bureau of Investigation (FBI) in the United States for analysis. Today the police conduct investigations without formal crime scene units to collect evidence. Not one explosives laboratory exists in Pakistan. There are also no ballistics experts, nor any firearms databases.

RESPONSIBILITY VERSUS CAPABILITY

Intelligence agencies arrest two-thirds of the terrorists, but they are not responsible for their prosecution in the courts. Alleged terrorists are arrested and handed over to police, who are to try them in the courts under the framework of substantive and procedural laws. As no legal authority backs the roles being performed by the agents of the military for carrying out internal security duties like arresting people, interrogating them, and gathering evidence, such facts cannot be presented before a court of law. This is a yawning gap between legal frameworks and ground realities that is filled by fabricated stories of backdated arrests, post-facto first information reports

(FIR) and subsequent recovery of weapons to camouflage the role of intelligence agencies. It is hardly surprising, then, that in many instances the beneficiaries of these inconsistencies are the accused as they are regularly acquitted by the courts.[27]

There is also no bridging in the efforts of intelligence and investigations. One important inquiry commented: "It is an admitted fact that the accused remained under probe with the agencies prior to the arrest (of the accused), but no positive information was passed on to the local police; thus the role played by the agencies could not be availed to probe the guilt of the accused. The police investigation and the preliminary inquiry of intelligence do not correspond, and this is due to lack of coordination and cooperation of the agencies."[28]

Substantive and procedural criminal codes are studded with multiple loopholes in tackling terrorism. Protective mechanisms in the current legal system for witnesses, police investigators, prosecutors, and Anti-Terrorism Court (ATC) judges are very weak.[29] Powers are concentrated in an individual police officer, the station house officer (SHO), in the PPC and Criminal Procedure Court but not in the investigation teams, such as the crime scene unit and the joint interrogation team (Hameed 2012). The Evidence Act, or Qanun-e-Shahadat, also has a number of lacunas. For example, evidence from public witnesses is not admissible if it does not corroborate the evidence of private witnesses. A lack of cybercrime laws and laws regarding DNA analysis also hampers investigations. The ATA lacks comprehensive definitions for the most recent kinds of terrorist acts. For instance, "there are no definitions of suicide attack, conspiracy or planning for a suicide attack, suicide bomber, armed insurgency and planning to cause wide spread disaffection against the state" (Hameed 2012). There are few thresholds that, if breached, are punishable in the ATA. For example, the ATA is silent on the number of weapons or the quantity of explosives that will qualify an act as terrorism versus a criminal offense. Moreover, there is no provision in the act that caters to attacks on nuclear installations, or the use of chemical, biological, and radiological weapons.[30] Additionally, the criminal justice system prefers to broadly apply the ATA to heinous crimes such as child molestation and stoning instead of specifically applying it to instances of terrorism.[31]

INFORMATION HOARDING

Law enforcement agencies operate in silos. The competition among institutions with overlapping jurisdictions leads to information hoarding. This lack of coordination among agencies was highlighted by the trial judge in the Gen. Mushtaq Beg case, the Pakistan Army's surgeon general who was killed in a suicide attack in Rawalpindi in 2008. The judge stated: "Such high profile cases require organized investigation not only by one investigating officer, rather, intelligence and investigation agencies should coordinate in the form of a joint investigation team. Otherwise, the real culprits will remain at large and innocent people will continue to suffer at the whim of terrorists."[32] A high-ranking official of the Karachi CID, Mushtaq Mahar, complained that in 2009 a thumb drive was recovered from a terrorist killed in an encounter with the police in Dera Ghazi Khan. In this thumb drive, the terrorists saved plans of high-profile attacks, including the attacks on the army headquarters in Rawalpindi and oil terminals in Karachi. However, the Punjab police failed to share this information with the Sindh police (Cheema 2011). Shortly after this encounter, terrorists mounted an attack on oil terminals in Karachi. At other times, when information is shared, it does not reach the concerned office or the designated leadership. When Master Riaz, the mastermind of a blast in a seminary in Mian Channu in Punjab, told investigators that the CID offices in Karachi would be targeted in future, the investigation failed to properly share this information, and CID offices were subsequently targeted in 2010.

DATABANKS

In the recent past, Pakistan has developed sophisticated software for data management. The National Database Registration Authority (NADRA) stores data on 92 million citizens of Pakistan while the Personal Identification Secure Comparison & Evaluation System of the FIA has a databank of 60 million travelers. Approximately eight hundred thousand ten-digit fingerprints of accused law offenders have also been entered in the Pakistan Automated Fingerprint Identification System.[33] These databases were helpful in identifying the terrorists involved in various acts of terrorism including the Mumbai attacks of November 2008, the suicide bombers of the Abdullah Shah Ghazi shrine in Karachi in 2010, and the attack on Federal Minister Amir Muqam in 2007. In spite of this obvious benefit of up-to-date databases, there are no national databases for weapons and vehicles. Terrorists continue to toy with unregistered weapons and vehicles that are available in the nooks and crannies of the country. Likewise, it is impossible to match DNA from body parts of suicide bombers because of the absence of DNA databases.

The Great Acquittals: The Lack of Investigative Skills

A recent report of the International Crisis Group observed, "Police investigations are undermined by the absence of professional autonomy, poor training and reliance on blunt investigative tools" (ICG 2010, 1). As a result, a number of terrorist attacks remain untraced: the attack on Benazir Bhutto at Karsaz, Karachi, in 2007, the attack on Awami National Party chief Asfandyar Wali Khan in Charsadda, KPK, in 2009, and the attack on the US consulate in Peshawar in 2010. Often owing to poor investigation, even traced masterminds cannot be arrested, as was the case with the Parade Lane attack in an area of predominantly military housing in Rawalpindi in 2009 and the attack on the Pearl Continental hotel in Peshawar in 2009. Some of the arrested militants even have to be released because they cannot be properly prosecuted and convicted with the available information. This happened with the perpetrators and masterminds of the 2008 Marriott Hotel attack in Islamabad, the 2004 assassination attempt on Prime Minister Shaukat Aziz in Fateh Jang, the 2008 attack on the Danish embassy in Islamabad, and the ISI Hamza Camp attack in 2007 (Mir 2011).

In analyzing cases brought forward for prosecution by the police, one inquiry officer of the Punjab prosecution department found that the foundations laid by the investigation officers were not up to the mark, allegedly containing several flaws and inconsistencies. These issues led to a belated examination of the prosecution witnesses and unserious attitudes of the senior officers in the investigation. Furthermore, the inquiry officer found that, in suicide attacks, the investigation failed to link the suicide bomber with the persons accused of conspiring, planning, and plotting the attack. One analysis carried out by the counterterrorism department of the Punjab Police observed that 74 percent of the total terrorist cases between 1990 and 2009 culminated with acquittals of the accused (S. Hussain 2011). One major flaw that the study identified was poor prosecution, which was in turn due to witnesses becoming hostile; the nonappearance of witnesses; compromises by witnesses; contradictions in witnesses' statements; or contradictions in medicolegal and ocular witnesses (S. Hussain 2011). Moreover, the concerned agencies did not exhibit any interest in the follow-up of the cases regarding the prosecution in the court of law. Unsurprisingly, the accused were generally acquitted because the case of the prosecution "throughout remained uncorroborated and unsubstantiated at the touch-stone of evidence," as observed by the ATC in a statement that would apply to most terrorism-related cases in Pakistan.[34] Following is a discussion of some glaring shortcomings observed in some of the most high-profile terrorist cases.

Benazir Bhutto's Assassination Case

On December 27, 2007, former prime minister of Pakistan Benazir Bhutto was assassinated at the end of a public gathering at Liaqat Bagh, Rawalpindi.

The report of the UN commission that probed this incident observed that "the crime scene was not cordoned off," and "within one hour and forty minutes of the blast, the police ordered fire and rescue officials present to wash the crime scene down with fire hoses" (UN 2010). The commission also found that even Bhutto's vehicle was cleaned so that the forensic analysis of the swabs taken from parts of the vehicle carried out later by Scotland Yard "yielded nothing" (UN 2010). The chief of the Rawalpindi police on three occasions refused permission to carry out a postmortem examination on Ms. Bhutto's remains as required by law.

The Manawan Attack

On the morning of March 30, 2009, several terrorists attacked a police training center at Manawan, Lahore. After struggling for more than five hours, the situation was brought under control with the loss of seven police officers. All but one terrorist was killed; the remaining one, Hijrat Ullah, was arrested alive. However, Hijrat Ullah, a poor, trash-collecting Afghan, was acquitted in the trial. In the trial, the judge and defense counsel conceded that the mode, manner, time, and place of occurrence were not disputed; however, they challenged the police version, which stated that the accused threw hand grenades from the northern boundary wall of the training center but that he was apprehended from the southern boundary wall (ATC-I 2009).[35] Some of the questions surrounding the logistics of the attack included the following: How did the accused terrorist travel from the northern side of the center from where he attacked to the extreme southern side of the center where he was apprehended while the whole area was cordoned off by the army, rangers, and police? Why did he attack using two hand grenades without a suicide jacket or firearms like other attackers did? Why were none of the police officers able to "apprehend Hijratullah for several hours when he became empty-handed allegedly after throwing two hand grenades?"[36] As the ATC judge concluded, the "prosecution has totally failed to produce any cogent and plausible evidence that who the police arrested was actually the accused, or whether Hijratullah was armed or possessed a cell phone or another instrument of connectivity (to act as a detonator) at the time of his alleged arrest."[37]

Gen. Mushtaq Beg's Assassination Case

On February 25, 2008, a suicide bomber from al-Qaeda targeted the surgeon general of the Pakistan Army, Lt. Gen. Mushtaq Beg, the highest-ranking military casualty in Pakistan's history of terrorism. During the trial, all of the nine people arrested in the case were acquitted. A learned judge of the ATC observed, "The investigation moved counter-clockwise by first identifying the accused by the star witness and then recording his statement. Whereas it should have been in the sequence of, first, recording the statement of the said witness at the earliest possible time after the occurrence, regarding his seeing of the occurrence, and then getting the identification of the accused by the star witness."[38] Moreover, the star witness allegedly stated, "Out of five persons responsible for the attack, one exploded himself; meaning thereby that four persons at the most appear to be accused in this case but the prosecution has indicted nine accused without an iota of evidence against others."[39] During the investigation of the case, five SHOs or inspectors of RA Bazaar Police Station in Rawalpindi were transferred from February 2008 until the submission of the *challan* (indictment) on May 6, 2009, thus creating additional complications for the prosecution.

Attempted Attack on Chief Justice Iftikhar Chaudhry

On July 17, 2007, a suicide bomber detonated himself in a gathering waiting to receive the chief justice of Pakistan. During the trial, the prosecution star witness, Altaf Khattak, was declared a "hostile witness" by the prosecution itself, and it was suggested that he had been won over by the accused persons.[40] He identified the accused during the identification parade held at the Faisalabad jail, but he expressed ignorance during the trial. There were flaws in the identification parade too. The prosecution only provided the names and the parentage, in spite of the requirement to also include the occupation, addresses, height, and age as well as the social status and the religion of the "dummies."[41] Also in this case, a subinspector conducted 90 percent of the investigation even though, as per the ATA of 1997, a police official below the rank of inspector is not considered competent enough to investigate this case (Punjab Public Prosecution Department 2010).[42]

The Marriott Bombing

On September 20, 2008, the largest truck bomb in Pakistan's history struck the five-star Marriott Hotel in Islamabad. State-of-the-art geo-fencing techniques were used to find and arrest the accused. However, the local police first chose a subinspector who had no experience in investigating even a conventional murder case, in spite of this being a high-profile case of terrorism.[43] Things became even worse when an inspector with a reputation as a hostile and unreliable witness in other terrorism cases was assigned to investigate the case.

Conclusion: Correcting Course

As long as regional issues that cause terrorism to flow from or to Pakistan are not addressed, the motivation for terrorism and, indeed, its incidence will continue. First, both the LoC and the Durand Line need to be transformed to bring collateral benefits instead of collateral damage. Second, Pakistan has three soft areas: FATA, PATA, and the "B" areas of Balochistan. Pakistan must bring these areas from extremes to the mean by extending the legal-constitutional blanket of the country to them. The ATA, the Customs Act, the income tax laws, CrPC, and PPC need to be extended to cover these undergoverned areas. Otherwise these regions will continue to radiate violence to other parts of Pakistan, and the law enforcement machinery will remain unable to tackle it. Pakistan cannot curb terrorism, separatism, and subnationalism from a law enforcement perspective while only partial constitutional cover persists in some parts of the country.

Next, Pakistan has to bring unity to its diverse law enforcement agencies. One option is to establish a joint terrorism task force at the divisional level. Instead of raising a reactive joint investigation team after each incident, an established task force should include permanent members from intelligence (ISI, IB, MI, and CID) and investigations (police, prosecution) departments. Pakistan could also create a new institution at the federal level that emulates the US Department of Homeland Security.[44]

Other key lacunas flow from the fact that military units perform a huge chunk of law enforcement functions. A senior police officer has suggested, sarcastically, that law enforcement should be made the fourth arm of the armed forces along with the army, navy, and air force if the current power balance, heavily skewed in favor of the military, cannot be altered (HRCP 2010a). A more sanguine policy would be to empower civilian LEOs constitutionally, legally, and administratively by providing CT facilities including communications interception, mobile-tracking systems (GSM), geolocators, and cellular calling data analysis to the provincial CIDs in order to make them more operationally autonomous. Moreover, civilian liaisons to the military establishment would be required to iron out matters pertaining to arrests, detentions, investigations, and prosecution of militants.

The state must also urgently redesign and revamp criminal procedural laws and substantive laws. Since the weapon of choice for terrorists has shifted from firearms to explosives, the ATA needs overhauling to acknowledge the new realities of suicide attacks, such as the types of explosives used and the penalties for each category of attack (S. Hussain 2011). Protective clauses must also be added to include witnesses, investigators, and the judges in the criminal procedural and penal codes, as was done in the fight against mafias in Italy and South America.[45] Moreover, Pakistan must amend its anti-terror laws to include the role of intelligence agencies in its ambit. This will make the testimonies of intelligence officials admissible in the courts and the evidence collected by them acceptable during trial. Additionally, it must also properly include provisions for technical evidence in penal and criminal procedural codes, along with provisions for eyewitnesses and circumstantial evidence for convictions. A conviction of life imprisonment means fourteen years in jail based on a life expectancy of almost a century ago. A judicial-legislative commission should suggest the necessary updates in the legal system required to bring these measures at par with the threats and requirements of today's Pakistan.

Finally, the quantitative and qualitative deficits of law enforcement need redressing. This must include the development of national databases on vehicles and weapons, state-of-the-art forensic labs with DNA capabilities, and the upgrading of techniques and equipment for wiretapping, geo-fencing, polygraph machines, fingerprinting, and voice data analysis.

Notes

1. "The Future of Energy: The End of the Oil Age," *Economist*, October 23, 2003, www.economist.com/node/2155717.
2. Tariq Pervez, ex-coordinator, National Counterterrorism Authority (NACTA), interviewed by author, Islamabad, January 2010.
3. See also "Failed States Index 2012," *Foreign Policy*, http://foreignpolicy.com/failed_states_index_2012_interactive.
4. "Terrorism Risk Index." Bath, United Kingdom: Maplecroft. Available at http://maplecroft.com.
5. "Frontier Police Writing Its History with Blood," *Express Tribune*, September 7, 2007, http://tribune.com.pk/multimedia/videos/47232/.
6. Analysis of terrorist acts by the Special Investigation Group (SIG) of the Federal Investigation Agency (FIA), 2010. The author was posted to SIG at the time.
7. Ibid.
8. Tariq Khosa, ex-director general of FIA, interviewed by author, Islamabad, March 2010.
9. The term "Great Game" is attributed to Arthur Conolly, intelligence officer of British East India Company's Sixth Bengal Light Infantry, but popularized by British novelist Rudyard Kipling in his 1901 novel *Kim*.
10. The British employed the Forward Policy in the tribal areas they forcibly occupied to counter Russian advances in Central Asia.
11. Khalid Qureshi, director Counter Terrorism Wing, FIA, interviewed by author, Islamabad, March 2010.
12. Saeed Wazir, police officer, interviewed by author, July 18, 2012.
13. SIG (Special Investigations Group), "FIA (Federal Investigation Agency) Analysis of Terrorist Attacks in Balochistan," 2010.

14. CID (Crime Investigation Department) Punjab, "Monthly Review: Terrorism Analysis," September 13, 2008.
15. Afzal Ali Shigri, ex–inspector general of police, interviewed by author, January 3, 2010.
16. Ibid.
17. SIG, "FIA Analysis of Terrorist Attacks in Balochistan."
18. Ibid.
19. Pakistan Rangers Ordinance, 1959 (W.P. Ordinance XIV of 1959), March 28, 1959, *Punjab Laws Online*, www.punjablaws.gov.pk/laws/106.html.
20. Ministry of Interior official, interviewed by author, June 5, 2010.
21. SIG, "FIA Analysis of Terrorist Attacks in Balochistan."
22. Officials of Home Department, interviewed by author, KPK, December 18, 2010.
23. SIG, "FIA Analysis of Terrorist Attacks in Balochistan."
24. Ibid.
25. Police lines are the district headquarters that serve as the logistics hub for the police, including accommodation for reserve police. Information regarding police without arms was ascertained through a presentation made by the governor of KPK to a group of civil servants in February 2008.
26. Shigri, interviewed by the author, Islamabad, July 13, 2012.
27. See chapter 6 in this book for more details of the legal problems in prosecuting and convicting the accused.
28. Enquiry report regarding the failure of investigation and prosecution in cases FIR no. 75/08 and 114/08, PS RA Bazar, Rawalpindi-Lt.Gen. Mushtaq Ahmad Beg case, Punjab Public Prosecution Department, 2010.
29. Qureshi, interviewed by author, Islamabad, March 26, 2010.
30. Shigri, interviewed by author, January 3, 2010.
31. Ibid.
32. ATC-II (Anti-Terrorism Court II), February 25, 2008. Case Number 3.
33. Sharif Virk, ex–inspector general of police, interviewed by author, August 10, 2010.
34. *State v Tipu*, FIR 245 (ATC-1, July 2007), Islamabad.
35. ATC-I (Anti-Terrorism Court I), March 30, 2009. Case Number 19.
36. Ibid.
37. Inter-Services Public Relations, Press Release No. 30, February 25, 2008.
38. ATC-II, February 25, 2008. Case Number 3.
39. Ibid.
40. ATC-I (Anti-Terrorism Court I), *State v. Fasiullah Tipu*, July 17, 2007.
41. Ibid.
42. Enquiry report, Punjab Public Prosecution Department.
43. Qureshi, interviewed by author, Islamabad, March 26, 2010.
44. Afzal Ali Shigri, ex-inspector general of police, interviewed by author, January 3, 2010.
45. Qureshi, interviewed by author, Islamabad, March 26, 2010.

CHAPTER 6

Legal Challenges to Military Operations in Pakistan

The Case of the Federally and Provincially Administered Tribal Areas

AHMER BILAL SOOFI

THIS CHAPTER highlights the deficiencies and shortcomings in Pakistan's existing criminal justice system regarding the conduct of military operations by the Pakistan Army against insurgent nonstate actors in Pakistan's northwestern Federally Administered Tribal Areas (FATA) and Provincially Administered Tribal Areas (PATA). In light of the current state of relevant municipal law or lack thereof, several proposals and suggestions for upgrading Pakistan's deficient criminal justice system are offered. The overarching purpose of this chapter, however, is to encourage debate and firmly move forward toward a much-needed overhaul of Pakistan's criminal justice system, which is vital for the safety of Pakistani people as well as the international community against nonstate actors and terrorists operating in Pakistan's tribal areas and beyond.

East of the Durand Line, within Pakistan, there are numerous groups and nonstate actors that can be broadly divided into two categories to facilitate a concise discussion of Pakistan's counterterrorism (CT) challenges. The first category, the Afghan Taliban, includes those who attack US forces within Afghanistan and take refuge in Pakistan. The second category, the allied groups and sympathizers of the Tehrik-e-Taliban Pakistan (TTP, or Pakistani Taliban), includes those attempting to assert unlawful control over Pakistan's territory by attacking its military and law enforcement personnel and infrastructure.

After six years of half-hearted attempts, Pakistan's government and its army launched in 2008 a comprehensive counterinsurgency (COIN) campaign against the TTP and other nonstate actors challenging the writ of the state of Pakistan.[1] While the Pakistan Army had previously been deployed to fight insurgent fighters, the 2008 declaration marked the first time the federal government formally called upon the army to aid civilian power by invoking the constitutional provision of article 245, which states that under the directions of the federal government and subject to law, the armed forces shall act in aid of civil power when called upon to do so (part XII, ch. 2). Thus far, the government of Pakistan has not initiated similar COIN offensives against the Afghan Taliban, and this inaction continues to be a thorny issue between Pakistan and the United States.

In terms of the territorial scope and the deployment of armed forces and related resources, the offensive against the TTP and its supporters marks one of the largest law enforcement operations anywhere in the world. The ongoing campaign has lasted for over five years. The Pakistan Army has wrested control from the militants in Bajaur and South Waziristan and in a number of other agencies in Pakistan's FATA, and Swat in the adjacent Khyber Pakhtunkhwa Province (KPK) (Lalwani 2010). Borrowing from the military lexicon, the army "cleared" or "secured" many areas and took complete control of the roads and important travel routes, which enabled the civilians to return to relative normalcy (ISPR 2009).[2] Pakistan's army intelligently and swiftly tailored its strategies and methodologies to more effectively weed out groups of militants. In a document prepared for the US Congress, the US Department of State duly recognized Pakistan's efforts and achievements in disrupting terrorist activities.[3]

Given the absence of an adequate and effective legal framework to process hundreds of detained militants, several legal issues such as the legality of detentions, the kind of legal evidence that could be collected against militants during COIN operations, minimum evidentiary standards for prosecution, and adequate safeguard of individual human rights arose as an unfortunate consequence of the military campaign. These issues highlighted the incapacity and inadequacy of the country's existing criminal justice system to meet new challenges and necessitated the creation of a new legal regime to effectively deal with these unique legal problems. (It is pertinent to mention that while this chapter focuses exclusively on legal issues arising as a direct consequence of military operations, these issues are also prevalent when militants are apprehended outside of military campaigns.)

Military operations are only one phase of CT efforts. Their success is fleeting and marginal in the absence of an effective judicial system to subsequently prosecute, try, and bring to justice all those arrested. If terror suspects are released due to limitations in detention legislation or procedures, or to faulty investigative techniques or weakness in laws of evidence, the utility of military operations is seriously diluted. It is not possible for Pakistan's intelligence agencies to keep track of those militants who are released due to the shortcomings of the country's criminal justice system. Once released, these individuals are free to travel anywhere inside or outside Pakistan, which is an alarming prospect with grave global consequences. Furthermore, a faulty legal framework negatively affects the morale of armed forces who risk their lives trying to bring the militants within the ambit of law and also wastes precious resources and time. Even in less challenging situations, where the law enforcement mechanism is far more advanced and well developed, terror suspects have been acquitted only to return with greater vengeance to strike at other civilian and military targets. Astonishingly, the perpetrators of some of the most destructive and gruesome attacks in Pakistan had previously been acquitted by the courts. Examples of these attacks include the Marriott Hotel bombing in Islamabad in September 2008, which killed 60 people including 4 foreigners and seriously injured another 200, the bombing of the motorcade of former Prime Minister Benazir Bhutto in Karachi in October 2007 that killed over 140 people, and the attack on the General Headquarters of the Pakistan Army in Rawalpindi carried out by Taliban gunmen in October 2009.[4] Given cognizance of this trend and the lack of incriminating evidence against them, yet desperate to contain such suspects, Pakistan's intelligence agencies are often forced to resort to clumsy and unlawful methods.

Unfortunately, there is greater proclivity for faulty legal practices in the country's remote regions where the military is conducting operations. In FATA, there are no functioning police stations, judges often go on leave to avoid assassination attempts, and the general governmental infrastructure is barely functional. Because there is no civilian infrastructure to receive those detained by the military or preserve evidence for trials, the army has in some cases allegedly declined to admit to the detention of the militants and, in order to avoid their release, has reported them as "missing persons."[5] Even more worrisome, because of frustration with the inability of the legal process to bring a militant or terrorist to justice, locals and military personnel might have a perverse incentive to commit extrajudicial killings. Indeed, there have been a series of allegations of such excesses by the military. For instance, Human Rights Watch reports more than two hundred cases of extrajudicial killings conducted by the Pakistani Army in Swat since September 2009 (HRW 2010).

Key Legal Impediments for Military Action against Terrorism in Pakistan

This section highlights the fundamental flaws of the existing legal framework that both compromise the military's use of force against terrorism and violate the fundamental rights of the alleged militants. Unfortunately, problems abound at several levels, from determining the very basis for use of military force to arrests and internment to compensation for victims.

The Legal Basis of Military Operations

Several politicians in Pakistan hold the view that the military is fighting the United States' proxy war.[6] Whereas this perception may be valid from a political standpoint, it must be highlighted that from a legal standpoint, the Pakistan Army has been requisitioned in FATA and the adjoining PATA in KPK by the federal government of Pakistan under Pakistan's constitution. The Pakistani civilian government's requisition was not undertaken in compliance with any US legislation.

According to Pakistan's constitution, the army cannot commence any military operation unless formally instructed to do so by the federal government. Article 245 of the constitution stipulates, "The Armed Forces shall, under the directions of the Federal Government, defend Pakistan against external aggression or threat of war, and, subject to law, act in aid of civil power when called upon to do so" (part XII, ch. 2). Because this is the only provision in the constitution that delineates how and when the armed forces may use force and carry out law enforcement operations, any military operation without prior legal authorization granted by the federal government would be unconstitutional.

Article 245, under which the COIN operations are being carried out in FATA and KPK, explicitly states that military force is "subject to law." In other words, any constitutional authorization of military force must be exercised in accordance with the "law" or "laws" to be separately enacted. Presently, only two laws provide brief procedures for conduct of armed forces in aid of civil power—the Criminal Procedure Code (CrPC) and the Anti-Terrorism Act (ATA) of 1997.

The problem lies in the fact that the CrPC and the ATA are inadequate within the context of the present scale and length of military operations. First, they do not clearly distinguish between the calling of the armed forces by the civilian authorities for a brief and short "CT action" and requisitioning them for a prolonged action against a sustained insurgency that involves direct military action and broader policies of "building" infested regions once they have been cleared. Second, the existing laws are primarily designed for surgical military operations to handle isolated or sporadic law and order incidents, which is why they do not address the manner in which the armed forces shall conduct themselves if asked to commit for a much longer or even indefinite duration.

Consequently, the armed forces have no regulatory law for a long-term engagement in an internal conflict and no guidelines for detaining and trying those captured. There is also no existing law for upholding human rights standards during a conflict and no obligation to conduct internal investigations in cases of excesses or abuses. Moreover, no law regulates the terms and conditions of detentions. In the absence of such laws, individual military officials cannot be held accountable. Equally troubling, without substantial laws detailing military operations and legitimizing detentions, militants are often released. In this regard, militants are the unintended beneficiaries of insufficient legislation and deficient legal codes.

To curtail abuses by military forces and the release of militants, the government of Pakistan must urgently frame laws that institute military accountability and provide legal parameters for detention and conviction of militants. It is also necessary for the political leadership to cooperate to enact laws that reflect a comprehensive "antiterrorism strategy." Military frustrations with the political leadership are legitimate and understandable given the parliament's inability to produce a single document detailing Pakistan's CT strategy. In the absence of a bipartisan consensus on a CT strategy, political leaders will be unable to guide a consistent military campaign.

The Legal Nature of the Military Operations in FATA

The legal nature of military operations in FATA remains blurred and indeterminate. Comments and analyses originating from outside Pakistan allege that military operations in Pakistan qualify as a "noninternational armed conflict" (NIAC) under international humanitarian law (IHL).[7] The categorization of any conflict as NIAC has legal repercussions. For example, for the duration of an NIAC, the International Committee of the Red Cross (ICRC) must be provided access to detainees and granted opportunity to evaluate the occurrence of war crimes. The Ministry of Foreign Affairs in Pakistan has reportedly denied the ICRC's requests to access detainees on the basis that the military operations in FATA and other regions of Pakistan do not constitute an NIAC.

There is no domestic law that either mandates the government or provides it with guidelines for making such a determination. It appears that both the Pakistani and the US authorities are not particularly interested in determining the precise status of the conflict. The government of Pakistan fears that the classification of the conflict as an NIAC might politically internationalize the issues and force Pakistan to provide access to foreign nongovernmental organizations like the ICRC. Consequently, the conflict has been variously classified as "war on terror," "COIN operation," "CT operation," "law and order situation," "conflict," "military operation," "armed conflict in FATA," and so on. The concern is beyond mere definitions, however; Pakistan is negatively affected by the lack of transparency surrounding its current COIN strategy. For one thing, it creates an alarming lack of trust between the civilians and the military. Furthermore, high collateral damage aggravates the already fragile relationship between the relevant stakeholders—civilian and military—and the state and society at large. Additionally, criticism of Pakistan's COIN strategy as ineffective in diminishing the terrorist activity (NDTV 2011) and establishing control over the concerned areas further fragments civil–military relations. It is important to note that the COIN strategy must include measures to promote constructive interaction between the civilians and military to advance rehabilitation and development in the region.

In this regard, the government of Pakistan needs to enact legislation mandating the state to determine the nature of any armed conflict. For example, in India, the Geneva Conventions Implementation Act (No. 6 of 1960) requires the federal secretary to make an administrative determination whether a CT or a COIN operation should be designated as NIAC. Pakistan needs a comparable mechanism.

Conduct of Military Operations

In addition to the legality and nature of military operations in Pakistan's northwestern territories, legislation applicable to the very conduct of the military in FATA and KPK is also insufficient. Currently, no specific federal or provincial enactment in Pakistan adequately regulates the conduct of military operations. The Pakistan Army Act (No. 34 of 1952) generally describes acceptable conduct for military personnel but only in the sense of defining a relationship among the commanders and their subordinates. The Army Act addresses issues such as when orders to mobilize will be issued (sec. 7), how orders will be passed on (sec. 2), who will issue the orders (sec. 4), and what the standard operating procedures (SOP) will be (sec. 9, 11, and 17). These codes of conduct relate to the internal management of the military forces but do not contain any provisions related to the conduct of military operations.

Additionally, besides nominal guidelines in the ATA and the provisions of the CrPC, there is no comprehensive federal law that defines parameters for the use of force by the Pakistan Army or any of Pakistan's law enforcement entities, and there is no delegated legislation under the Army Act (1952) or the Police Order (2002) prescribing the means and methods of using force during prolonged military campaigns within the country.[8]

The absence of a code of conduct for military personnel during CT and COIN operations is an unfortunate and glaring omission, especially in light of the global importance of Pakistan's success against insurgents and terrorists. That said, the absence of any law regulating the conduct of armed conflict does not give Pakistan's armed forces free rein to use force at will during military operations. Every military commander is under a general duty, even in the absence of a specific law, to exercise care when using force during operations in aid of civil power. If he violates this principle, he is liable to sanctions under the military law that include various punishments, including court-martial. In fact, in terms of state practice, law enforcement agencies of Pakistan and the army have largely conformed well to the principles of IHL.[9]

Yet these blanket provisions seldom prove sufficient. In Pakistan's case, a number of incidents of IHL violations have come to the fore. In October 2009, a video was publicly circulated that showed people in military uniforms but without identification roughing up TTP suspects (Hasan 2009). In Quetta in May 2011, the Frontier Constabulary and locals killed five innocent foreigners who were rushing toward a check post because they were mistakenly identified as suicide bombers.[10] Witnesses confirmed seeing human rights activist Siddique Eido and his friend Yousaf Nazar Baloch being abducted on December 21, 2010, by men in plain clothes accompanied by the paramilitary Frontier Corps. The dead bodies of the two men bore signs of torture and abuse when they were found in April 2011.[11] The body of prominent Baloch nationalist activist Abdul Ghaffar Lango was discovered in a hotel room in the town of Gadani in Lasbela, Balochistan. He had been kidnapped from Karachi in 2009 by security agencies. Hanif Baloch, an activist and member of the Baloch Students Organizations (Azad), was kidnapped from Lasbela on July 4, 2011. His body, which had been subject to brutal treatment, was found two days later (HRW 2011a). Such gruesome incidents threaten the legitimacy of the operations in the eyes of the local population. At the very least, the army's treatment of accused militants negatively dents its image of a disciplined force. Moreover, if the accused are found to be innocent, the local populace often retaliates and ends its cooperation with security officials, which considerably hurts the state's fighting campaign. Thus, there is an urgent need for the enactment of legislation that makes the military both accountable and responsible for its actions during the conduct of its operations. Given the general credibility deficit of the Pakistani state's institutions in the eyes of the average citizen, military sanctions alone would not dispel the mistrust prevailing in the local populace over the operations, and judicial military proceedings concerning misconduct would be viewed as farcical by the people.

Sustained military operations like the ones carried out in KPK merit comprehensive legislation that institutionalizes and mandates discipline in the application and use of force. Pakistan's criminal law and the military's internal regulations need to be synchronized to ensure the military's transparency and accountability and to support and guide COIN and CT operations across the country. The civilian government and military leadership also need to regulate the Pakistan Army's SOPs and establish a comprehensive accountability mechanism for their proper conduct during military operations. In other countries, it is not uncommon for the civilian government and military institutions to determine the SOPs that are consistent across all divisions of the armed forces, that are known to the public, and that signify a sense of responsibility on the part of the civilian and military leadership. For example, India, the United States, and the United Nations have issued guidelines on the use of force and firearms.[12]

In addition to passing regulatory legislation, a comprehensive accountability mechanism within law enforcement agencies and the army is needed to deter excessive and unjustified action that will undoubtedly arrest the public's negative perceptions about the military operations. Such legislation shall compel the armed forces to use force with caution, reduce collateral damage, and provide civilians with information that could safeguard their well-being.

Arrests during Operations against Terrorists

Perhaps the most challenging political and legal aspect of military operations in KPK has been the treatment of the captured persons. Several questions have been raised about the legal basis of retaining persons who give up their weapons or who surrender to the army. These questions include determining the law under which individuals who surrendered or were captured can be held in the army's custody, prescribing the permissible length of detention time, and identifying the personnel exercising direct authority for custody.

Unfortunately, Pakistan's government has thus far never provided an exact number of militants captured in military operations since 2008. However, it is suspected that there are close to three thousand militants who have been captured and retained in various confinement centers.

According to CrPC, under normal circumstances or in times of peace, a person who is arrested must be produced before a magistrate within twenty-four hours (sec. 61). Article 9 of the Constitution of Pakistan confers on every individual the right to liberty, and article 10 provides a detailed procedural mechanism of safeguards against a person's arrest and detention. Preventive detention, although allowed, is subject to monitoring by a review board constituted pursuant to the constitution.[13] Moreover, in a positive move, a comprehensive legal framework for arrests during full-fledged COIN operations in which the armed forces of Pakistan are committed to a large portion of territory and for much longer durations to aid civilian power has been provided for in the recently enacted Action in Aid of Civil Power (AACP) Regulations 2011, which set legal parameters for retention of militants during COIN operations.

AACP Regulations correctly distinguish between a "constitutional detainee," a person detained for ordinary infractions when the state is not fighting an insurgency or terrorism, and an "armed conflict (COIN) detainee," a person who has joined a private army to wage war against the state. Whether someone is a terrorist or an ordinary civil law offender, any person arrested during times of peace is entitled to full protection under the constitution, including his or her fundamental right to be presented before a judicial authority within twenty-four hours.

According to article 10 of the constitution, the twenty-four-hour deadline applies to situations in which there is no conflict or armed action and in which the law enforcement and judicial apparatuses are operating jointly. However, the correct protocol during intrastate conflicts is fuzzy. Is a miscreant who attacks the state and has designs to assert unlawful control over its territories entitled to the protection of the constitution? Or should he be treated under an exceptional and distinguishable category of an "armed conflict detainee"? Should the twenty-four-hour deadline to present detained offenders apply during an intrastate conflict?

The current circumstances in FATA are not peaceful and resemble a conflict-like situation. Therefore, it is a reasonable assumption that the judicial and law enforcement apparatuses are not operating effectively. Without a properly functioning civilian infrastructure that can accept the custody of a detained militant, the twenty-four-hour detention limit is not executable. In other words, if the armed forces were to strictly adhere to the twenty-four-hour limit, as mandated by the constitution, the army would have no choice but to release many militants, thereby effectively limiting the progress of the military campaign. Thus, given the conflict environment and the nonfunctionality of the civilian infrastructure in FATA, the armed forces have rightly been granted the legal cover under AACP Regulations by authorizing retention until the end of the conflict.

Pakistan had been under pressure to enact legislation that would address the legal retention of militants in conformity with international human rights standards since Pakistan has ratified the International Covenant on Civil and Political Rights (ICCPR). Furthermore, human rights protections are now also entrenched as customary international law. Preventive detention for security reasons as provided for by AACP Regulations is permissible under human rights law as the primary route to incapacitation of threats and mitigation of threats to society (Bellinger and Padmanabhan 2011). Even the European Convention on Human Rights (ECHR), generally regarded as the most rights-respecting of all international human rights instruments, would permit AACP Regulations' administrative detention for security purposes because the requirements for derogation from the convention are met. Since the state of Pakistan is under attack from the insurgents-cum-terrorists and faces an existential threat, article 15 of the convention would allow derogation and permit administrative detention for security purposes.[14]

The framers of Pakistan's constitution were mindful of the fact that in the event of military deployments in aid of civil power, derogations from the fundamental rights would be necessary. Therefore, Pakistan's parliament has the legal space under article 245 of the constitution to implement legislation that legalizes the retention of militants during a conflict. In fact, the constitution restricts the High Courts from enforcing fundamental rights during actions like COIN operations undertaken in aid of civil power. This "constitutional pause" in the enforcement of fundamental rights during an internal armed action signifies that the fundamental right granted in article 10 with a timeline of twenty-four hours may also not be implementable during a conflict of this scale. Since the AACP Regulations are consistent with the aforementioned constitutional framework, they cannot be held unconstitutional.

Law for Internment

The state's right to "intern" a militant during a conflict is necessary to curtail activities that can be considered war efforts against the state itself. Internment is not "detention" in the constitutional sense but a measure to temporarily incapacitate the miscreant. The practical outcome may be the same as detention—that is, the person may not be allowed to leave a compound or a house or any specific premises and so on—but legal principles applicable to "detention" and "internment" are completely different.

Under the AACP Regulations, a miscreant taken into custody during COIN operations in FATA and PATA is aptly categorized as an "armed conflict detainee" rather than a "constitutional detainee." AACP Regulations extend constitutional protection only to the "constitutional detainee" and not to an "armed conflict detainee" for whom separate time-bound or event-linked legal authorization for formal internment is mandated.

The difference between these two situations and their legal treatments is straightforward. During any conflict, every member of the enemy force contributes to its strength and thus adds to the extension of the overall duration of the conflict. Alternatively, an individual arrested in peacetime has no such effect upon the state or its security. Therefore, the thesis to maintain uniformity and consistency in the obligations of the state toward the constitutional detainee and the armed conflict detainee ought to be revisited.

There are both international and municipal law precedents for internment legislation similar to AACP Regulations. Article 245 of Pakistan's constitution, which regulates actions in "aid of civil power," provides the necessary legal space to enact internment legislation at a time of a "constitutional pause." In a recent case, *Pakistan Muslim League-N v. Federation of Pakistan*, the Supreme Court reiterated that the security of the state takes precedence over all fundamental rights in Pakistan.

With respect to international law, internment as a regime is permissible under article 78 of Geneva Convention IV of 1949.[15] More recently, "internment" as a possible legal solution to incapacitate internal security threats has gained acceptability among scholars of IHL as well. It is now accepted that IHL provides parties to a conflict the power to capture persons that pose a serious security threat (ICRC 2008).

Under UN law, the United Nations Security Council (UNSC) has created a precedent of sanctioning internment in Iraq.[16] UNSC resolution 1546/2004 specifically authorizes "a broad range of tasks to contribute to the maintenance of security and to ensure force protection" (annex, para. 4), including internment. The length of internment is not determined by any regulatory framework but instead by the length of the conflict itself. Clearly, therefore, internment as laid down in AACP Regulations is permissible. It has legislative precedent in Pakistan's municipal law—The Foreigners Act of 1946—and is also acceptable in selective circumstances under international law.

AACP Regulations also address the procedural issues related to internment by providing mechanisms of supervision and periodic assessment by impartial administrative boards. They also provide the legal basis for the state to collect, preserve, or bring evidence against the internee.

With regard to the length of internment laid down in the AACP Regulations, precedents exist in international law. Pakistan's government has called on the army to initiate action against those who have challenged the constitution and laws of the state because it is unable to control them through civilian law enforcement means. The action in aid of civil power needs to continue as long as the rebellious elements proclaiming to exert control over the state's territory are eliminated or forced to surrender, or their threat is considerably reduced. IHL does not prescribe a specific length for retaining a prisoner of war (POW) because the duration of internment of a POW is proportional to the duration of the conflict itself.[17] The purpose of this detention is to weaken the enemy force by diluting the strength of its fighting arm.

Significantly, in order to ensure that the enabling power to intern suspected militants is not misused or abused, AACP Regulations incorporate clear obligations to account for the militants arrested, allow access to their relatives, provide health care, and ensure decent conditions of detention. It is imperative that the state takes the implementation of these regulations seriously and sincerely.

Prosecution Issues

If, at the conclusion of or during the conflict, the internees are handed over to the law enforcement agencies, the law under which those agencies should operate must be delineated. "Laws for prosecution," comprise the procedural law that governs the procedural aspects of the trial as well as the substantive law that determines the individual criminal liability and the nature of charges or indictment. The appropriate framework for procedural law is fairly simple. The CrPC, which is widely applicable throughout Pakistan, ought to guide the proceedings of insurgents' trials and govern their various stages and conduct. However, in certain cases, the prosecution could opt to conduct the legal proceedings against the militants under the Frontier Crimes Regulations 1901, which is specific to Pakistan's tribal belt of FATA.[18]

There is greater difficulty in delineating the substantive law required to appropriately frame the charges. Due to the nuanced nature of insurgent operations, the provincial governments and the law enforcement agencies could charge militants with many different crimes, and their respective choices could have legal and political repercussions. There are two major statutes under which charges can be framed: the ATA and section 121 of the Pakistan Penal Code (PPC). Additional charges for carrying an unlicensed weapon could be filed under the Surrender of Illicit Arms Act of 1991 or under the Explosive Substances Act of 1884 and several other ancillary laws, such as provisions of PPC relating to abetment, unlawful assembly, murder etc.[19]

In the case of shooting with the intent to kill law enforcement agents, the accused could be charged prima facie under the provisions of ATA. However, the ATA was enacted to address isolated incidents of breakdown of law and order or sectarian violence. Thus, it is more applicable in times of peace and has limited application during an ongoing conflict involving armed forces. Although the attacks on the Marriot Hotel in Islamabad, the General Headquarters of the army, the Police Training Center in Manawan near Lahore, and the Sri Lankan cricket team in Lahore qualify as terrorism under the ATA, these terrorist attacks were not conducted in conflict zones and thus present a slightly different challenge.

Alternatively, the accused could be charged with waging war against the state for shooting at law enforcement agents and engaging them in serious level of combat. In this context, the state could try the accused according to offenses under section 121 of the PPC. Those who raise arms against the state and challenge its writ are engaged in a rebellion, which is clearly distinguishable from terrorism in legal terms. The purpose of a rebellion is to challenge the state's constitution, assume control of its territories, and establish alternate state structures. Conversely, terrorists use violence to intimidate or coerce a population for political purposes, but are not often concerned about acquiring full control of the state.

Unfortunately, distinguishing between acts of terrorism and rebellion is not as straightforward as the ATA and PPC might suggest. As discussed in the introductory chapter to this volume, insurgents in Pakistan have regularly used terrorism as a strategy for undermining state control during the course of their rebellion. In this context, the government and the state's prosecution have difficulty distinguishing between a rebel and a terrorist. While the ATA, under sections 17 and 21-M, allows other offenses to be tried in conjunction with terrorist charges, it does not expressly endorse the PPC. Issues related to deciphering legal jurisdiction coupled with the inability to distinguish between a rebel and terrorist are frequently an obstacle for prosecutors and undermine efforts to effectively bring the militants to justice (C. Hussain 2010).

There are two circumstances that limit the allegations presented in court against rebels and force the prosecution to secure convictions on hard-to-prove terrorism charges. First, because the ATA does not clarify how to bring additional charges against the accused, law enforcement officers file a *challan*, or indictment, that does not incorporate offenses related to waging war against the state. Second, to ameliorate the negative effects of legal disarray and possibly as a result of political pressure resonating from the international war on terror, the prosecution often limits its focus to individual terrorism charges that are attributable to the rebels and charges them with committing a "terrorist act."

Recent reports reveal that police and other law enforcement agencies in KPK are frustrated with an increase in terrorist acquittals due to a lack of evidence (Gul 2011a). A report in Pakistan's *Dawn* on March 24, 2011, released the following statements of government officials, "We are heading for a paralysis," and "the entire effort to catch these scums is going for [a] six. You catch them and the next thing you know is they are out and back in business."[20] Indeed, the recent surge in terrorist attacks in KPK is attributable to the acquittal of militants by antiterrorism courts. The aforementioned news report revealed that about two thousand suspected militants were captured in the Pakistan Army's Swat Operation in May 2009, and although half of them were declared to be extremely dangerous, prosecutors have faced various obstacles in framing a legitimate case against the accused. Overlapping laws, poorly drafted legislation, and a lack of charging and sentencing guidelines are sources of increasing confusion for the prosecution and work to the militants' advantage.

Charges related to acts of terrorism require more detailed evidence to secure a conviction than do offenses related to "committing an offense against the state." With respect to framing charges under section 121 of the PPC, the prosecution must establish that the law enforcement action was ongoing, that the suspect was arrested or taken into custody during the said operation, and that the suspect was armed and had hostile intentions or was party to the insurrection. Evidence of these requirements for conviction is relatively easy to establish during military operations. However, if the same suspect were tried under the ATA, the prosecution would have to establish and prove the actual act of terrorism and provide admissible evidence to link the accused to the terrorist act. Further, independent evidence is required to corroborate the role of the accused. Because capacity constraints are significant, these requirements make it difficult for the prosecution to establish its case.

According to the ATA, there must be a record documenting the circumstances of how the accused was captured. The prosecution faces many difficulties in verifying the lawfulness of a defendant's capture because the defendant is often in the military's custody for longer than twenty-four hours. Therefore, unless the prosecutor can justify it, the detention is deemed unlawful and results in the release of the accused. Moreover, often the evidence that forms the case against the accused is lost during the prolonged custody. There is no possibility of searching the premises or seizing his personal belongings because the site has been destroyed. The eyewitness account is also difficult to obtain as the witnesses from the community might have moved elsewhere or be intimidated into silence by accomplices of the arrested militants. Such hurdles and difficulties faced by the prosecutors might make them hesitant to move for trial. Therefore, in order to strengthen the prosecution's case, there is a pressing need for law delineating the collection and preservation of evidence during operations in aid of civil power. Terrorism offenses do not result in a sufficiently harsh sentence for militants. Those who are found guilty of crimes including terrorism, conspiracy, and sedition under section 124-A of CrPC are sentenced to three years to life in prison, whereas punishment for waging war against the state is imprisonment for life or execution. A three-year prison sentence is inappropriately lenient and would seriously undermine the long-term effectiveness of military operations. More often than not, in military theaters where operations continue for years—FATA being a case in point—a three-year term implies that the convicted militants are released in time to rejoin active militancy against the state.

One option is that those captured during an armed conflict and then interned should be prosecuted under the chapter in the PPC titled "Offences against the State." It includes section 121, titled "Waging War against the State," which states the following: "Whoever wages war against Pakistan or attempts to wage such war, or abets the waging of such war, shall be punished with death, or imprisonment for life, and shall also be liable to fine." It would be more appropriate and effective to try the rebels or militants who are waging war against the state under section 121 in conjunction with the relevant provisions of the ATA.

The prosecutor must be mindful of the territorial application of both procedural and substantive laws. Before initiating prosecution, he must take into account the venue of the prosecution as the choice of forum may affect the applicability of laws. This is important because, in FATA and PATA, it has to be determined if the laws are applied formally under article 247 of the constitution, which states that no act of parliament shall apply to FATA unless the president so directs, and no act of parliament shall apply in PATA unless the governor of that province so directs.

Pakistan's Troubled Court System

Pakistan's judicial system is overburdened by large caseload. Serious doubts therefore persist over the system's capacity to handle the load of trials and appeals of high-profile terrorists. The Supreme Court alone has approximately 19,000 pending cases (LJCP 2009). Compared to the US Supreme Court's eighty cases in a calendar year, this is staggering. The combined number of pending cases in the High Courts of Punjab, Sindh, KPK, and Balochistan is more than 140,000, and trial courts or the courts of first instance throughout Pakistan have more than 1.3 million pending cases. On an average, a civil judge has at least 100 cases on his daily roster.

Terrorism trials can take place in ordinary criminal courts or before the specialized courts established under the ATA. The ATA courts were supposed to handle only those cases that relate to state terrorism. However, over time, the ATA courts have been overrun with cases involving personal or clan enmity. It is proposed that the ATA courts should only try cases involving high-profile terrorists that are referred to them by the Home Department and not those based on the report of the officer in charge of any police station. This would prevent the evolution of these courts into a parallel judicial system.[21]

Independent prosecutions play a decisive role in any court of law. The experiment of creating an independent prosecution service in provinces such as Punjab (the Public Criminal Prosecution Service) along the lines of the UK's Crown Prosecution Service, however, did not fare too well because the new service recruited a fresh batch of lawyers with little experience to be prosecutors while laying off veteran prosecutors (Bukhari 2011b). Consequently, the crucial consultative process between prosecutors and investigators before the filing of a case suffered enormously.

Pakistan's investigating officers are also overburdened. Often investigating officers are not given adequate time to collect sufficient evidence. Foreign capacity-building efforts aimed at expanding Pakistan's investigatory capacities mostly focus on senior police officers. However, the investigating officers who are directly tasked to handle investigations are often lower-level police officials. There is a need for instituting capacity-building programs that focus on training and skill development of those directly engaged in investigations.

Judges and witnesses are also reluctant to participate in terrorism trials due to threats and assassination attempts on their lives. Current measures taken to protect judges and witnesses are minimal. Witness protection programs require the witness to completely disengage from her entire clan, something that is not culturally permissible for several ethnic groups in Pakistan.

Addressing the Fallout of Weak Criminal Justice and Antiterrorism Legislation

The many lacunas in Pakistan's criminal justice and antiterrorism legislation have impacted the state's ability to counter terrorism in multiple ways. This section highlights the principal concomitant issues and concerns that have emerged as a result of the adverse effects of deficient criminal justice system and antiterrorism legislation.

The "Missing Persons" and the Human Rights Issue

Pakistan's "missing persons" are a serious concern for human rights organizations who have constantly berated Pakistan's armed forces and intelligence agencies over this issue. The Human Rights Commission of Pakistan has documented persons who have disappeared (HRCP 2010b), and the Supreme Court has exercised its inherent jurisdiction in taking notice of this issue. According to various cases pending in court, there are hundreds of cases of missing persons.[22]

With the aim of curbing antistate activities, the Supreme Court formed a commission headed by Justice Javed Iqbal to recommend legislation that would grant armed forces the option to detain and arrest under special circumstances.[23] In this context, the AACP Regulations enable the law enforcement and intelligence agencies to intern the insurgents through a lawful regime of preventive detention for security purposes. Furthermore, by mandating that the armed forces conducting military operations in the tribal areas must account for all the arrests they make and by defining parameters for the lawful use of force by the armed forces during such operations, the AACP Regulations provide an effective legal check over the perverse incentives of armed forces and intelligence agencies to engage in enforced disappearances and extrajudicial killings.

Refugees and Internally Displaced Persons

Today, Pakistan houses nearly 1.7 million refugees, mostly from Afghanistan (UNHCR 2012).[24] Afghan refugees are often subject to investigations following terrorist attacks if they are unable to give proper accounts of their whereabouts on initial questioning. The National Database and Registration Authority (NADRA) has recently renewed efforts to maintain a database of Afghan refugees and to issue identification cards to them.[25]

It would be useful for Pakistan to take into account the implications of ratifying the UN Convention on Refugees while installing a domestic law regime regulating the actions and movements of Afghan refugees. By ratifying the UN Convention on Refugees, the government would have options of distinguishing between genuine refugees and unlawful infiltrators and would be able to create a corresponding regime that regulates Afghan economic migrants, users of easement rights across the Durand Line, and those Afghans wishing to seek asylum or wanting to acquire Pakistani citizenship. There is no clarity on the status of Afghan refugees at the moment, as a number of them have acquired Pakistani identity cards while others simply remain undocumented. Consequently, authorities invariably end up questioning them injudiciously in the aftermath of major terrorist attacks.

Pakistan must also regulate treatment of internally displaced persons (IDP) through the passage of national legislation. More than 3 million Pakistanis were displaced as a result of military operations in the country's northwest in 2009–10 because insurgents had embedded themselves among the population, and the military's strategy hinged on clearing the areas of civilians and using heavy force to target the militants in their hideouts. Just in the Rah-e-Rast operation in Swat in 2009, upward of 2 million Pakistanis were displaced, the largest internal displacement since the Rwandan genocide of

1994. The administrative and legal treatment of IDPs was also ad hoc. NADRA was mobilized to document the fleeing population in order to identify future terrorists masquerading as IDPs. However, NADRA's documentation did nothing to address the crisis or needs of thousands of displaced people.

Pakistan does not have a legal regime to regulate the treatment of and address the issues of IDPs. While the West Pakistan National Calamities (Prevention and Relief) Act provides legal cover for relief activities, it does not address displaced persons and issues that are peculiar to them. Legislation is needed to protect the property interests of the temporarily displaced persons, provide them with protection, and regulate their right to receive temporary accommodations. A failure on the part of the state to treat the IDPs respectfully also causes resentment among them and creates fertile ground for the terrorist enclave to take advantage by creating greater antistate sentiment, and in some cases even recruit from residents of the IDP camps.

Compensation for Affected Civilians

Irrespective of displacement, law enforcement operations accrue heavy costs that include property damage, injuries, loss of civilian life and destruction of state infrastructure. Compensation to civilians in such events is generally viewed as good practice.

While the provincial governments and the Pakistan Army often provide compensation to civilians in lieu of their lost property, there is a need of a comprehensive legislative framework that ensures that compensation is awarded in a systematic manner and that delineates a well-defined procedure for the affected locals to apply and receive compensation in due course. Given that Pakistan's forces are likely to face terrorist violence for some time to come, the state would do well to demonstrate a genuine concern for the distress suffered by its people by administering legal procedures for providing objective, transparent, and efficient measures for compensation. Such a compensation mechanism would also reduce the space in which the popularity of the militants could grow.

Correcting Course: The Way Forward

It is high time that the government of Pakistan issues a clear mission statement for the military operations against the insurgent-cum-terrorist threat. For a country beset with multiple militant threats and one that is certain to be embroiled in the whirlpool of terrorism for the foreseeable future, the absence of a clear mission statement is unsustainable and imprudent. The mission statement should illustrate the rationale of the operations to the people of Pakistan who are currently confused about the real objectives and purposes of the military campaigns. Many Pakistanis perceive that Pakistan's civilian government and its armed forces are fighting the United States' proxy war. In order to dispel this perception, the government authorities need to publicize and articulate how military operations are critical to Pakistan's interests and domestic security. The people of Pakistan deserve to know facts, figures, and political or religious arguments that legitimize military operations as a last and necessary resort to secure civilian power and domestic stability. In this regard, Army Chief General Kayani's Independence Day 2012 speech in which he categorically refuted the view that the battle against extremism and terrorism was America's war and acknowledged that the fight was "our war" was a welcome start.[26]

Next, Pakistan's president needs to authorize the creation of a committee comprising politicians from all parties and a selective group of experts to draft CT and deradicalization strategies. The document should incorporate conceptual insights of a progressive Pakistan and operational mandates for governmental organs and ministries. The final product should determine the roles of madrassa (seminary) boards, religious ministries, the powers and jurisdictions of law enforcement agencies, and the role of the armed forces. Additionally, it should distinguish or redefine the roles of the Ministry of Interior and the Ministry of Law to curtail frustrations that arise from current jurisdictional overlaps. Finally, the committee should propose guidelines for the provincial ministries concerning law and order issues. The lamentable lack of concern for reforming and creating a CT policy is further evident from the fact that the amendments urgently required in the ATA for improving conviction rates have been pending in the Senate for several months.

Pakistan's civilian government must revise their laissez-faire relationship with the armed forces. It must address measures to regulate the conduct of the security forces' personnel. The government needs to enlist the necessary parties, civilian and military, to create comprehensive federal legislation institutionalizing the manner and method in which domestic kinetic operations are conducted. Such legislation should be prepared while keeping in view the range of actions that the armed forces may be called upon to perform. For instance, the proposed legislation should suffice for both a CT operation and for a much more extensive and prolonged COIN campaign. The proposed law should also be consistent with the obligations of international human rights law and IHL. The AACP Regulations are at best a stopgap arrangement that does not subsume all legal concerns related to use of military force against terrorism and insurgency and is limited in geographical scope to FATA and PATA. The aspects of arrest and internment that it does cover must be adapted to the national context, and its remit extended throughout.

Legal statutes concerning terrorism and rebellion need to be revised to most effectively indict offenders, secure convictions, and justly punish those found guilty of rebellion against the state. In order to ease the courts' caseload, Pakistan's legal sector should explore the possibility of conducting collective trials for groups of militants. Those arrested on similar counts of waging war against the state could be tried together to expedite the judicial process.

Finally, the state must deal with the fallout of its past operations and remain prepared to deal with displacements of large swaths of population in future instances. Adequate compensation should be awarded to the civilians who have been affected by the operations. Pakistan needs legislation to protect the property titles and rights of locals displaced by military operations. Presently, compensation is ad hoc at best and is not formally part of the government's political or military strategy. In areas where antigovernment sentiments trump national loyalty, streamlined compensation mechanisms may also prove useful in strengthening the legitimacy of the government, reducing support for rebellious groups, and forging relationships with locals who could provide state law enforcement and intelligence agencies with useful assistance.

Notes

1. Following the declaration of this offensive, the army's public relations directorate (the Inter-Services Public Relations) referred to the aggressive nonstate fighters as "militants." Thus, "miscreant" is now widely used by the government and the media as a collective reference to "terrorists," "rebels," or "nonstate actors."

2. ISPR (Inter-Services Public Relations), Press Release No. 156, Rawalpindi, May 25, 2009.

3. US Department of State report to US Congress, pursuant to Section 2042 of the Implementing Recommendations of the 9/11 Commission Act of 2007 (P.L. 110-53), stated: "The Pakistani Government stationed military and paramilitary forces along the border with Afghanistan, and security operations in the FATA disrupted terrorist activity by targeting and raiding Al Qaeda and other militant safe havens."

4. "Czech Ambassador and Two US Marines among 53 Killed," *Dawn*, September 22, 2008, http://archives.dawn.com/2008/09/22/top1.htm; "Attack on Bhutto Convoy Kills 130," *BBC World News*, October 19, 2007, http://news.bbc.co.uk/2/hi/7051804.stm; and Rao 2009.

5. See, generally, Amnesty International, *Annual Report 2011: Pakistan*. www.amnesty.org/en/region/pakistan/report-2011.

6. The Pakistan Tehrik-e-Insaaf chief Imran Khan and members of Jamaat-e-Islami, for instance, have adopted this stance publicly.

7. "International humanitarian law (IHL) is a set of rules which seek, for humanitarian reasons, to limit the effects of armed conflict. It protects persons who are not or are no longer participating in the hostilities and restricts the means and methods of warfare. The Geneva Conventions and the Hague Conventions are the main examples. Usually called international humanitarian law, it is also known as the law of war or the law of armed conflict" (ICRC 2004).

8. The Pakistan Police Order (2002) was enacted to reconstruct and regulate police with respect to their "obligation and duty to function according to the Constitution, law, and democratic aspiration of the people." A version is available at www.npb.gov.pk/police_order/Police_order_2002_with_amendment_ordinance_2006.pdf.

9. According to the Lauterpacht Centre for International Law (LCIL) on state practice, evidence of state practice can be found in government press releases; declarations, statements, and other papers on foreign ministry websites; and websites of organizations of governments. For more information on state practice in different country contexts, see Sahl 2007. Some studies have documented Pakistan's compliance with IHL during military operations in the northwest. See, for example, Henckaerts and Doswald-Beck 2005.

10. "Kharotabad Incident: Chechens Were Not Carrying Suicide Vests," *Express Tribune*, May 21, 2011, http://tribune.com.pk/story/173223/kharotabad-incident-chechens-were-t-carrying-suicide-vests-explosives/.

11. Amnesty International, *Annual Report 2012: Pakistan*, www.amnesty.org/en/region/pakistan/report-2012.

12. Armed Forces Special Powers Act (AFSP), 1958, "Special Power of the Armed Forces;" UN 2008; and *Naga People's Movement of Human Rights v. Union of India*, SC (Supreme Court) 431, AIR 2008.

13. Explanation I of article 10 of the Constitution of Pakistan defines "the appropriate Review Board" as follows:

(i) In the case of a person detained under a Federal law, a Board appointed by the Chief Justice of Pakistan and consisting of a Chairman and two other persons, each of whom is or has been a Judge of the Supreme Court or a High Court; and

(ii) In the case of a Person detained under a Provincial law, a Board appointed by the Chief Justice of the High Court concerned and consisting of a Chairman and two other persons, each of whom is or has been a Judge of a High Court.

14. ECHR (European Convention for the Protection of Human Rights and Fundamental Freedoms), 1950, Art. 15, ETS No. 5, 213 UNTS 221.

15. Article 78 of the Geneva Convention (1949) reads as follows: "If the Occupying Power considers it necessary, for imperative reasons of security, to take safety measures concerning protected persons, it may, at the most, subject them to assigned residence or to internment."

16. The law in particular is propounded by the UNSC through various binding resolutions under chapter 7 of the UN Charter.

17. Article 5 of the Geneva Convention (1949) reads as follows: "The present Convention shall apply to the persons referred to in Article 4 from the time they fall into the power of the enemy and until their final release and repatriation."

18. The Frontier Crimes Regulations (FCR) are a set of laws that are applicable in the semiautonomous region of FATA. Enacted by the British to maintain order in the restive tribal areas, these laws provide relatively weak procedural safeguards.

19. These include the following: sec. 141, ch. VIII, of Offences against the Public Tranquility, Pakistan Penal Code, 1860 (Act No. XLV of 1860); sec. 300, 302, ch. XVI, of Offences Affecting Human Body, Pakistan Penal Code, 1860 (Act No. XLV of 1860); and sec. 109, ch. V, of Abetment, Pakistan Penal Code, 1860 (Act No. XLV of 1860).

20. "Row over Release of Suspects by ATC," *Dawn*, March 24, 2011, http://dawn.com/2011/03/24/row-over-release-of-suspects-by-atcs/.

21. See, generally, Bukhari 2011b.

22. "Pakistan Court Accuses Security Force over Missing People." *Agence France Press*, July 11, 2012, www.google.com/hostednews/afp/article/ALeqM5jBlNf63MHgtixlM4ceYZi9HzpJ0g?docId=CNG.23164f646e2ead3dcadd9bef7f2d23e0.671; HRW 2011b.

23. The commission passed an order dated December 31, 2010.

24. UNHCR, "Pakistan," UNHCR Global Appeal 2012–2013: 182–85.

25. This project is formally known as RIPAC (Registration Information Project for Afghan Citizens). The project is a collaboration between the United Nations High Commissioner for Refugees and the government of Pakistan for the registration/update/modification/correction of information of Afghan refugees in Pakistan and previously issued proof of registration cards.

26. "Militancy Poses Risk of Civil War, Warns Gen Kayani," *Express Tribune*, August 14, 2012, http://tribune.com.pk/story/421855/militancy-poses-risk-of-civil-war-warns-gen-kayani/.

CHAPTER 7

Choking Financing for Militants in Pakistan

MUHAMMAD AMIR RANA

THE MILITANT LANDSCAPE of Pakistan is a complex one, with numerous groups from different backgrounds pursuing multiple agendas. The militants have diverse financial sources, both formal and informal. They receive public donations like other religious organizations, religious seminaries, and charities in Pakistan; at the same time, they generate financial resources through criminal activities and illegal financial channels.

Tracking and curbing the sources of their financing is a critical challenge, and the Pakistani state apparatus is yet to develop a comprehensive mechanism to do so. Although the state has taken some initiatives, including banning militant organizations, freezing bank accounts, and enforcing an anti–money laundering law, these have not proved to be entirely effective. This is mainly because militant groups do not rely on the formal financial sector, for the most part, and the state has failed to implement a comprehensive counterterrorism (CT) approach that checks the informal channels. Moreover, the state's efforts to curb the militants' financial flows focus mainly on the formally banned militant organizations, even though Pakistan faces threats of terrorism from other quarters, such as Afghan Taliban groups and terrorist cells that have recently emerged in the Punjab and Sindh provinces; the former are referred to as the Punjabi Taliban.

This chapter maps the resources and avenues of financing for militants in Pakistan and the traditional and nontraditional methods they have used to sustain their finances. Most important, it analyzes how the government is working to choke militants' access to funds and resources. In Pakistan, very little real analytical work has been done on the issue. This chapter thus relies on media reports and literature published by militant organizations as well as on consultations with members of religious and militant groups and senior security officials, both serving and retired, who have dealt with the issue first-hand.

Trends in Militant Fund-Raising and Funding Sources

This section outlines the trends in militant financing in Pakistan and then details the various methods and sources of revenue generation for militant groups.

Trends in Organization and Survival

A number of structured and organized militant groups in Pakistan were formed in the 1980s and 1990s. After 9/11, many of these groups faced government restrictions, so they devised new ways to survive and keep their financial channels intact. The state proscribed most of these groups in 2002 and 2003, including Jaish-e-Mohammed (JeM), Harkat-ul-Jihad-e-Islami (HuJI), Harkat-ul-Mujahideen (HuM), Sipah-e-Sahaba Pakistan (SSP), Lashkar-e-Taiba (LeT), Jamaat-ud-Dawa (JuD), Hizb-ul-Mujahideen (HM), Jamaat-ul-Mujahideen (JM), and Al-Badar Mujahideen (BM).

Since then, all of these militant groups have established "public welfare wings" as a front for their activities, or they have resurfaced after the ban as "charity organizations" to boost their image among the people and circumvent government restrictions. This ploy has not only helped them gain social acceptance, it has also enabled them to expand their support base and ultimately add to their financial resources. Some militant groups, in an attempt to diversify their assets, have set up commercial ventures such as English-medium schools, health care centers, transportation companies, residential projects, and media groups; some have also acquired farmland on a large scale. While the militant groups have kept the supply line for their financing in the country intact, many of these groups have also found ways to cultivate and consolidate financial resources abroad. Not only do they use bank transactions, they also use informal *hawala* channels and other illegal means to bring funds into Pakistan.[1] Some groups have even set up their own currency exchange networks, while others continue to use smugglers' networks to bring in funds from abroad.

Al-Qaeda and foreign militants based in Pakistani tribal areas rely on funds mainly from Arab countries and from cybercrimes. With regard to crime, smaller terrorist cells like Jundullah's in Karachi generate their revenue through criminal activities such as bank robberies and abduction for ransom.

Karachi is especially lucrative for terrorists, where their involvement in bank robberies has increased tremendously in recent years.[2]

The Pakistani Taliban, or the Tehrik-e-Taliban Pakistan (TTP), as they are formally known, rely on multiple financial sources. They raise money through levying fines or a "toll tax," as it is referred to in some parts of the country, receiving *zakat*, and even raising money through criminal activities such as abduction for ransom.[3] Evidence of this is visible in the undocumented tribal economy, which is considered an important factor in the rise of insurgency in Pakistan's Federally Administered Tribal Areas (FATA) bordering Afghanistan (Mian 2009). The undocumented aspect of the tribal economy accounts for more than 50 percent of the total economic output in the area, and it mainly constitutes the smuggling of electronic goods, sophisticated weapons, luxury vehicles, timber, minerals, and drugs (Mian 2009). According to a report, "A number of actors in the conflict-hit areas are striving to safeguard existing economic interests and relatively new players [Taliban] are fighting for a stronger position and to wrest control of economic resources" (Mian 2009, 1). Some of these funding avenues are discussed in greater detail in the following.

Traditional Funding Sources

DIRECT PRIVATE DONATIONS

Raising finances through donations has been one of the most important sources of funding for militant groups. Such donations are not the same as *zakat* or *ushr*.[4] Although the precise extent has never been quantified, there is a trend among Pakistanis, particularly in Punjab, Khyber Pakhtunkhwa Province (KPK), and the adjacent FATA, to donate in the name of religion and jihad. Militant groups based in Pakistan's mainland and the TTP raise between 55 percent and 65 percent of their funds from local sponsors.[5] Sympathetic Muslim donors in European and Persian Gulf states also send huge sums of money to them.[6] According to a media report, there is a trend in Karachi and KPK to donate money indirectly to jihad organizations—where the donors do not know the destination of their funds and the groups are not aware of the sources of the donations they receive.[7] A number of organizations working as charities or seminaries (madrassas) collect donations from commercial centers and via door-to-door campaigns, ostensibly for charitable pursuits, but quite often they are operating as fund-raising organs for militant organizations. People respond generously to such drives, especially in the holy month of Ramadan. Militant groups claim to raise millions of dollars in this manner every year. For example, the JuD claimed that it collected $1.9

million through private donations in 2006.[8] The JuD organizes hundreds of public meetings, religious congregations, and welfare activities such as free medical camps where collection boxes are placed at prominent places and members and visitors are encouraged to donate for JuD activities.

The capacity of militant groups and affiliated organizations to raise private donations supposedly for relief efforts has traditionally witnessed a sharp increase after natural disasters, such as earthquakes, floods, and famine. After the 2005 earthquake in Kashmir and KPK, the Al-Rasheed Trust raised $9.7 million for relief work within a span of five months.[9] It used the funds for welfare activities, including providing food and medical treatment for the affected population and reconstructing damaged madrassas and mosques. The Al Rehmat Trust, a charity associated with the JeM, raised $6.1 million in funds and supplies after the earthquake.[10] The Al-Asar Trust, affiliated with the HuM, was a new and relatively unknown welfare organization when the 2005 earthquake struck, but it still managed to raise $2.9 million in the months following the earthquake. It is not clear how much of the collections it spent on relief activities, but such activities have certainly earned it goodwill among the masses.

Major religious charities, including the Al-Khidmat Trust of the Jamaat-e-Islami (JI) and the Idara Khidmat-e-Khalq of the JuD, claim to have raised millions of dollars in private donations overall.[11] It is important to note that these claims were made in the post-9/11 scenario, with government sanctions in place and militant organizations officially barred from raising funds. The situation was totally different before 9/11. In 2001, LeT had collected over $918,000 from direct private donations and had a very organized jihad fund collection system across the country (Rana 2002, 243). It had placed thirteen thousand "jihad fund boxes" at important markets and public places across the country, and the average daily income from each box was $5, amounting to a whopping $65,000 a day for the organization. The LeT had employed a team of five hundred persons to manage the jihad fund boxes.[12] Most of these boxes were removed after the ban, but they later reappeared with the charities' tag. The JeM, established in March 2000, was even more successful in jihad fund collection in its first year of existence.[13]

Overall, while militant groups still raise direct funds to this day, their campaigns lack the pace of the pre-ban years and they have been forced to increasingly use charity organizations as a cover. That said, even before 9/11, militant organizations had begun to introduce innovative ways of campaigning to raise funds that went beyond collection boxes and the like. The HM and Al-Badr, Kashmiri militant groups affiliated with the JI, are two examples of this. The HM launched a substantial jihad fund campaign in 1998 in collaboration with Pasban, a youth organization affiliated with the JI, when they organized "jihad shows" around the country. These shows included staged plays; videos of jihad training and operations; live addresses of militant commanders from Afghanistan, Kashmir, and other parts of the world; and jihadi anthems. According to Ejaz Gillani, an HM member interviewed by the author in Islamabad in 2007, the group raised $3.5 million in funds during the campaign while the shows cost less than $50,000. According to a former member of the outfit, Al-Badr organized a countrywide road show in 1999 during the Kargil conflict between India and Pakistan.[14] The HM imitated this approach and brought along parents of fighters killed in Indian Kashmir for the countrywide road shows. These shows also met with a fair amount of success.

ZAKAT, USHR, FITRANA, AND ANIMAL HIDES

During Ramadan, Muslims pay two levies (*zakat/ushr* and *fitrana*[15]), while on Eid-al Azha, the annual celebration of the completion of the Muslim pilgrimage in Makkah, they sacrifice animals and donate animal hides for charitable purposes. On both occasions, religious and social charities, religious political parties, madrassas, and militant groups launch campaigns to collect as high a portion of the religious levy and hides as they can. In fact, *zakat*, *ushr*, and *fitrana* and animal hides are the most attractive traditional sources of funds for the militant organizations.

Intelligence agencies investigating the collection of animal hides on Eid-al Azha have found links between organized money laundering and banned militant groups. Militant groups use animal hides as a cover to legitimize funds received from abroad—by showing that the money has been generated by selling the hides (Siddiqui 2007). In 2003, the JuD collected 1.2 million animal hides on Eid-al Azha worth an estimated $7.2 million, while the Al Rehmat Trust collected hides worth more than $400,000 (Rana and Khattak 2004). An investigation by Pakistani intelligence agencies in 2004 showed that between 1999 and 2002, the Al-Akhtar Trust, which was banned after 9/11 because of its alleged links with militant groups, received around $100 million from hide sales in bank accounts it maintained in Karachi (Rana and Khattak 2004). Even after their accounts in Karachi were frozen, the Al-Akhtar and Al-Rashid trusts received $10 million each in 2006 in other bank accounts from a UK-based organization that sacrificed animals on Eid-al Azha for thousands of British Muslims.[16]

SUPPORT FROM LOCAL BUSINESS COMMUNITIES AND BUSINESS ENTERPRISES

Pockets of the business community have also not been immune to the lure of the militant networks' drive to acquire funding. In Lahore, the JuD secretly formed the Dawa Traders' Wing in 2002, which collected donations from traders. The outfit now operates openly in spite of its parent organization being banned. Hundreds of businessmen have also been donating money to the SSP since the early 1990s, mainly in major urban centers in Punjab. Traders started funding the outfit in 1992 when a paper merchant initiated a fundraiser for the SSP in collaboration with traders from Lahore's business hubs of Hall Road and Beadon Road. Later, a number of traders from Urdu Bazaar, Anarkali, Badami Bag, and other leading business centers in Lahore also started supporting them. Worryingly, many of these businessmen did so because they believed in the SSP's anti-Shia sectarian agenda (Rana 2008b).

Militants have also managed to make tremendous gains through business enterprises that appeal to religious sections of the society. After the US invasions of Afghanistan and Iraq, a move to boycott products of American and European multinationals was launched across the Muslim world. In Pakistan, local industrialists tried to benefit from the boycott by introducing "Islamic products" as an alternative. There was a flood of locally made toothpastes, shampoos, soaps, and cold drinks in mid-2002, but only cola drinks survived in the market. At least thirty-two local cola brands were registered after the US invasion of Afghanistan and Iraq. Interestingly, these cola brands did not launch any major campaign in mainstream media; instead, brand owners were able to penetrate the market through advertising in religious and jihadi media publications (Rana 2005a).[17] These cola enterprises provided funding to different religious charities such as the Al-Rasheed Trust and the Al-Akhtar Trust, and to militant organizations to ensure that they would continue to appeal to their target market, which was made up essentially of the religiously inclined. Many of the cola brands have since gone out of business, but a number of them, including Zam Zam Cola and Mecca-Cola, have captured a significant market share.

TRADING COMPANIES AND MONEY LAUNDERING

While there is little specific information on how widely trade is used to launder money for militancy, the trade sector can provide militant organizations with opportunities to transfer money and goods through seemingly legitimate trading activity. At least one major case of successful use of trade has been uncovered. On March 10, 2005, a CT unit discovered that a company that allegedly had links with remnants of the Afghan Taliban was selling sugar in Pakistan.The special investigation group (SIG) of the Federal Investigation Agency (FIA) found that Abdul Bari, the owner of the Afghanistan-based trading company Fazal Karim Maidanwal Limited, imported sugar in Pakistan for the commodity's eventual delivery to Afghanistan. Bari had made transactions of over $600,000 in 2006 in the name of Taliban leaders, who frequently shuttled between Pakistan and Afghanistan. According to FIA sources, detailed investigations found that Abdul Bari was a close associate and business partner of Afghan Taliban chief Mullah Mohammed Omar. They established that Bari was providing funds to the Taliban through their commanders in Pakistan. A raid was conducted on his Naz Cinema Road office in Peshawar, where documents showed details of transactions in the name of Taliban commanders after 2001. The money was allegedly given to a Taliban commander who ran a madrassa in North Waziristan Agency, one of the seven Pakistani tribal districts in FATA. Government agencies also seized records of transactions worth nearly $60,000—made from the Muslim Commercial Bank (MCB) Miranshah (North Waziristan Agency) branch to the MCB Yadgar Chowk branch, Peshawar—that were carried out by Guladar Khan in the name of Din Mohammad. Khan was an aide of Afghan Taliban commander Jalaluddin Haqqani and Din Mohammad, son of Abdul Bari. The SIG froze thirty-two bank accounts of Abdul Bari, his brother Abdul Baqi, and their sons on charges of funneling money to the Afghan Taliban (Imtiaz 2006; Ahmed 2006).

THE USE OF PIRACY RACKETS

Despite the fact that Pakistan is a signatory to various intellectual property rights conventions, the piracy of CDs, DVDs, and other such products is commonplace. In November 2007, a US Federal Bureau of Investigation (FBI) team visited Pakistan to investigate some top bankers on charges of money laundering for al-Qaeda. The FBI team seemed more interested in the money laundering aspect because it suspected that al-Qaeda and criminal mafias were transferring money through organized groups making and dealing in pirated CDs and DVDs. Pakistani police officials, who agreed to be quoted only on condition of anonymity, said the FBI team inquired about organized piracy operations' foreign currency accounts in Pakistan and abroad and about the actual quantum of earning through the sale of pirated CDs and DVDs and other sources to determine the extent of funds funneled to al-Qaeda.

Police officials who had facilitated the FBI probe are convinced that members of the piracy rackets provide facilities to LeT, JeM, and al-Qaeda for mass production of CDs even though they have no ideological affinity with the outlawed militant groups. The services are provided on a commercial basis. They hold that the JeM and SSP send their religious material, including audiocassettes and CDs, to Africa through different channels, mainly employing the organized piracy setup.[18]

CDs and DVDs promoting and glorifying jihad have emerged as another business of militant organizations that cater to a receptive audience in Pakistan's tribal areas and KPK. These CDs and DVDs contain videos of militants' training drills, operations against security forces including beheadings and bombings, sermons delivered by militant leaders, and documentaries glorifying jihad. The industry has flourished, and such CDs and DVDs are easily available in the markets of the tribal areas and KPK for between thirty cents and fifty cents. Peshawar-based journalist Aqeel Yousfazai, in an interview with the author in Peshawar in December 2008, noted that almost every Taliban-affiliated group now has a multimedia section that produces jihad CDs to spread their message as well as to generate funds. He estimates that thousands, and at times tens of thousands, of copies of every such CD or DVD are launched with each new release.

Nontraditional Funding Sources

Militant groups also rely on legitimate business operations to generate funds. These include construction firms, restaurants, shops, schools, health care facilities, and media groups. These ventures ensure uninterrupted base funds even as other sources continue to be used to provide the bulk of the finances. This section discusses nontraditional financing sources that are relatively common and for which credible information is available.

SCHOOL CHAINS

Investment in the education sector is an attractive prospect for religious organizations and militant groups. It offers them dual benefits of educating students according to their own ideology as well as safe investment with a good rate of return. Several religious organizations and militant groups are currently running their own English-medium school chains where the courses have a specific religious bent. The JI, or people affiliated with it, runs three school chains, Al-Suffa, Ghazali, and Dar-e-Arqam, which employ more than one thousand people. The number of the JuD's "model schools" has risen to more than four hundred, and the English-medium Islamic school network, Iqra Rozatul Atfaal of Al-Rasheed Trust and Jamia Binori Town, Karachi, has spread across the country, establishing seven hundred branches between 2005 and 2007 (PIPS 2008). These schools, which market themselves as offering an Islamic academic environment, have a fee structure similar to regular English-medium schools in the country.

HEALTH CARE FACILITIES

Almost every militant group maintains a medical wing. These wings not only serve organizational purposes and enhance the group's image and social acceptance but they also serve as a means for militant outfits to generate funds by citing their medical wing's activities and financial needs. The Idara Khidmat-e-Khalq of the JuD and the Al Rehmat Trust of JeM are prime examples. The Al-Rasheed Trust, the Al-Akhtar Trust, JI's Medical Mission, and other small militant and sectarian groups hold so-called free medical camps across the country throughout the year. They place collection boxes on the camp premises and usually get considerably more through donations than the cost of arranging the camp. According to JuD spokesman Yahya Mujahid, the group organized two thousand medical camps in 2006; donations covered the expenses incurred on arranging the camps, and the camps also earned hundreds of thousands of dollars in profits. According to Mujahid, JuD members and other donors contribute substantial amounts of money for the organization's free medical activities.[19]

HOUSING PROJECTS

Religious and militant groups have also invested in housing projects, which they deem a major source of building organizational assets. These projects help them establish their own turf and support base in a specific area, usually in walled-off communities, where they aspire to live according to their beliefs, something they claim is denied to them otherwise. Residence or acquisition of property in these projects is not open to all; it is usually by invitation only. The number of such projects is on the rise across the country. In Lahore alone, Pakistan's second-largest city, there are at least twelve such schemes (Rana 2003). In fact, various religious sects and parties have launched housing schemes in the city with residence rights reserved for members of the sect or party. The JuD's Markaz in Muridke, the Tanzeemul Akhwan's Owassia Housing Society, and the Al-Rasheed Trust's sponsored housing schemes in Karachi and Lahore are a few examples. These projects house the party secretariats and serve residential communities.

MEDIA GROUPS

Overall, jihadi media has acted as perhaps the most important tool for militant groups in Pakistan, serving as a device to generate funds, spread propaganda, and recruit militants. It is not an overstatement to say that jihadi print media has emerged as alternative print media in the last two decades with the explicit aim of promoting jihad and radical views. Jihad media has wide readership in the country and some jihadi publishers even claim they could replace the mainstream media overnight if given a free hand by the state.[20] Around twenty jihad periodicals continue to be published regularly, including some with wide circulation, like the *Daily Islam* and weeklies *Zerb-e-Momin* of the Al-Rasheed Trust, *Ghazwa Times* and *Al-Qalam* of the JeM, and *Al-Harmeen* of the JuD.

According to official statistics, there are around sixteen thousand madrassas in Pakistan, and two thousand regularly publish to project their activities to attract admissions and generate funds. Around 50 percent of these publications promote jihad and radicalization and back Taliban and other militant groups (Rana 2008a). After government curbs were imposed, the banned jihad organizations' publications had to improvise to ensure continued circulation. Banned publications are now sold or distributed, often for free, mainly outside mosques after weekly Friday congregations, or they are available at madrassas and select newsstands. A few groups have formed special units that go door to door preaching jihad, collecting funds, and selling their publications. In this manner they have managed to avoid some restrictions imposed by the government.

International Sources

As briefly mentioned earlier, in addition to local funding, Pakistani and foreign militant groups also receive money from abroad, collecting funds from individuals and institutions in different countries and funneling them to Pakistan through established arrangements.

Much before 9/11, militant organizations had launched fund-raising operations in a number of countries. At one time during the 1990s, the JI and the LeT had launched six different jihad funds for Afghanistan, Kashmir, Palestine, Bosnia, Kosovo, and Myanmar. They launched specific fund-raising campaigns for each country, but the campaign for Kashmir generated the largest amount of money. In 2005, SSP chief Maulana Ahmed Ludhianvi boasted that the funds collected in the name of Kashmir by various groups were enough to buy all the land in Kashmir and a few other regions in India.[21]

Funds for Pakistani and foreign militant groups are still pouring in from abroad, especially the Persian Gulf states, where the Pakistani community and Arab donors are able to send donations through banks and money transfers through services such as Western Union, or through illegal *hawala* channels. Wealthy Arabs in the Gulf states are very particular about paying *zakat* and try to give the annual levy on Muslims to those who are really in need. They deem madrassas in Pakistan, Afghanistan, India, and Bangladesh as deserving of their help. They usually assess their *zakat* before Ramadan and engage the services of local religious scholars to deliver the amount to the deserving. The Pakistani madrassas and religious parties remain in contact with the scholars, who keep them on the list of the deserving and distribute the *zakat* money among them. Scholars from these countries either visit countries such as Pakistan themselves or send their representatives to investigate who is the most deserving of *zakat*. Maulana Ahmed Sheraj, for example, a Pakistan-born religious scholar settled in Kuwait, visited Pakistan in September 2004. A religious scholar from Peshawar claims that Sheraj had brought with him *zakat* money for Pakistani madrassas and organizations. Jihadi sources say an administration of leading madrassas, jihadi organizations, and religious parties sought to arrange meetings with Sheraj.[22]

Militant groups and religious seminaries also send their representatives abroad to raise funds, especially in the month of Ramadan. They send designated members not only to the Gulf states but also to Africa and Europe. Madrassas and other organizations also engage these persons and other businessmen to transfer funds to Pakistan.[23] Foreign currency exchange concerns, especially in Karachi, have direct links with the money changers in Dubai, and they travel once or twice between the two cities on a daily basis. Militant organizations, madrassas, and religious parties also hire their services to bring in their money. One such foiled attempt was the 2004 arrest of personnel from HH Exchanges, a foreign currency exchange company. Pakistani security agencies arrested two HH Exchanges employees who had arrived from Dubai at the Karachi airport carrying US dollars, euros, and riyals worth nearly $390,000. According to intelligence officials, the money was meant for al-Qaeda in Pakistan (*Nida-e-Millat* 2004), and al-Qaeda member Abu Faraj was involved in the illegal money transactions (Maqbool 2004).

Recent Trends: The Role of Criminal Networking, Drug Cartels, and Forced Levies in Fund-Raising

As the Taliban-led insurgency in Pakistan has expanded, it has increasingly taken advantage of the state's shrinking writ by using crime and drug cartels as a source of income. In areas where the insurgency runs parallel governance structures, it has even instituted levies that are collected from the local public. The discussion that follows captures these relatively recent trends in militant financing.

Money through Criminal Activities

As terrorists' infrastructures and ambitions grow, they face a serious financial crisis (Z. Khan 2011). As military operations in tribal areas and some state initiatives have contributed to blocking the flow of funds to them, they have continuously looked for new ways to generate money. With that aim, militant groups have increased links with criminals in recent years. Terrorists are involved in abductions for ransom across Pakistan (Azeem 2011). Reports also suggest that terrorists, mainly al-Qaeda and its affiliated terrorist cells, are aiding criminals in their activities, usually bank robberies and abductions for ransom. These groups, which cannot operate publicly, include factions of the Punjabi Taliban, factions of the LeJ, the Sipah-e-Mohammed, and the Jundullah in Karachi. They have developed a nexus with criminal groups in Karachi, Punjab, and KPK (Munawer 2010; Rana 2012). According to some investigative reports, terrorists were found to be involved in major bank robberies within the last three years.[24] For instance, a small terrorist cell led by Dr. Abdullah, a former member of JI, confessed to robbing seven banks in Karachi. The money was spent on buying weapons and explosives for terrorist attacks.[25]

Militant groups that are not completely underground, such as the LeT, the Al-Umar Mujahideen, and the HuM, are also reportedly involved in criminal activities. These groups were notorious for extorting money from shopping centers and markets in Azad Jammu Kashmir.[26] The SSP was known to raise funds in such a manner from the Jhang, Sargodha, and Lahore districts in the Punjab province.[27] The TTP and its affiliates resort to similar tactics in the tribal areas and the adjacent parts of the KPK. According to police sources, thirty-five complaints of robbery were received against Taliban members for robbing people in Bannu district of the KPK between January and June 2007, a time when the militants were in ascendency.

Law enforcement agencies have also arrested many people for harassing citizens and forcing them to pay money on behalf of the TTP. The police arrested one such person in Tank on January 8, 2007, when he was collecting money from the people by posing as a Pakistani Taliban member. He allegedly forced a man to pay him five hundred dollars.[28] Similarly, a youth was arrested in the Dera Ismail Khan district of KPK on March 3, 2007, for threatening a local trader of consequences if he did not pay ten thousand dollars. The youth wanted to use the money to buy weapons for the TTP.[29] A gang of armed militants looted twenty-four thousand dollars in computers and telephone sets from Mirali Bazaar branch of MCB in North Waziristan on May 30, 2006.[30]

Pakistani Taliban members, highly influenced by Wahabism, also destroy the shrines of other religious groups, such as the Sufis, and loot donations and offerings by devotees. In April 2004, local Taliban destroyed the shrine of Malik Arshad Baba in Tapi, South Waziristan, in FATA, and they looted the money donated to the shrine. They warned the local people against rebuilding the shrine and asked them to donate money for jihad instead.[31]

Drug Money/Smuggling

The Pakistani and Afghan Taliban and al-Qaeda are also involved in human trafficking and drug and arms smuggling, and they use the proceeds to finance their operations. The consequences of uncontrolled poppy cultivation in Afghanistan are evident in the neighboring countries today, where terrorists use proceeds from the drug trade to further their agenda. Analysts believe the Taliban are using drug money to sustain their activities in Pakistan's tribal areas and in Afghanistan.[32]

Drugs and deadly weapons are transported from Afghanistan via Balochistan to Sindh province and to the southern districts of Punjab. Afghan refugee camps in the Pakistani border tribal areas act as de facto base camps for weapon smugglers. Approximately 720 miles of the Pakistan–Afghanistan border area is effectively unguarded, so smugglers move freely between the two countries. Their task is made easier by the fact that families of most smugglers are settled along the border. Weapons traffickers have reduced reliance on traditional smuggling routes and have switched to new ones on the outskirts of Quetta, Balochistan province's capital, through refugee camps of Khorotabad and Gulistan, Basti Pir Jangle Alizai, Mehmand Khel, Saranan, and Pishin. Through these routes, weapons are supplied to urban metropolises like Karachi. Weapons are also smuggled into interior Sindh and southern Punjab through the southwestern regions of Chaghi and Noshki districts in Balochistan.

Smugglers in the Pakistan–Afghanistan border region have been providing assistance and shelter to Taliban and al-Qaeda for both drug and weapon smuggling activities for several years. Smugglers' networks also help al-Qaeda and Taliban operatives reach major urban centers such as Karachi, Quetta, Peshawar, and Lahore (Rana and Gunaratna 2008, 15). The Pakistani government has been trying to regulate weapons manufacturing and trade in Darra Adam Khel—a KPK town renowned for manufacturing of firearms, from revolvers to antiaircraft guns, by craftsmen using traditional manufacturing techniques. However, the government's efforts have not succeeded so far because of the influx of militants in the area. In recent years militant groups have smuggled weapons from Darra Adam Khel to Afghanistan, Kashmir, Karachi, and Balochistan. The TTP is also highly active in the area. Indeed, Darra acts as a hub of trade of local- and foreign-made arms and weapons.

"Sharia Tax," Levies, and Penalties in Tribal Areas

In all tribal areas where they exert some control, the TTP and its affiliates have introduced "Sharia taxes," which provide them the resources to continue their activities and pay salaries to their foot soldiers. Local tribesmen confirm that Taliban collect "taxes" on houses, vehicles, transportation, petrol pumps, big shops, and dispensaries.[33] In some Taliban-controlled areas, when locals have any problem or dispute, they pay some money to the Taliban office and then the Taliban issue notices to parties. *Qazis* (judges) are appointed through the *jirga* to resolve the issue, and the tribesmen follow the decision of the *qazi*.

In October 2006, the Taliban in Miranshah, headquarters of North Waziristan tribal agency, decreed that the people pay them various sums of money they referred to as "taxes."[34] They issued an extensive "tax schedule" and distributed it through pamphlets. The pamphlets referred to the tax as a "donation." There was no mention of how the money would be spent, although its use was stated to be at the sole discretion of the Taliban Shura. When the Shura was formed in November 2006, its head, Mullah Nazir, issued edicts and a declaration to curb crimes in Waziristan. One clause of the declaration read: "A joint committee would accept donations and maintain their record and no individual or group would be allowed to demand or collect donations."[35] Moreover, in 2009, the Taliban gave Sikhs and Hindus in the tribal areas under their control an ultimatum—leave the land of their forefathers or pay *jizya*, a tax on non-Muslim subjects of an Islamic state. While some paid the tax, four hundred Sikh and fifty-seven Hindu families migrated from Khyber Agency.[36] They could afford the twelve-dollar-per-person annual jizya but feared for their lives living in Taliban-controlled areas.[37]

The Taliban also managed to receive some money by imposing penalties. A ban on adult male Muslims shaving their beards was extended to parts of FATA, including Bajaur Agency, in February 2007. Violators were subject to a fine of fifty dollars.[38] The ban was imposed after the local Taliban distributed pamphlets that warned Muslim males against shaving their beards, and warned barbers against offering the service.

The Pakistani Government's Response

The government has engaged in diverse efforts to choke the financial resources of militant groups, but most of these efforts are confined only to banned militant groups. A more comprehensive policy is lacking. Between 2002 and 2012, the government took the following major steps.

The Banking Sector

The State Bank of Pakistan (SBP) supports global efforts to check money laundering, a vital tool for the militant groups to fund terrorist activities. The SBP has taken steps to prevent the use of banks to transfer criminally obtained proceeds, measures that fall under the anti–money laundering ordinance, which was promulgated in 2007. In conjunction with this, the SBP has developed a regulatory framework by issuing prudential regulations for banks and development finance institutions. Implementation of these regulations is ensured through on-site examination and off-site surveillance. This framework is working well because the SBP's inspectors specifically verify the adequacy of "know-your-client" policies and other anti–money laundering safeguards.

The SBP has been instrumental in freezing bank accounts of proscribed entities and individuals in accordance with UN Security Council resolutions since 2005. Periodic reports on such measures are sought from the banks, and records of frozen accounts are maintained. But no data is available on the effectiveness of the initiatives. To overcome this issue, the federal Interior Ministry has decided to consult with Interpol databases on criminals and terrorists.[39] The memorandums of understanding that the SBP has signed with a number of central banks for exchange of information and expertise also include efforts targeting money laundering and financing of terrorism.

In May 2002, the SBP prohibited the issuance of Rupee Traveler Cheques in denominations exceeding one hundred dollars. In the same year in September, the Anti–Money Laundering Ordinance, 2007—promulgated by then-president Pervez Musharraf—made the offence of money laundering punishable with rigorous imprisonment for a term of at least one year and a maximum of ten years, and with a maximum fine of ten thousand dollars as well as forfeiture of the property involved in money laundering. But this ordinance expired on November 28, 2009, and took more than a year to be repromulgated due to the fact that, under the 18th constitutional amendment passed shortly thereafter, the president no longer has the power to repromulgate the ordinance without the National Assembly's approval. The lapse deprived the state of certain powers that are crucial to dealing with terrorism, such as a ban on banks and financial institutions on providing loans or financial support to members of proscribed outfits. Similarly, it was this ordinance that barred members of banned organizations from obtaining passports and traveling abroad. When the government finally extended the ordinance in March 2010 (now termed the Anti–Money Laundering Act 2010), it introduced a clause that declared any financial assistance to a terrorist group a crime.[40]

The FIA also has a CT wing that includes a section on financing to monitor all remittances coming into the country through money exchanges and wire services. The FIA authorities are confident that the section is working well, although there is little independent verification of this claim.[41]

Implementation of Antiterror Financing Measures

In December 2010, the Securities and Exchange Commission of Pakistan directed stock exchanges and more than six hundred financial companies to implement antiterror financing measures outlined by the international Financial Action Task Force. Progress is visible as the amount of remittances being channeled through banks rather than *hawala* channels is on the rise (Yusuf 2010). Between 2008–9 and 2012, home remittances surged from $7.8 billion to $13.2 billion following the tough measures against money laundering (Iqbal 2013).

Militant/Madrassa Monitoring

The government has also closely monitored madrassas due to the financial links of some seminaries with the militants. In May 2006, state funding for madrassas under the Madaris Reforms Program was stopped when provincial governments failed to provide reporting on the use of $5 million allotted by the federal government for distribution to registered madrassas (Ghauri 2006).

Moreover, the government issues directions every year to provincial and local governments to ensure checks on banned militant groups that collect animal hides sacrificed on Eid-al Azha. But these orders have been largely ineffective so far (Malik 2006). When the federal and provincial security departments failed to enforce these and other directives, the government decided to engage the Auqaf departments, which are responsible for the management of mosques. On January 15, 2007, the federal government directed the central and provincial Auqaf departments to implement a ban on collection of funds being defied by registered mosques and madrassas, particularly on Fridays. Intelligence agencies were also monitoring the bank accounts of mosques, nongovernmental organizations, and madrassas for links with militant groups. The Auqaf departments were also directed to gather the records of registered and unregistered mosques and madrassas that had encroached on private land (Siddiqui 2007). Even these campaigns have not proved successful largely because of the increasing political leverage that the clergy enjoys in Pakistan. Government officials are afraid to take action against them. According to a media report, in the capital city of Islamabad alone, 61 mosques and madrassas out of a total of 372 were constructed illegally, but officials hesitate to take strict measures for fear of provoking a confrontation (Gishkori 2011).

Border Security

Pakistan has established eight hundred check-posts and deployed about seventy-five thousand troops along its border with Afghanistan—a major route for militants as well as for the trafficking of weapons and drugs—to check infiltrations. But this deployment was never meant to continue, and even as a secondary objective, it has been ineffective in checking militant financing due to the large volume of regular and legal movement across the border by members of tribal groups with relatives living on the other side of the border. The Durand Line, as this border is called, is often believed to be unmanageable.

Strengthening Financial Curbs on Militants

The government's efforts, while commendable, demonstrate an overriding focus on the formal financial sector. Even here, most of the initiatives were undertaken due to international pressure. The challenge the state faces is far bigger, and it demands more robust resolve and efforts. Even in the formal financial sector, attempts to stop financial flows to militants have not been up to the mark. The major reason is the lack of training of as well as lack of focus by law enforcement agencies on the financial trail behind terror-related crimes. Media reports suggest that around ten thousand people or facilitation centers still operate in Pakistan, where such illegal transactions continue to take place (Siddiqui 2010).

There is little doubt that finances remain available to militant groups in Pakistan despite years of government curbs. The government has not yet paid attention to the nontraditional sources of financing for small terrorist cells, the TTP, and al-Qaeda. The involvement of these groups in crime, especially in abduction for ransom and robberies is increasing. The challenge will keep growing unless a comprehensive strategy is evolved. There is the risk that militant groups will become even more involved in crime if the government's determination to choke their finances is not as resolute as the will of militant groups to wreak havoc in Pakistan. The tribal area–based militants have also emerged as one of the major beneficiaries of the traditional tribal economy by charging various "taxes" on local businessmen. Weapons and narcotics smuggling is also occurring at a greater pace.

Clearly, Pakistan is in need of a more comprehensive CT policy to curb the financial flows of militants. Experts suggest that in the formal financial sector, the SBP can be empowered to revitalize its intelligence unit and the capacity of law enforcement agencies can be enhanced to conduct financial investigations (Yusuf 2010). Another imperative step to combat terror financing is regulating the *hawala* channel and other informal financial sectors. The trend of mobile banking is on the rise in Pakistan, which reduces the opportunities for illegal funds transfers because cellular connections are under increased regulation. The government should encourage and facilitate the expansion of this endeavor.

Militant organizations have changed tactics to survive government restrictions; these organizations are seeking to diversify their funding sources to sustain their operations, and the government's actions must keep pace with these changes. The government must move beyond conventional restrictions and evolve a strategy to block new avenues for militant financing. This is only possible through a vigilant monitoring mechanism.

Charity organizations must not be allowed to operate unregulated since many militant organizations now operate in the garb of charities. The activities of these organizations must be monitored and their assets promptly frozen if any link to militants is found. Individuals linked to banned organizations must also be prosecuted instead of being allowed to start another organization, conducting the same activities under a different name. These objectives cannot be achieved unless the capacity of law enforcement agencies, mainly the police, is increased.

There is also an urgent need to devise coordinated CT finance strategies not only at the level of the law enforcement agencies but also at the policy level, with input from civil society, which can play an important role to educate the people about the motives of the militants, their methods to raise money, and the use of that money to spread chaos in Pakistan and beyond. Finally, the rise of militancy in Pakistan has a substantial regional dimension as well. The growing concern among policymakers and experts over external support for transnational militants and their involvement in the illegal drug and weapons trade is understandable. Despite the complex political landscape of the region, Islamabad needs to develop collaborative strategies with neighboring countries as well as with its international partners in the war on terror to counter the problem at a regional level. Substantial progress in overcoming militancy in Pakistan will remain elusive in the absence of these measures.

Notes

1. Informal *hawala* channels provide anonymity and rapid transfer of funds from one country to another without any documentation.

2. "Row over Release of Suspects by ATC," *Dawn*, March 24, 2011, http://dawn.com/2011/03/24/row-over-release-of-suspects-by-atcs/.

3. *Zakat* is an annual obligatory tax required of Muslims with assets in excess of need. *Zakat* is payable after one year's possession of the assets. It is a prescribed charity for public welfare.

4. Literally meaning "one-tenth," *ushr* is a tax on agricultural produce.

5. The estimates are based on claims made by militant organizations in their publications or during interviews with the author.

6. No official figures are available, and militant groups only concede off the record that funds from abroad are still pouring in, and only on the condition that their groups' names are not cited.

7. "Jihadists Collecting Funds in the Cover of Charities," *Daily Jang* (Rawalpindi), September 17, 2007.

8. The Jamaat-ud-Dawa official interviewed preferred to remain anonymous. Interview with author, Lahore, March 2008.

9. After imposition of sanctions by the state in 2007, the Al-Rashid Trust is operating under the name of the Maymar Trust.

10. "Al-Rehmat Trust Raised Rs. 600 Million for Earthquake Relief," *Daily Islam* (Lahore), February 19, 2007.

11. Anonymous JuD member, interview with author, Lahore, March 2008.

12. Anonymous JuD member, interview with author, Lahore, March 2008.

13. "One Year of Jiash-e-Muhammad," [Editorial] *Fortnightly Jaish-e-Mohammed* (Karachi), March 2001.

14. Jaanisar, a former member of Al-Badr, interview with author, Lahore, 2003.

15. *Fitrana* is an amount of charity—in the form of staple food or its equivalent price—that all Muslims of means are required to pay at the conclusion of Ramadan.

16. Ahmed Maqbool, "In the Name of God," *Herald* (Karachi), October 2008; and "Banned Charities Asked to Provide Funding Details," *South Asia Terrorism Portal*, February 1, 2006. www.satp.org/satporgtp/detailed_news.asp?date1 = 1/2/2006&id = 17.

17. For instance, banned Jamatul Furqan's monthly journal *Tadbeer-e-Nau* (June 2003) advertised that buying products made by multinationals amounted to "throttling ourselves."

18. This was ascertained through personal interviews with shopkeepers in Karachi, 2004.

19. Interview with the author, Lahore, May 2008.

20. Quote from Ameer Hamza's address at a seminar in Karachi, *Ghazwa Times* (Lahore), September 22–28, 2006.

21. "SSP Launched Earthquake Relief," *Daily Islam* (Islamabad), June 11, 2005.

22. Ibid.

23. Maulana Syed Yousaf Shah, Jamia Akora Khattak, interviewed by author, Nowshera, KPK, March 2008.

24. "New Wave of Sectarian Killings: Bank Robberies Become Major Source of Banned Organizations," *Daily Ummat* (Karachi), June 12, 2010.

25. "Banned Organizations Intensifying Financial Sources," *Daily Ummat* (Karachi), June 8, 2010.

26. Mir Dawood, Jammu Kashmir Liberation Front, interview with author, Muzaffarabad, Azad Kashmir, 2007.

27. "Banned Organizations Are Still Collecting Funds," *Daily Mashriq* (Peshawar), April 7, 2007.

28. "A Forged Taliban Arrested," *Daily Mashriq* (Peshawar), January 9, 2007.

29. "Business on the Name of Taliban," *Daily Jinnah* (Lahore), March 4, 2007.

30. "Bank Robbed in Mirali Bazaar," *Dawn* (Lahore), May 31, 2006.

31. "Taliban Warned Not to Build Demolished Shrine," *Daily Mashriq* (Peshawar), January 9, 2007.

32. For an excellent analysis of the Afghan Taliban's use of drug smuggling and narcotrafficking, see Peters 2009, 2010.

33. Aqeel Yousafzai, interview with author, Peshawar, December 2010.

34. "Taliban Slap Taxes in Miranshah," *Dawn* (Lahore), October 23, 2006.

35. "Mujahideen Shura Resolves to Enforce Shariat," *News* (Lahore), November 6, 2006, www.thenews.com.pk/TodaysPrintDetail.aspx?ID=30779&Cat=2&dt=11/6/2006.

36. "Sikhs, Hindus Dread Taliban Tax," *Daily Times* (Lahore), July 28, 2009.

37. Ibid.

38. "Ban on Beard-Shaving Extended across Bajaur: Shaving Beard to Cost Rs. 5,000," *Daily Times* (Lahore), February 15, 2007.

39. "Interpol SG Calls on Rehman Malik," *Daily Times*, January 30, 2012.

40. Anti–Money Laundering Act, Act VII of 2010, March 26, www.sbp.org.pk/about/act/Anti-Act-2010.pdf.

41. "Interview, Ahmed Waseem—FIA Director General," *Express Tribune*, November 10, 2010.

CHAPTER 8

Cyberia

A New War Zone for Pakistan's Islamists

ZAFARULLAH KHAN

TIME AND AGAIN, militants have demonstrated their expertise at catching people and their governments off guard. However, the policy responses to check these challenges have been lukewarm. The latest addition to the militants' toolkit is the use of modern gadgets and technology to propagate their medieval ideology. Ostensibly operating from rough terrains in comparatively less-developed areas, they have exhibited an amazing level of sophistication in wielding their "digital sword" (Blunt 2003, 25). They use and abuse information and communication technologies (ICT) in several ways: (a) to occupy normative communication and social spaces to present, project, and promote their narratives; (b) to create their own spaces to disseminate unfiltered propaganda based on their worldview; and (c) as tools to communicate, train, and network for waging global jihad.

The focus of this chapter is these "technologies of liberation" (Diamond 2010) that aid extremists in establishing their own "Cyberia" with dangerous digital trenches. The chapter examines the overarching context that facilitates the militants' use of Cyberia to pursue their agendas in Pakistan, the specific tools and technologies they employ, and the weakness of the state's response that are allowing greater space to militants for actions linked to cybercrime and cyberterrorism.

This is a crucial and grossly neglected aspect of counterterrorism (CT) as far as the Pakistani state apparatus is concerned. Besides the question of will, there is no coherent legal regime or a corresponding institutional capacity to check the threat of cyber militancy. The communication vectors among existing institutions with a mandate to check abuses—for example, the Pakistan

Telecommunication Authority (PTA), the Pakistan Electronic Media Regulatory Authority (PEMRA), and the Cyber Crimes Wing of the Federal Investigation Agency (FIA)—are very weak. Therefore, most of the efforts to curtail the resources available to terrorists—in this instance, technology—have produced little success in Pakistan.

The Context: Militant Organizations and the Use of Media

The South Asian region witnessed a proliferation of militant organizations during the first Afghan conflict (1979–89) against the Soviet Union; after the Soviet withdrawal, the sphere of their violent activities expanded to Pakistan as well. The Pakistani security establishment tolerated, and in a large number of cases actively supported, militant outfits as tools of its foreign policy in Afghanistan and Indian Kashmir. It only hardened its attitude toward these jihadi proxies after they became a domestic sectarian problem in the latter half of the 1990s.

Pakistan had started banning militant sectarian organizations prior to 9/11. While it banned various Islamist outfits with varying agendas and activities, some under international pressure and others of its own accord, these bans have largely proved ineffective.[1] First, the mere banning of an organization does not signal a complete closure or an end to their activities because monitoring every member of the organization is impossible. Also, the larger phenomenon of militancy and the aura of ideological ambivalence with respect to the legitimacy of violence in the name of religion in Pakistan add to the difficulties in structuring a CT strategy that targets the use of technology and the internet by terrorist groups. Huge governance gaps and the failure of the Pakistani state to provide basic social services to its citizens further add to the conundrum; they allow space for these militant outfits to run schools, charities, ambulance services, and so on—all activities that come across as innocent social work and that help knit a vibrant community of radicals who are able to earn the trust of people by providing humanitarian services.

Like any other institution, the media is also a microcosm of the society in which it exists. The media ecology is influenced by popular discourses and narratives that prevail in any given context. The use of media in Pakistan has always reflected its internal dynamics, especially those surrounding religion. Since its birth, the country has experienced an intellectual struggle over its ideological foundations; at its core, the debate has been between modernists and traditionalists. The country's mainstream population is conservative, and selective readings of history through textbooks have created public discourses and worldviews in the idiom of Islam (Nayyar and Salim 2005). The media professionals are drawn from the same sociology. The emergence of the press in the subcontinent during the colonial period was part of the nationalism project, but after sixty-five years of independence, the media has expanded in terms of size, scale, and scope. Beginning in 2002, following the liberalization of electronic media in Pakistan, there has been an explosion of media outlets. As many as 106 FM radio stations, 89 private satellite television channels, and 2,500-plus cable operators with a license from PEMRA have flooded the market. There are also more than 352 active newspapers across Pakistan.[2]

To influence this mainstream media, religious political parties continue to use institutional mechanisms and national policymaking processes to create structures and spaces that are conducive to their worldviews. A report on publicity media (1962–93) prepared by the government-run constitutional body, the Council of Islamic Ideology, contains recommendations on how to include an Islamic ethos in media discourse, how to check obscenity, and how to inscribe notions of Kalmia-e-Tayyba (Muslim creed) and Allah-Hu-Akbar (God Is Great) on the Pakistani flag; many of these groups hope that symbols like these will inspire Pakistanis to join the jihad and embrace martyrdom.[3]

Scholars and media professionals subscribing to this point of view have continuously pleaded for a genre of Islami Sahafat, or Islamic journalism (Zani 1988), to mold Pakistani society according to an Islamic ethos on the basis of "Amr bil Ma'roof wa Nahi Anil Munkir" (commanding right and forbidding wrong). These notions often appear in the public manifestations of many jihadi militant outfits. First, partially influenced by these narratives, many Pakistanis view the use of ICTs to propagate militant points of view couched in Islamic idioms, including jihad, to counter Western propaganda as a legitimate preaching enterprise. Second, such a discourse lumps the plight of specific Muslim groups like Kashmiris with the struggles of other Muslim polities, such as Palestine. This communalization of the narrative of victimhood blurs the line between ideological and literal support to these disturbed Muslim theaters, motivating many young people to join jihad. Moreover, many religious political parties and militant outfits own vibrant publishing houses that produce various media products to promote these points of view and create a cohesive community of passionate followers.

In strategic terms, the paradigm of "jihadi journalism" (Khan 2001) was put to test during the Afghan–Soviet war (1979–88) as the militant media machinery was carefully crafted to eulogize jihad. This included the establishment of an Afghan media resource center, an essential part of the overall security apparatus and "jihadizing" textbooks.[4] These institutions, especially the Afghan Islamic Press, and the jihadized textbooks were used by the Taliban regime in Afghanistan. From 1989 until 2001, the focus of this methodology also shifted to Kashmir-specific propaganda (Gan, Gomez, and Johannen 2004) where the Pakistani intelligence agencies were supporting an armed jihad.

After 9/11, the ownership and contents of militant media machinery have changed drastically. Today one can find the effective use of audiocassettes, CDs, DVDs, FM radios, cellular mobile phones, and the internet in a militant's arsenal. The producers, audience, and consumers of these products are spread all over the world in the shape of a horizontal, mostly privatized, and freelance network run by outfits such as al-Qaeda and its affiliates. Overall, in the presence of a nonhostile, if not sympathetic, context for militants successfully using religious dialects to conflate their true agendas and in the absence of an effective legal regime and the vigilance of law enforcement, the Pakistani situation provides an ideal opportunity for technology-savvy militant outfits seeking to use Cyberia to further their agendas.

Defining Cyberterrorism

Pakistan has struggled to find an effective legal regime to fight cybercrime. The Prevention of Electronic Crimes Ordinance has been promulgated at least three times since 2007, but it was allowed to lapse every time after its legal life span of 120 days. It has now been blocked in the Standing Committee on Information Technology of the National Assembly since January 28, 2009, on the pretext that it is too wide-ranging and potentially detrimental to people's fundamental rights. Even after two and a half years, there have been no serious efforts to address the concerns and adopt it.

The expired ordinance and the proposed law define cyberterrorism as "any person, group or organization who, with terroristic intent utilizes, accesses or causes to be accessed a computer or computer network or electronic system or electronic device or by any available means, and thereby knowingly engages in or attempts to engage in a terroristic act commits the offence of cyber terrorism."[5] It explains terroristic intent as the intent to "alarm, frighten, disrupt, harm, damage or carry out an act of violence against any segment of the population, the government or entity associated therewith."

For the purposes of this section, the proposed law explains that the expression of a "terroristic act" includes, but is not limited to:

> (a) Altering by addition, deletion, or attempting to alter information that may result in the imminent injury, sickness, or death to any segment of the population;

> (b) Transmitting or attempting to transmit a harmful program with the purpose of substantially disrupting or disabling any computer network operated by the Government or any public entity;
> (c) Aiding the commission of or attempting to aid the commission of an act of violence against the sovereignty of Pakistan, whether or not the commission of such act of violence is actually completed; or
> (d) Stealing or copying, or attempting to steal or copy, or secure classified information or data necessary to manufacture any form of chemical, biological or nuclear weapon, or any other weapon of mass destruction.[6]

The law proposes that whoever commits the offence of cyberterrorism and causes the death of any person shall be punished by death or imprisonment for life plus a fine, and in any other case, he shall be punished with imprisonment of a term that may extend to ten years, or by a fine not less than ten million rupees, or with both. The law will extend to the whole of Pakistan, and it aspires to apply to every person irrespective of his nationality or citizenship and locale outside or inside Pakistan. The law calls for the establishment of a specialized cell within the FIA to investigate and prosecute cybercrime offences. The law also proposes the constitution of an ICT tribunal.

Globally, the US Federal Bureau of Investigation (FBI) defines cyberterrorism as "the premeditated, politically motivated attack against information, computer systems, computer programs and data which results in violence against noncombatant targets by sub-national groups or clandestine agents" (Pollitt 1997). The US National Infrastructure Protection Center defines it as "a criminal act perpetrated by the use of computers and telecommunications capabilities, resulting in violence, destruction and/or disruption of services to create fear by causing confusion and uncertainty within a given population, with the goal of influencing a government or population to conform to particular political, social or ideological agenda" (Elmusharaf 2004).

Keeping these definitions in mind, and looking at internet sociology and the way it has been manipulated and abused by extremist militant individuals and groups, cybercrime can be categorized in the following way:

- *Cyberactivism*: Propaganda to win hearts and minds, hate speech, recruitment, sharing of training manuals and planning terrorist plots, and so on;
- *Hacktivism*: Reverse engineering through viruses, denial of service attacks, hacking and defacing websites; and
- *Cyberterrorism*: Disruption or destruction of services, taking control of vital operations/institutions.

As of today, militants in Pakistan have successfully climbed the first two rungs of this ladder. Their maximum abuse falls in the category of cyberactivism. The Pakistan Hackers Club, including portals like "Doctor Nuker" and "GForce Pakistan" are primarily known to deface Indian and Israeli websites, and they have occasionally tried to hack websites in the United States with little success. There also exists a talent among Pakistani hackers to generate viruses and infect global computer networks. Hackers linked to al-Qaeda dispersed in various parts of the world have tried to propel the jihad mindset elusively through the internet; Pakistanis are among them.

Prior to his death, the world's "most wanted" terrorist, Osama bin Laden, used offline computer services. His couriers disseminated his messages with the help of portable flash drives and online services available at internet cafes (Goldman and Apuzzo 2011a). They also used cell phones to coordinate terrorist plots and occasionally used them as detonators. Jihad-inspired cyberactivists in Pakistan not only use these possibilities to forward their agenda; they also occasionally use vigilante tactics to disrupt the internet, shut down cyber cafes, burn or confiscate CDs, and terrorize television networks.[7] Interestingly, the "cyber troops" for Pakistan focused on checking India are considered quite legitimate. On July 20, 2009, a militant ideologue, Zaid Hamid, wrote an open letter to Pakistanis across the globe. The letter stated, "Pakistan needs you today. We are inviting you to become cyber troops for Pakistan, wherever you might be, whatever you might be doing. From your homes and offices, you can protect, defend and dignify Pakistan and respond to Indian propaganda" (Hamid 2009). The letter describes cyberspace as a solid defense and line of attack. In terms of the language of preference, al-Qaeda produces its content in Arabic and English primarily for an audience in the Middle East and the Western world, respectively. Their Pakistani affiliates by and large focus on Urdu and Pashto languages.

While militants still prefer to communicate primarily through traditional modes such as individual couriers, face-to-face communication, and trusted emissaries who help them dodge domestic and international forms of law enforcement, they have clearly exhibited more sophisticated approaches toward Cyberia in recent years. Prominent jihadi media organizations such as As-Sahab Media, Labayk Media, Jundullah Media, Islam Awazi Information Center, Ummat Studio, Badr at-Tawheed Media, and Manba al-Jihad Media have direct or indirect links to al-Qaeda and its affiliates. Many freelance supporters of militant outfits also run covert and overt websites, blogs, and e-lists along with occupying spaces on social media websites such as Facebook, Orkut, and YouTube.

In Pakistan indigenous jihadi groups such as Lashkar-e-Taiba (LeT), Jamaat-ud-Dawa (JuD), Jaish-e-Muhammad (JeM), and Harkat-ul-Mujahideen (HuM) took advantage of ICTs to push their agenda and propaganda before being proscribed by the state. The media products of these militant outfits multiplied and, after appearing on the radar of law enforcement, resurfaced with camouflaged identities. For example, these days JeM promotes its ideology through a website, www.alqalamonline.com. The TTP, besides publishing some magazines in Pashto, mostly relies on hand-written letters, handbills, pamphlets, CDs, FM radios, cell phones, and e-mails. Most militant outfits also try to occupy space in mainstream media through their formally designated spokespersons and audio-visual messages to present their claims and points of view on various issues.

Militants' ICT-Based Arsenals

Like the rest of the world, Pakistani militants are also finding increasing opportunities to use ICT-based arsenals to support and conduct terrorism. Pakistan's telecommunication and media boom and fast-increasing internet penetration coupled with weak state capacity and regulation provides an appealing environment for technology-savvy militants to operate in. The discussion below captures the major avenues that militants in Pakistan have managed to exploit.

Cell Phones

The penetration of cellular phones in Pakistan has increased tremendously over the past decade. From 5 million users in 2003–4, the number increased to 105.15 million in 2011. Out of these, around 14.4 million people have internet services on their handsets. This infrastructure potentially provides militants with an opportunity to browse Google Earth maps to identify, locate, and learn about possible targets. However, the abuse is not limited to this capability. In terms of SMS (short messaging service) traffic through cell phones, Pakistan ranks fourth in the world. SMS messages are an equally convenient way to communicate and coordinate for militants.

Al-Qaeda and its Pakistani affiliates, including the TTP, have made effective use of this amazingly popular medium not only as a communication device but also as detonators to conduct blasts and as cameras to visually capture the scope of their brutal activities. According to a media report, the Afghan Taliban has also established a Twitter feed, @alemarahweb (Boone 2011).

The easy availability of cellular phone SIMs (subscriber identity modules), especially prepaid SIMs (including on other peoples' national identity cards), has enabled militants to camouflage their identities and abandon used SIM cards successfully. Only after terrorists were tracked through the SIM recovered from the scene of attack on former president Gen. Pervez Musharraf in Rawalpindi in 2003 did the PTA direct all five Pakistani service providers to verify their SIM card records. Incidentally, Osama bin Laden's discovery in Pakistan was also tracked through the use of a cellular phone by one of his personal messengers (Goldman and Apuzzo 2011b).

In the wake of the recent wave of terrorism, the issuing of prepaid SIMs has become more stringent, and the PTA has developed the SIM Information and Verification System-668 to address associated risks on security and to ensure subscription regulations in the cellular sector. The objective of the project is to provide a consumer-based facility to mobile subscribers in Pakistan by which they would be able to find out the total number of SIMs registered against their respective computerized national identity card number with each mobile operator. The PTA has blocked about 3.5 million unverified SIMs in this process. In November 2011, the PTA also issued a list of about 1,500 English and Urdu words to be filtered in text messaging (Popalzai and Haque 2011). Within a week the decision was withdrawn because the list had more words to police morality than to check militancy (Ghauri 2011b).

CDs and DVDs

On the one hand, militants have burned down several music and CD shops in Pakistan, especially in FATA and KPK, declaring them factories of obscenity, while on the other, they have used CDs, audiocassettes, and DVDs to spread their propaganda messages, glorify their so-called victories on the battlefield, share final motivational messages of suicide bombers, disseminate messages from hostages, and capture gory beheadings. CDs and DVDs are a prominent medium through which jihadi militants conduct their public relations campaign, including providing recorded messages and videos of their missions to the media.

We can envision that they use these CDs and DVDs along the lines of distance learning materials of an open university of jihad-inspired militancy, with most of them offering practical, step-by-step training manuals on bomb making and preparing suicide jackets. Militant communities also frequently exchange these products without leaving any digital fingerprints. CDs and DVDs like these are publicly sold, especially at religious congregations by seminaries and organizations sympathetic to militancy. Militants also upload their CDs and DVDs on websites and deliver them to mainstream media organizations. Moreover, jihadi inspirational songs are also available in the format of CDs and DVDs. Militants upload videos sharing this genre of music on social networking websites like YouTube as well.

FM Radio

Militants in the FATA and Swat in KPK province, both hotbeds of the TTP, extensively use unlicensed illegal FM radios to propagate their worldviews and jihadi propaganda. According to a conservative estimate, more than 150 pirate FM radio stations have operated in these areas. Maulana Fazlullah of Swat, the chief instigator of the antistate militancy in the region in 2008, earned the nickname of "Mullah Radio," while Mangal Bagh, the chief of Khyber agency in the FATA-based militant organization Lashkar-e-Islam, used to deliver regular sermons on his FM radio to terrorize the tribal society, recruit new fighters, and issue fatwas (religious edicts) against his opponents. FM radios used in this manner continue to broadcast anti-American, antigovernment, and antidemocracy sermons.

FM radio channels enable fierce orators to offer extreme versions of religion in order to infuse the jihadi spirit into the Pashtun social milieu. They remain a popular, culturally relevant, and less expensive medium in illiterate and religiously conservative communities. Jihadi magazines report that women in the Swat who respond to Fazlullah's calls for donations on the air even donated their jewelry as the Mullah Radio couched his message in terms of revival of Islamic values and challenging the corrupt system and values of the state (Khaliq 2010). This is an apt example of the deliberate conflation of issues that militants regularly employ to gain the sympathy of the public.

In legal terms, the PEMRA issues broadcast licenses, and the Frequency Allocation Board allots frequencies to legal licensees while also checking the abuse of country's airwaves. However, they failed to assert their authority over militants' FM radio stations for some time. It was only during and after the army's Operation Rah-e-Rast in Swat in 2009, which ended Pakistan Taliban's control of the Swat Valley, that they dismantled the illegal infrastructure of these FM radios.

The Internet

Pakistan's internet penetration has grown steadily in recent years. Over 25 million Pakistanis now have access to internet of varying quality (Ameen 2012). Al-Qaeda and its Pakistani affiliates are some of the early adaptors of ICTs and were thus well positioned as increasing number of Pakistanis gained access to the World Wide Web. A website, www.azzam.com, created to pay tribute to Abdullah Yusuf Azzam—the teacher and mentor of Osama bin Laden—strongly urged Muslim Web professionals to spread and disseminate news and information about jihad through e-mail lists, discussion groups, and their own websites.

After post-9/11 military operations in Pakistan squeezed the physical space available to militant outfits, they expanded their virtual presence. They used the internet to influence, incite, recruit, and raise resources. Many militant outfits have woven a web of volunteers through this medium. In this way, unregulated cyberspace has become an innovative battlefield with anonymous soldiers in its virtual trenches. Along with their own websites, militants have successfully intruded on a lot of cyberspace through social networking sites and blogs. After the brutal assassination of Salmaan Taseer, the governor of Punjab, by his own security guard in Islamabad in January 2011 over Taseer's opposition to the blasphemy legislation, a Facebook group eulogizing the killer was created, which attracted more than three thousand sympathizers within four hours.

Many websites of jihadi militant organizations with Pakistani URLs were shut down after 9/11. However some militant organizations and their sympathizer *madrassas* (religious seminaries) still have functional websites hosted abroad, as their URLs testify. Maulana Masood Azhar of the defunct JeM offers a wide range of publications for understanding jihad "theology" and accessing Islamic literature for Muslim children and women at his website, www.AlQalamOnline.com. Interestingly, the website also solicits contributions for a charity, the Al-Rehmat Trust. To prevent the website from being blocked, the enterprise has secured numerous other URLs, such as www.Fathuljawwad.com and www.Musalmanbachay.com.

The Lal Masjid (Red Mosque) group in the federal capital that created a lot of mayhem in 2007 by openly defying the state's writ also runs many websites. For instance, www.lalmasjid.2truth.com offers the last will of Maulana Abdur Rasheed Ghazi, the brother of the mosque's chief cleric, who was killed in the paramilitary-cum-commando operation at the mosque in July 2007. The website even provides a blueprint of Islamization in Pakistan. Its sister seminary for females, Jamia Hafsa, has a separate website, www.Jamiahhafsa.com, with a message that states, "You can kill the body, but you cannot kill the passion." Another website of Jamia Hafsa is www.Jhuf.net, which claims to support online the mujahideen (Muslim fighters) worldwide. It states, "Our struggle is for our thousands of Muslim sisters, mothers and daughters who are in the prisons of *kuffar* (infidels). We also aim to get the Muslim *ummah* together under the flag of jihad *feesabilillah* (holy war in the name of God)." The site also offers links to other jihadi websites. Materials about Dr. Afia Siddiqui, Abu Musab al-Zarqawi, videos related to the Taliban in Afghanistan, jihad in Iraq, and many other jihadi publications are available at the click of a mouse. The Pakistan chapter of Hizb ut-Tahrir, another banned organization, operates its own website, www.Hizb-pakistan.com, which advocates for a caring global caliphate, and demonizes democracy as a Western project to enslave Muslims.

The internet in Pakistan provides ample space to jihadi militants to connect their local operations with their global counterparts. Jihadi websites also serve the purpose of linking members of the Pakistani diaspora with jihadi militants to donate toward and participate in their activities.

It is important to note that while jihadi websites continue to operate and promote radicalism, in May 2010, on the direction of the Ministry of Information and Technology and in light of a decision by the Lahore High Court, the PTA shut down YouTube and Facebook, along with 450 other sites, in view of the growing militant nature of their contents.[8] Although this suggests that authorities could do more, it still reflects a sense of will toward more stringent action on militant abuse of cyberspace. On the other hand, the PTA, the internet-governing body in the country, released a list of thirteen thousand websites to more than fifty internet service providers to be blocked on grounds of immorality—not militancy (Haque 2012). In March 2012, the National ICT Research and Development Fund of the Ministry of Information Technology invited proposals for the development, deployment, and operation of a national-level URL filtering and blocking system. Even before what would have been the biggest firewall in Pakistan could be judged effective for checking militant activities in cyberspace, the Ministry's request for proposals was withdrawn. Such reversals tie the thread back to the fundamental underlying contextual anomaly that Pakistan is operating under: the ambivalence and reluctance to oppose outright any source that uses religious idioms to promote its message.

Television

Since 2002, Pakistan has had a vibrant industry of privately owned independent television channels. PEMRA has licensed eighty-nine channels, with more than thirty of them producing news and current affairs–related content. Pakistan has also experienced a revolution in cable-distribution networks, which implies that these TV channels can now penetrate deep into Pakistan's countryside. Indeed, survey after survey has shown that TV has trumped radio and other outlets as the number one information source for Pakistanis, including the youth.[9] Religious programs, while not compulsory, inevitably find substantial air time on TV transmissions of virtually all channels. The cable-distribution network can also operate low-cost CDs and DVDs based on local channels, and jihadi militants have not ignored this avenue.

In April of 2010, PEMRA took action against more than one hundred illegal and unregistered satellite television channels aired through cable-distribution networks throughout the country. These channels not only violated PEMRA laws but they also led to huge financial losses for the government exchequer by blocking space, which, according to the law, is a legal right of registered satellite TV channels (Rahman 2010). Many religious channels, including Peace TV, Iqra, and Q-TV, were also blocked, but within days, on the orders of the prime minister, PEMRA issued verbal instructions to cable operators to reopen these unlicensed channels. Again, this reinforces the notion that illegality in the name of religion remains permissible in Pakistan even if it dilutes rule of law.

Presently, there are at least seven religious TV channels operating in the country. They include QTV, Hadi TV, Haq TV, Labaik TV, Madni TV, Such TV, and Azan TV. Some of these channels broadcast sectarian programs that serve as fertile ground to implant jihadi ideology in the viewers' minds.

Besides maintaining a presence on purely religious channels, the militant mindset makes every effort to remain visible within the mainstream media as well. Even though the media is not a monolithic entity, the vernacular media often has a conservative—and sometimes even sectarian—bent. The institution of the professional editor is weak, and many gatekeepers fail to block texts and narratives that glorify extremism or violence. The ultraright is extremely organized and persistent; using phone and e-mail communication, they maintain constant outreach to sympathetic individuals within media outlets through seemingly benign fronts. These sympathetic media operators consciously or unconsciously end up providing the "oxygen of publicity" (Thatcher 1985) to extremists and militants.

The reporting about militant organizations in the mainstream media speaks volumes of the success of the Islamist enclave in blunting what could otherwise be a potent force multiplier in terms of building public consensus against their violent actions. As Azam (2008) notes, "news regarding the stance of banned militant and religious organizations are reported frequently. All they [media] do is add the word 'banned' before mentioning their names" (2). A majority of the newsrooms in Pakistan's media industry even shy away from using the term "extremist" or "terrorist" to describe the Taliban militants.

In essence, the journalists are often sandwiched between the competing narratives of militant outfits and law enforcement. "The media is blamed for publishing anti-Islamic materials if something is published against radicals"

(Azam 2008, 3). The logical outcome is either a "spiral of silence" or self-censorship in a hostile environment experiencing full-scale militancy. A survey conducted by the Pakistan Institute for Peace Studies in 2008 revealed that 87 percent of Pakistani journalists acknowledged the impact of radicalization on the media (Azam 2008, 10).

The ability of the militant enclave to force the media to circumvent the state's dictates is obvious from the fact that the TTP has arranged journalist trips to their operational areas and their designated spin-doctors have effectively liaised with many news channels. Alarmed by this, PEMRA warned all channels not to air the activities of the proscribed TTP, or to interview anyone affiliated with it. Within three months of this development, PEMRA had to issue at least ten notices to various mainstream channels for airing interviews of TTP leaders, including their now-killed leader, Baitullah Mehsud, and other senior figures like Muslim Khan and Maulvi Umar. In total, PEMRA issued sixty-four notices; of these, thirty-four pertained to the coverage of terrorism-related events.[10]

After these violations, the government attempted to cobble together a basic and viable voluntary code of conduct for the electronic media on the coverage of terrorism, but it failed (H. Khan 2010). Interestingly, though, the Lal Masjid group and the TTP have come up with their own code and set of recommendations for the mainstream media, imploring them not to ignore their positions and points of view.

The Missing Legal Regime

Cyberspace and electronic media are realities the world will have to live with. So is the fact that, just like states and private law-abiding citizens, violators of law, including militants, will also attempt to use this space to their advantage. Laws designed to check militant use of cyberspace therefore become pivotal for states and international bodies seeking to counter technology-savvy militant outfits. These laws may not be sufficient given that the fight against ideologically driven terrorism of the kind Pakistan faces requires far more. But laws are nonetheless a necessary ingredient of the recipe for success.

Pakistan's legal regime to check the "new terrorist" is quite weak, in part because it is diffuse. The absence of an overarching cyberterrorism-specific law has already been mentioned. Therefore, even though the cybercrime wing of the FIA is supposed to check cybercrime, the legal cover for this, the Electronic Crimes Ordinance of 2007, is no longer valid. A special investigation group has also served as a CT unit in the FIA since July 2007, and it is mandated to detect, seize, and prosecute hate material through computers and cell phones. Checking FM radios falls under the ambit of PEMRA and the Frequency Allocation Board. The PTA is responsible for checking illegal SIMs and the abuse of cellular phone services. The district administration is in charge of checking and confiscating objectionable print materials. There is no formal institutional mechanism to coordinate all these efforts under a larger umbrella. Pakistan tried to establish an effective National Counterterrorism Authority as the overarching coordinating body, but the attempt remains abortive.

Moreover, jihadis never existed as a threat in the imagination of Pakistani law enforcement agencies, especially those groups that were active in Kashmir. Rather, they were systematically used as proxies to promote the doctrines such as "bleed India" and "strategic depth" in Afghanistan. This was despite the fact that their very existence is explicitly banned in Pakistan's constitution, which maintains that "no private organization capable of functioning as a military organization shall be formed, and any such organization shall be illegal" (art. 256, ch. 4). Although it may not publicly manifest itself as much, this mentality still exists within some quarters and is evident in the reluctance to systematically weed out all militant outfits in the country. Cybercrime, with its rather virtual and intangible nature and effects, becomes the first casualty in terms of lack of will.

The state adopted a full-fledged Anti-Terrorism Act (ATA) in 1997 to check increasing violence in Pakistan. The law was later amended in 1999 and 2002. The act has not yielded the desired results to combat terrorism because the country's criminal justice system is not geared to respond adequately. Therefore, even though about twenty-five organizations and institutions have been banned under the ATA since 1998, most of them either reappeared with new names or continued their operations in violation of the law.

Admittedly, the law enforcement agencies have gradually begun to act against militant use of cyberspace. PEMRA has recently started fining private channels that cover the activities of banned extremist outfits (PEMRA 2010). The PTA also started blocking unverified cellular phone SIM cards since 2010, and ordered in late 2012 that all SIM cards be delivered directly by service providers to the physical addresses listed on the national identity cards of the users. It also banned mobile phone number portability, which allowed users to switch service providers while retaining their numbers, on the pretext that such portability made it harder to track down terrorists using cellular phones as part of their activity (Baloch 2012). Most recently, the Fair Trial Bill 2012 has been passed into law in February 2013—after extensive delay. This bill allows the intelligence outfits to monitor electronic communication and makes evidence gathered in the process admissible in courts of law.[11] While these are significant advances, the measures for the most part appear to be a weak response to various terrorist attacks instead of a thought-out policy to weed out militant organizations and their communication infrastructure.

Conclusion

Pakistan has been part of the global effort to combat terrorism since 2001, and it has paid a huge price for its involvement, in both terms of human lives and resources. However, it has failed to structure a coherent policy to address this challenge, or to cut off vital resources to its militants, such as ICTs.

For the first time, in October 2008 the Pakistani parliament came up with a fourteen-point resolution to reject extremism, militancy, and terrorism in all forms as well as manifestations that pose a grave danger to the stability and integrity of the country. The resolution called for framing of laws and building of institutions to protect citizens from violence and to eradicate terror at its roots.

Subsequently, a seventeen-member special committee of the parliament was constituted under the leadership of Senator Mian Raza Rabbani. The committee included the representation of thirteen political parties and an independent group from the FATA. The committee came up with a detailed set of sixty-six recommendations that address each point of this resolution. However, after more than two years, very little has been achieved in tangible terms, even though the Islamist threat has become truly existential.

Policies require corresponding structures to translate intentions into meaningful actions. Unfortunately, Pakistanis have largely become a nation ridden with claims that fall short on delivery. Along with inflicting violence and terror, al-Qaeda, the Afghan and Pakistani Taliban, and their affiliates epitomize a mindset that has gradually found resonance among large segments of the Pakistani society. Since the days of the Cold War, many Pakistanis have grown up under a single narrative woven around the illusion of superiority immersed in an Islamic ethos. The propaganda promoted by the militant media machinery has influenced many who now feel that the entire world is conspiring against Islam and Pakistan and its nuclear assets.

Within this climate of opinion, extremists gain a lot of publicity from mainstream media. This is evident from the June 2011 issue of *Ab-e-Hayat*, a monthly magazine of the defunct SSP, which added an editorial to its collection of articles from mainstream newspapers on the US raid that killed Osama bin Laden in Abbottabad, Pakistan, in May 2011.

In order to contain militancy and its psychology, Pakistan needs to reform its textbooks, facilitate media trainings, and evolve a voluntary code of conduct to drive myopic ideologies from normative public and discursive spaces.[12] This is the only way to develop an alternative discourse that will disinfect society from virulent extremism. Otherwise both modern and traditional media will continue to be abused by the medieval mindsets of militants.

Specifically in terms of Cyberia, Pakistan needs to adopt a comprehensive cybercrime law after consultation with the relevant stakeholders. Once the law has been adopted, an effort must be made to improve the communication and coordination necessary to effectively enforce it. To put this into effect, the spirit of the law needs to be internalized, which in turn will foster the institutional capacity to effectively deprive militants of their cyber safe havens.

Pakistan exhibited a unique capacity to block Facebook and other websites in 2010 on the order of Lahore High Court when these sites announced a cartoon competition on the Prophet of Islam.[13] In 2012, YouTube was again blocked when it posted parts of a film that was disrespectful to Islam and its Prophet. This is one indication that the state is capable of acting against those who hurt its citizens, emotionally in this case. Pakistan needs to be more imaginative in realizing threats of extremists. The legislative framework and regulatory regime in Pakistan must check extremist elements in cyberspace for if jihadis continue to abuse these spaces with impunity, the risk remains that Pakistani youth—a population that is increasingly consumed by new media—will be more vulnerable to their propaganda. As a country that has already paid a huge price in the "war on terror," Pakistan must deny safe havens to extremists not only in the physical but also in the virtual world.

Notes

1. On August 14, 2001, the state banned Lashkar-e-Jhangvi (LeJ) and Sipah-e-Mohammad (SeM), Sunni and Shia sectarian militant groups, respectively. Later in 2002, in response to global pressures and domestic concerns, Pakistan banned Jaish-e-Mohammad (JeM), Lashkar-e-Taiba (LeT), Sipah-e-Sahaba Pakistan (SSP), Tehreek-e-Nafaz-e-Shariat-e-Mohammadi (TNSM), and Tehrik-e-Jafaria Pakistan (TJP), Islamist outfits with varying agendas and targets. Al-Qaeda was formally banned in 2003, as were Millat-e-Islamia, Khudaamul Islam, Jamiatul Ansar, Jamiatul Furqan, and Hizbul Tehrir. In 2004, the Khairun Naas Trust was banned; in 2006, the government banned the Balochistan Liberation Army and the Islamic Student Movement of Pakistan; and in 2008, bans were imposed on Lashkar-e-Islam, Ansar ul-Islam, the Haji Namdar group, and Pakistan's avowed enemy, the Tehrik-e-Taliban Pakistan (TTP). In the wake of the Mumbai terrorist attacks of November 2008, the Jamaat-ud-Dawa (JuD), a charity arm of the LeT,

and other charities linked to militant organizations, for example, Al-Akhtar Trust and Al-Rasheed Trust, were scrutinized in the light of the Indian request to the UN Security Council on December 10, 2008, to declare the JuD a terrorist organization ("Govt Cracks Down on Daawa after UN Ban," *The News*, December 12, 2008, www.thenews.com.pk/TodaysPrintDetail.aspx?ID = 18899&Cat = 13&dt = 12/12/2008). However, Pakistani courts acquitted the JuD leaders soon thereafter and the group continues to operate in the public sphere with impunity, running its charity, the Falah-e-Insaniyat (Betterment of Humanity).

2. "UIS Data Centre," UNESCO Institute for Statistics, Montreal, Canada, 2008, http://data.un.org/Browse.aspx?d = UNESCO.

3. The report was published on February 24, 1993, by the Council of Islamic Ideology, Government of Pakistan.

4. According to its official website, the Afghan Islamic Press was established in 1982. Later, Professor Nick Mills of the journalism department of Boston University worked with the Afghan Resistance and was a founder of the Afghan Media Resource Center in Peshawar, Pakistan, in 1987. The textbook project was housed at the University of Nebraska and led by Thomas Gouttierre.

5. "President's Orders and Regulations, Ordinance No LXXII of 2007," *Gazette of Pakistan* (Islamabad), December 31, 2007.

6. Ibid.

7. Such episodes are frequent in FATA and other strongholds of the militants. Their followers burn TV sets in public. There are also instances of blasts at CD shops in Swat, Peshawar, and FATA.

8. "Religious Intolerance: LHC Orders Ban on Hate Spreading Websites," *Express Tribune*, September 20, 2011, http://tribune.com.pk/story/256152/religious-intolerance-lhc-orders-ban-on-hate-spreading-websites/.

9. "Youth Speak," *Herald* 41, no. 1, January, 2010.

10. The author collected copies of these notices from relevant sources.

11. The text of the Fair Trial Bill that was introduced into the national assembly is available at www.na.gov.pk/uploads/documents/1349757295_711.pdf.

12. In 2010 the government constituted a committee, headed by Justice (retired) Fakhruddin G. Ebrahim, to evolve a voluntary code for private media channels. The author was a member of the committee. The media has constantly resisted any regulation formulated by the government; therefore, this committee was an attempt to present a code to be adopted voluntarily rather than through an official decree.

13. According to an article in the *Tribune*, the Lahore High Court on September 19, 2011, ordered the Ministry of Information Technology to block access to all websites that were spreading religious hatred. Justice Azmat Saeed, however, made it clear that no search engine, including Google, would be blocked. The court also directed the ministry to submit a compliance report in this regard. "Religious Intolerance," *Express Tribune*, September 20, 2011.

CHAPTER 9

Pakistan's Paradoxical Survival

ANATOL LIEVEN

THIS CHAPTER addresses the puzzle of Pakistan's survival in the face of the Islamist insurgency-cum-terrorism threat coupled with internal weakness and the possibility of domestic revolution. Discussing the central dilemmas of the United States and Pakistani governments, the chapter demonstrates the strengths and weaknesses of the Pakistani state, specifically the entrenched systems of patronage that preserve the state even as they prevent positive transformation. It argues that the likelihood of the state being overthrown from within is minimal—mass urban uprisings appear unlikely and the Islamist insurgency (though not terrorism) is geographically contained. As a result, internal collapse hinges on the cohesion and loyalty of the army, where a mutiny on Pakistani soil is unlikely in the absence of a major military offensive by the United States.

The Wild Card: Pakistan's Relationship with the United States

In the "war on terror," Pakistan faces a basic dilemma: By doing what the United States wants, Pakistan stirs up unrest among its own population and, more importantly, its soldiers—as has indeed happened since 9/11—to the point that the Pakistani state system may be in danger of being overthrown. On the other hand, refusing cooperation with the United States would endanger Pakistan's survival as a state. US policy toward Pakistan also faces an inescapable paradox: The United States is discontented with a lack of Pakistani help against the Afghan Taliban, and many Americans would like to take tough action against Pakistan in response. However, Pakistan has been of essential help in preventing Pakistan-based terrorist attacks against the US and British homelands. The collapse of the Pakistani state would therefore be a catastrophe that would exponentially increase the terrorist threat to the West.

So far, because of this US dilemma, Pakistan has been able to get away with not taking action against the Afghan Taliban, although mutual distrust has skyrocketed as a result of public anger over intensified drone attacks on suspected al-Qaeda and Taliban commanders in Pakistan's tribal belt; the killing of two Pakistanis by CIA contractor Raymond Davis in Lahore and his subsequent release (Friedman 2011);[1] the US raid that killed Osama bin Laden, which outraged both Pakistani and American public opinion; and the NATO airstrike in November 2011 that killed twenty-four Pakistani soldiers, who were apparently mistaken for Taliban fighters who had been attacking Afghan National Army soldiers in the area. However, in early 2012, the United States and Pakistan moved closer on Afghanistan, participating in tentative talks with the Taliban in Qatar. Differences remain, however: Pakistani civilian and military establishments are wary of being drawn into participation into an Afghan peace process the goals of which they may not share—especially since, if the process fails, they may be treated by Washington as scapegoats. This wariness has not changed as a result of the May 2013 national elections in Pakistan that have thrown up the right-of-center Pakistan Muslim League-Nawaz (PML-N) as the country's leader. PML-N's leadership shares this view entirely.

In this setting, what threat does the current situation in Afghanistan pose to Pakistan? The first is the Islamist rebellion in Pakistan itself, inspired by the jihad in Afghanistan and by seeing itself as waging an allied struggle. This insurgency (though not the accompanying terrorism) can probably be contained in the Pashtun tribal areas unless the United States takes actions that infuriate the entire population and undermine military discipline to the point that the soldiers ally with the insurgents to fight against the United States. For this to happen, there would most probably have to be a major terrorist attack by Pakistanis within the United States itself. The Pakistani state and military can be expected to go on doing everything possible to prevent such attacks precisely because they know that they would risk dooming Pakistan to destruction. As discussed in chapter 1 of this volume, serious action by Pakistan on behalf of the United States against the Afghan Taliban is a very different matter. Neither the military nor the population supports this.

In the West, Pakistan's failure to act against the Afghan Taliban is attributed chiefly to the strategic calculations and machinations of the Pakistani military and its intelligence service, which are dedicated above all to increasing Pakistani influence in Afghanistan and creating a barrier against Indian influence there. This is not wrong—the obsession with the Indian threat colors everything that the Pakistani army does, and fear of Indian influence in Afghanistan is a very major factor in Pakistani policy there.[2] However, judging by the public statements of Chief of Army Staff General Kayani and my private conversations with senior generals, the military high command now sees domestic militancy, not India, as the greatest threat to the Pakistani state. They no longer wish to see the Afghan Taliban win an overall victory in Afghanistan, fearing that the Afghan Taliban would then be free to turn on Pakistan, raising the old Afghan cry of the abolition of the Durand Line between Afghanistan and Pakistan, and creating a greater Afghanistan including the Pashtuns of Pakistan. Compared to before, the Afghan Taliban would be in a stronger position—they could do so under the banner of Islamic revolution, with formidable armed allies among the Pakistani Taliban.

Most Pakistanis feel differently. Judging by my own extensive interviews in Pakistan, the overwhelming majority of the population regards the Afghan Taliban as akin in essential respects to the Afghan mujahideen of the 1980s: cruel and fanatical perhaps (though not corrupt and factionalized, like the mujahideen), but nonetheless waging a "defensive jihad" (or, in Western terms, legitimate resistance struggle) against an illegal foreign occupation of their country. This feeling is stronger among the Pashtuns (because of their ethnic links to the Pashtuns of Afghanistan who provide the backbone of the Afghan Taliban's support) than elsewhere in Pakistan, and is strongest of all among the Pashtun tribes of Federally Administered Tribal Areas (FATA) and northern Balochistan, which actually straddle the Afghan border; but it exists to some degree throughout Pakistan.[3]

Sympathy for a perceived war of resistance in Afghanistan does not translate into support for an Islamist revolution within Pakistan. While Islamist terrorism is taking place across Pakistan, insurgency has been confined to some of the Pashtun areas in the northwest, and even there it has been pushed back a long way by the Pakistani army since 2009. The military's success against the Pakistani Taliban owes much to the growing realization that they are enemies of the Pakistani state and not just of the Americans.

The Survival of Pakistan: Guaranteed by Its Internal Paradoxes?

If Pakistan's role in the war on terror is full of paradoxes, so too are the reasons for Pakistan's survival.[4] In the face of both internal and external pressures, Pakistan is strong in part precisely because it is weak. Moreover, those social, economic, and cultural forces within Pakistan that help make Pakistan resilient as a country also make it weak as a state.

Internally, most local elites and a number of ordinary people know that the overthrow of the existing state would lead to anarchy and a range of vicious civil wars between different nationalities and ethnoreligious groups, possibly encouraged by India. This is in contradiction to Iran, for example, where the overthrow of the shah was succeeded by an effective new state. No similar uniting forces exist in Pakistan. The overthrow of the existing state would lead not to a new revolutionary state but to unending chaos: Somalia on a vastly larger scale.

Building on this, the fear of India is of great importance in Pakistan, especially in Punjab. An Indian attack on Pakistan (in the aftermath of a terrorist attack on India) is not a clear-cut threat as far as Pakistan's survival is concerned. A full-scale war may lead to the destruction of the Pakistan armed forces or a nuclear exchange with India, but it may unify most Pakistanis, especially the Pakistani military.

The real threat—Islamist revolution (indeed, any revolution)—is opposed by powerful, entrenched social and economic elites in Pakistan: not so much by the great "feudal" and industrial families at the apex of the social pyramid (like the Bhutto-Zardaris and the Sharifs) as by networks of small local landowner politicians and urban bosses who usually base their strength not only on land and property but also on their leadership of local kinship networks. This allows them to get elected to national or provincial assemblies, and to use their elected positions to extract corrupt patronage that they employ to strengthen their local support (Lyon 2002; Lieven 2011; Ahmad 1977; Roniger and Gunes-Ayata 1994; Eglar 1960; Fischer 1991). This circular movement of money has proved extremely durable over time, largely because a high proportion of the proceeds spreads downward through society in order for the local notables to keep their local support—a crucial barrier to the spread of Islamist revolution.

However, since the whole system depends on extracting money and favors from the state, it prevents successful development of the country, especially in the crucial areas of water and energy infrastructure but also in every area of state services: education, health, pay for the police, and so on. This in turn keeps Pakistan miserably weak economically, providing the basis for Islamist discontent in parts of the country—another of the paradoxes that define Pakistan's extremely complicated situation.

Pakistan's economic situation has worsened markedly since 2007, thereby increasing Pakistani economic dependence on the United States. This is not because of US economic aid to Pakistan, which, at around $1.5 billion a year (much of which is in fact not delivered), is barely one-tenth of remittances from Pakistani workers in the Persian Gulf. Of far greater importance is US goodwill at the International Monetary Fund and World Bank in shaping their policy toward loans for Pakistan; in 2011, 38 percent of Pakistan's federal budget was devoted to debt servicing. Above all, the Pakistani establishment fears that if the US–Pakistani relationship were to collapse altogether, Washington might impose trade sanctions on Pakistan. The closing of the biggest international market for Pakistani textiles would have a shattering effect on Pakistan's most important industrial sector, a role other allies—such as China—cannot replace.

Economic hardship combines with misgovernment to produce a permanent state of social tension in Pakistan, which regularly breaks out in urban rioting. This tension has often been exploited by the political opposition to stir up protests against the government in power, but it has not led to any kind of serious urban revolutionary movement. The new government formed by Nawaz Sharif and his PML-N party after the May 2013 election may improve Pakistan's economic prospects—it seems likely to introduce some valuable reforms in the fields of privatization and energy strategy. However, reducing corruption and increasing tax collection would require a radical assault on Sharif's own key allies, an unlikely prospect.

Adding to this, the Pakistani state remains essentially the British colonial state. This means that, while it has not collapsed, unlike states in parts of Africa, it has also not developed beyond its colonial forms and limitations. It is reasonably good at repression, the co-option of local elites, and the maintenance of basic infrastructure.[5] It is very poor at social, economic, and educational development in part because—like the colonial state—it does not dare intervene in social traditions, especially when it comes to those governing the family. It has not controlled the birth rate, and a massively growing population has swamped whatever development has taken place.

Pakistan does, however, contain one remarkably strong and effective state institution: the army. Within its narrow spheres (military action and disaster relief) the Pakistan Army is fairly good at what it does. Contrary to the repeated dreams of much of Pakistani society (and some observers in the West), though, military rule can never succeed in transforming the country as a whole. A large part of the resources of a country of more than 180 million people has been transferred to some 600,000 of those people. Total military expenditures are up to around 26 percent of the budget (Fazl-e-Haider 2011). Coupled with genuine elements of discipline, ethics, and esprit de corps, this money keeps the army disciplined, loyal, and efficient. As soon as the military takes power, however, the virtues of the well-paid, well-trained, well-equipped 0.16 percent of the population inevitably vanish without trace amid the rest of the 99.84 percent. Military rule is not usually worse than civilian rule in Pakistan—on the record, that would be pretty hard to achieve—but it is also not usually any better, and the reason is that military and civilian rule are essentially *the same*. Whoever rules in Islamabad has to do so in the provinces and districts through the existing elites and the existing state structures that the elites dominate.

Given the current political situation, then, the real question for Pakistan is, will the junior officers, noncommissioned officers, and rank-and-file *jawans* (literally, "young men") of the army remain loyal to their commanders and the existing Pakistani state, or might they mutiny or at least stand aside and let the state collapse?

Military coups in Pakistan have always been carried out by the serving army chief of staff with the support of the great majority of senior generals. They have never occurred from below. If such a revolt did occur, Pakistan as a country could be destroyed in very short order as the military split and every malcontent in society joined the mutineers. So far, military discipline has held, underpinned by the great material benefits of military service, by a very strong military ethos, and by a strong and accurate belief that mutiny would mean the destruction of Pakistan and the triumph of India.

However, despite the best efforts of the military, soldiers cannot be completely isolated from society, and condemnation of their alliance with the United States in their home communities and families has wounded many of them deeply. This would seem to be the case from my own experiences traveling in the towns and villages of the Potwar region of northwestern Punjab, from which a majority of the army's rank and file is still recruited. The great majority of them—like the overwhelming majority of ordinary Pakistanis with whom I have spoken—believe the grotesque fantasy that 9/11 was not the work of al-Qaeda but of a CIA or Israeli conspiracy to give the United States the excuse to invade and subjugate Muslim countries.

The extent of specific radicalization within the army is difficult to gauge; there has been a demonstrable increase in the size of the army over the decades, and the officer corps has swelled to take in more and more sons of the lower middle classes, from traditionally conservative religious backgrounds. The proportion of the old Westernized aristocratic officers has declined radically (Nawaz 2008).[6] These are soldiers who may not be willing to risk their lives in America's "war on terror," but they *will* fight to defend Pakistan against threats from within and without, including Islamist radical threats—though their willingness will also depend on the form that Islamist unrest takes.

The Islamist Threat and Pakistan's Survival

To understand the threat from Islamist extremism in Pakistan, it is necessary to understand its nature, its limits, and the precise circumstances in which it might succeed—briefly and partially, for as already explained, the consequence would not be a national revolution along the lines of Iran or the Afghan Taliban but would be a bloody and unending civil war.

The first critical distinction is between terrorism on the one hand and insurgency and revolution on the other. Terrorism is now a grave and, alas, probably permanent menace across Pakistan—but to the best of my knowledge, no state has ever been overthrown by terrorism or by a movement acting chiefly through terrorism. On the contrary, by angering the population and legitimizing state repression, terrorism can sometimes even make states grow stronger. To overthrow a state from within, you need at least one of three things, and preferably a combination of them: widespread insurgency in the countryside, a mass movement on the streets of the cities, and mutiny in the army. The Vietminh in Vietnam, the National Liberation Front in Algeria, and other anticolonial rebellions took place on the basis of the first element: rural insurgency. The Russian and Iranian revolutions and the recent successful uprisings in Tunisia and Egypt took place as a result of a combination of the second and third elements, when mass demonstrations in the cities led to collapse of the police and the army being called in to quell the protests—and the soldiers refusing to open fire on the crowds.

How likely are any of these scenarios in Pakistan? Insurgency has been going on in some of the Pashtun areas over the past decade, but this insurgency does not in itself threaten the existence of Pakistan. After all, it was not for nothing that this region was known as "yaghestan," the land of unrest (corresponding to the "bled-es-siba" of the Maghreb).[7] The British, the Sikhs, and the Mughals all faced repeated rebellions among the Pashtun tribes without this threatening the heartland of their power.

These Pashtun insurgencies looked much more menacing in the years before 2009 because of their apparent ability to spread from one area to another without the army being able to stop them, and because of apparent unwillingness of some soldiers to fight (especially in the Pashtun-recruited Frontier Corps, or FC), which led to a number of cases of units surrendering en masse to the insurgents. However, since the army counteroffensive in Swat in 2009, the military has demonstrated that it is willing and able to push the insurgents back. In this, the military was only demonstrating once again its proven historical record of determination to defend Pakistan against local insurgents, as demonstrated in the past in Balochistan, Sindh, and East Pakistan.[8] The disproportionate number of Pashtuns in the military has made action against Pashtun insurgents more difficult for the army, but not impossibly so.

Prior to the May 2013 elections, the PML-N and the Pakistan Tehrik-e-Insaf (PTI) led by Imran Khan have repeatedly promised that, if elected, they would seek a peace settlement with the Pakistani Taliban. At the time of writing, it is impossible to say where or how far this may lead, but Pakistani generals and security analysts are seriously concerned that there may be a return of the policy of the Pervez Musharraf and Asif Ali Zardari administrations before the spring of 2009, a policy of alternating between limited offensives against the militants and truces with them. The result of these truces tended to be not only that any ground won from the militants was lost again but also that the militants promptly killed or expelled any local people who were identified as having worked with the army and the police against the militants. The result was to destroy the entire local basis of Pakistani administration and, of course, the military and police system of local informers.

Fears that this experience may be repeated have been increased by the very strong circumstantial evidence of a covert truce between the PML-N government of Punjab and sectarian terrorist groups between 2008 and 2009. It is alleged that this was created by the Punjab interior minister, Rana Sanaullah, who frequently appeared at political rallies with leaders of the Sipah-e-Sahaba Pakistan (SSP), an anti-Shia militant outfit, in order to win Sunni sectarian votes for the PML-N. It is suggested that there was also a covert agreement with the Lashkar-e-Jhangvi (LeJ) sectarian terrorist group whereby the Punjab police would turn a blind eye to their activities as long as they did not carry out terrorism in Punjab. And in the years immediately leading up to 2013, there has indeed been surprisingly little sectarian terrorism in Punjab, whereas the rate of attacks has grown in other provinces.

Like the PML-N, Imran Khan and the PTI were spared from militant attacks during the 2013 election campaign because of their calls for a peace settlement, whereas left-of-center parties suffered severely. The PTI in particular has adopted this position not from fear but because it corresponds to the very real desire of a large majority of Pashtuns in KPK, where the PTI won their greatest victory and where they now form the government. My own informal polls on the streets of Peshawar in 2008–12, and conversations with Imran Khan's Pashtun supporters during the 2013 election campaign, made very clear the desire of most Pashtuns for peace.

According to opinion polls, over the past decade, majorities—often very large majorities—of Pakistani citizens have supported peace talks with the Pakistani militants. The only exception was the period from the spring of 2009 to 2011, when a determined propaganda campaign by the military and the government succeeded in rallying a majority of the population behind military operations. The success of this propaganda was tremendously helped by the way in which the militants broke the Nizam-e-Adl (System of Justice) peace deal that established Sharia rule in Swat and used the resulting truce to seize control of the neighboring district of Buner. Several authors in this volume have rightly mentioned this episode as the turning point for the Pakistani state's campaign against the insurgency in the northwest.

The Nizam-e-Adl agreement was reached by the new "secular" governments in Islamabad and Peshawar, the Pakistan People's Party (PPP) under President Zardari, and the Awami National Party (ANP). During their first year in power (2008–9) the ANP resisted military action against the Pakistani militants—until the growing power and ruthlessness of the Pakistani Taliban and their allies made it clear that further compromises would ensure the destruction of their own government and endanger the survival of Pakistan. Very strangely and depressingly, this was also true of ANP activists, even after several of their own leaders had been killed by the Taliban; the unpopularity of the ANP's alliance with the army against the Taliban appears to be a key reason for the absolutely crushing defeat that they suffered at the hands of the PTI in the 2013 elections.

Even at its strongest, support among Pakistani Pashtuns for military operations against the Pakistani Taliban never exceeded 60 percent (Pew Research Center 2012). Nationally, the majority for military action between 2009 and 2011 later dissipated partly, it would seem, as a result of growing anger with US actions and growing opposition to anything that could be seen as Pakistani collaboration with the war on terror. By the spring of 2013, immediately before the elections, opinion polls suggested that large majorities were for negotiations. Gallup Pakistan's results showed 47 percent of Pakistanis in favor of negotiations with the Pakistani militants, 34 percent for a mixture of negotiations and military action, and only 15 percent for military action alone.[9] So, in running on a platform of negotiations in the 2013 elections, the PML-N and PTI were undoubtedly tapping into the dominant public mood. Once again, a desire for peace with the Pakistani Taliban is most definitely not the same thing as a desire for Taliban rule over Pakistan, something for which every poll suggests only extremely limited support, even among Pashtuns.

There is a very real risk, however, that even if—as seems overwhelmingly probable on the basis of the past record—peace deals with the Pakistani Taliban fail and the national and provincial governments eventually take up the fight against the militants, severe damage will have been done in the meantime to the struggle against militancy in Pakistan. Fearing this, Pakistani generals have told me privately that they would draw strict red lines against giving up territory that they had reconquered from the Taliban at such a dreadful cost in military and civilian lives. It may be difficult, however, for the military to stick to this position if—as seems likely from my research—it appears that much of the rank and file also favors peace settlements.

This is the truly crucial question: whether and in what circumstances the soldiers will fight. The most dangerous factor, however (which has worsened considerably as a result of the events of 2011), is the growth of bitter hostility to America in the lower ranks of the armed forces, something that is clear to me from my travels in areas of military recruitment. Actions by the United States on Pakistani soil have been felt by the soldiers as a bitter humiliation. This feeling is increased when soldiers go on leave and are asked by members of their local communities—and even by members of their own families—why they are taking American money to kill fellow Muslims. A real risk now exists that if Pakistani soldiers encounter US soldiers on what they believe to be Pakistani territory, they will fight; and if their generals order them not to fight, they will mutiny.

As to the threat of mass protest by the civilian population, by the same token this will only become a really serious threat to the state if that unrest spreads to the areas of military recruitment in northern Punjab, not in the form of insurgency—the flat, open plains of this region are hardly the right kind of terrain for that—but of massive protests in the cities. The reasons for this are obvious. Punjab has some 56 percent of Pakistan's population and 70 percent of its industry; above all, the province, especially the northwestern districts of the Potwar plateau, provide a majority of Pakistan's soldiers, especially its infantry. They have demonstrated again and again their willingness to shoot down members of other Pakistani ethnicities, but would they shoot down fellow Punjabis?[10]

The classic scene goes as follows. It has appeared in a number of films, but in a messier way and with local variations, it has also occurred on numerous occasions in reality, from Russia in 1917 to the Middle East in 2011. A massive demonstration seizes control of the streets. The police run away. A line of soldiers confronts the demonstrators. A voice cries out from the crowd (usually an elderly female one): "Soldiers! Do you want to kill your mothers and sisters?" The rifle barrels begin to waver. The soldiers retire to their barracks or join the crowd. Game over.

Or is it? To assess the chances of this happening in Lahore and Rawalpindi, it is necessary to suggest answers to a number of questions: Which groups could organize such mass demonstrations? Failing that, what events could occur that would send masses of ordinary people onto the street without prior organization? Would the generals ever put their men in a position where this could happen? And when the government had fallen—as it would in these circumstances—what would happen next?

To seek provisional answers to these questions requires an understanding both of the nature of Islam and Islamism in Pakistan and of the workings of what in Pakistan is called "democracy." Even under military rule, with brief exceptions, Pakistan has always been far more of a parliamentary system than the autocracies of the Arab world. And while Pakistani democracy has been horribly bad at producing good government or even defending the human rights of its citizens, it has been, like the Indian system, fairly good at co-opting local elites—including new ones—thereby defusing mass revolt from below. Moreover, Pakistani democracy ensures that there is generally an organized and legal opposition party ready to take power if the existing government falls. Unlike in the Arab world, therefore, the overthrow of a given government does not risk the destruction of the entire governing system.

It is thus possible that we will one day see massive demonstrations in Pakistan against the new PML-N government, perhaps (as against both Musharraf and Zardari) in the form of another "long march" on Islamabad.[11] The raw material for such protests is always present in the miserable lives of ordinary Pakistanis and in the miserable quality of their government, and it is easy to see how a catalyst could be provided either by US actions or by moves by the PML-N government to follow through on Nawaz Sharif's promise of improved relations with India. But there is no way that Pakistan's generals would order their men to open fire on such protests.

Would such mass unrest lead to an Islamist revolution and the destruction of the state? Almost certainly not. In the first place, Pakistan's democratic system gives the population a safety valve denied to the peoples of Arab dictatorships. Despite the disillusionment with democracy and politicians among Pakistani youth displayed in a British Council survey of early 2013, the elections two months later still showed the highest voter turnout in almost a generation.[12] Pakistan's system allows the overthrow of a government without forcing the entire system to pack up. Second, as the 2013 elections showed, Pakistanis disillusioned both with the PPP-led government in Islamabad and the ANP government in Peshawar have not flocked to radical Islamist parties. Instead, they were threatening to vote either for the old conservative establishment party, the PML-N, or for Imran Khan, a populist member of the same establishment.

Imran Khan has adopted a platform of strong hostility to the United States and the US "occupation" of Afghanistan, support for peace talks with the Afghan and Pakistani Taliban, and condemnation of the corruption of the political elites. This appeal has been very successful because most Pakistanis agree with him on all three points. In the 2013 elections, the PTI did not do as well as it had hoped it would in Punjab, but it won in KPK and beat the PPP into third place in the national vote, giving the PTI a real chance to become the long-term chief party of opposition to the PML-N and the Sharifs. However, this does not in any way make Imran Khan an Islamist revolutionary. He is a wealthy hereditary aristocrat who turned to a Sufi-influenced, nondenominational form of Islam in his middle age. The limited success of

Imran Khan's PTI therefore marks a reshuffle within the existing system, not a political revolution.[13]

For mass protests to lead to revolution and the collapse of the existing order, an organized revolutionary force capable of leading the masses to seize the institutions of government would be required, and then the force must take control of those institutions—something like the Muslim Brotherhood in Egypt, or the Islamic Salvation Front in Algeria in the early 1990s. In Pakistan, such a movement would need two things: a genuinely revolutionary spirit and program, including a willingness to use ruthless force; and deep roots in the province of Punjab.

A glance at Pakistan's Islamist groups makes clear how difficult this would be for all of them to achieve, above all because of Pakistan's deep ethnic differences and Punjab's deep religious ones. Of the two Islamist political parties, the Jamiat Ulema-e-Islam (JUI) is overwhelmingly Pashtun with very little Punjabi support. The Jamaat-e-Islami (JI) does have Punjabi support, but it is restricted to relatively narrow social strata in the towns. JI's religious culture is alien to the Punjabi masses; even more importantly, like the JUI, the JI's decades in and out of government and parliamentary politics have led many people to see it not as a force for Islamist revolution but as just another patronage-based party. Its more moderate elements have tended to drift away to join the PML-N in a search for much better chances of patronage and its more radical elements, to join the militants.

As to the militants, their problems in mobilizing masses of Punjabis are also formidable. The groups making up the Pakistani Taliban (Tehrik-e-Taliban Pakistan, or TTP), like the JUI, are overwhelmingly Pashtun and highly localized and tribal-based. The biggest autonomous group within the TTP, the Tehreek-e-Nafaz-e-Shariat-e-Mohammadi, is almost exclusively from Swat in KPK province. People from northwest Punjab have strong cultural affinities with the Pashtuns, of course, but considerable distrust also exists between the provinces.

The chief militant allies that the TTP has found in Punjab are the old anti-Shia sectarian parties, the SSP, and its even more violent offshoot, the LeJ. These groups want to attack the state because they have themselves been subject to periods of intense state repression since the mid-1990s and have intermittently struck at state targets (as well as Shia ones) in response (Rana 2005b, 192–213). However, the mass appeal of the sectarian groups is limited to central and southern Punjab and certain parts of Karachi and KPK (although they have enough support elsewhere to carry out savage acts of terrorism). They are hated not only by the Shia but also by the devotees of Sunni shrines linked to the Shia, and they have no wider prestige in Pakistan or in the Muslim world.

The groups that do have such prestige are the militants who took part in the jihad in Kashmir against India, a cause that has very great public sympathy in northern Punjab. By far, the greatest danger of the spread of radical Islamist revolution in Pakistan would be if enough of these groups could be persuaded to ally with the Pakistani Taliban. Some have indeed done so. A majority of these groups and their members still seem loyal to the existing Pakistani state, however, and much more importantly to the army—which for so long armed, trained, and funded them to fight first in Afghanistan and then in Kashmir.

Of these groups, the most powerful is Lashkar-e-Taiba (LeT) and its official (though also now proscribed) wing, Jamaat-ud-Dawa (JuD).[14] LeT's terrorist skills (developed by the Pakistani Inter-Services Intelligence, or ISI) were demonstrated by their attack on Mumbai in November 2008, which killed more than 160 people. Equally important, the LeT has a very extensive network of educational and social welfare institutions that give it considerable influence in Punjabi society, and it gained considerable prestige both from its actions against India and from its relief work after the 2005 earthquake in northern Pakistan and Pakistani Kashmir. Pakistani officials and security officers dread the idea of this group joining the TTP rebellion, and they say that this is why they did not dare launch the crackdown on the group demanded by India and the West after the Mumbai attack.

So far, however, the Pakistani military have been able to keep the LeT from joining the Islamist rebellion in Pakistan, not by the threat of repression if they do but as a result of an explicit or implicit deal on certain terms. These terms go to the heart of the dilemmas confronting Pakistan and the West when it comes to Pakistan's role in the struggle against terrorism.

As far as India is concerned, since the Mumbai attacks of 2008, the LeT has been held in reserve and has carried out no further attacks even though internal developments within Indian-controlled Kashmir have provided ample opportunities to rekindle the jihad. It may be that the leaders of the LeT have been persuaded that further attacks would bring a response in kind from both the United States and India and would risk the destruction of Pakistan, but it also seems highly likely that the army has promised them that one day they will be able to resume the jihad with military support. For the moment, however, the military high command has no desire at all for a crisis with India. They are already faced with overstretched resources in the battle with militancy and have to contemplate the possibility of another military intervention to control the growing ethnic, sectarian, and militant violence in Karachi. That city now has more than 20 million people and could easily swallow every last man of Pakistan's remaining military reserves. While the United States has been publicly telling the Pakistani military not to resume terrorist attacks on India, according to my conversations with both Pakistani and Chinese officials, China has been privately telling them the same thing.

As for terrorism against targets in the West, the Pakistani military seems to have been able to persuade the LeT and JuD leadership that attacking Western targets would be absolutely catastrophic, bringing with them the certainty of massive US retaliation against Pakistan. On the other hand, the LeT appears to have been given free rein to send its activists to fight against the United States and its allies in Afghanistan; more than that, in at least one major operation (the attack on the Indian embassy in Kabul in 2008), there seems strong evidence to suggest that the ISI helped the Haqqani network plan and carry out this attack with the assistance of specialist volunteers from the LeT (Tankel 2011, 199).

Whether this strategy is correct depends mainly on whether the LeT and its political/social welfare organization, JuD, are as strong as Pakistani officers and officials profess to believe, and whether it would, if attacked, become a serious threat to Pakistan and the West; conversely, as critics of the Pakistani military believe, the military may be able to suppress them with relative ease and is simply using this fear as an excuse to sustain the LeT and other groups for future use against India.

It is impossible to answer this question definitively. Two things can be said, however. The first is that not just the military but Pakistani civilian officials and politicians with no love for the military are also genuinely scared of the consequences if the LeT goes into rebellion.[15] The second is that so far this approach on the part of the Pakistani military has in fact been successful both in preventing the LeT from rebelling against the Pakistani state and army and in preventing LeT terrorist attacks against the United States and the United Kingdom. And as mentioned, since the Mumbai terrorist attacks of 2008, the LeT has also not carried out attacks on India.

Thus far, the situation has on balance therefore been good for both Pakistan and the West. The price for not going after the LeT has been continued help to the Afghan Taliban from the LeT and other Pakistani groups as well as continued shelter for the Afghan Taliban in Pakistan—and, therefore, increased losses for Western forces in Afghanistan. One can well understand why, despite Pakistan's strategy benefits of the LeT not turning against the Pakistani state, Pakistani strategy is hardly welcome to Western soldiers or to any analyst who places more importance in the future of Afghanistan than that of Pakistan. However, this would seem to be a strategic error, given the far greater size of Pakistan, and the far greater potential terrorist threat that Pakistan poses to the West. This will remain the case long after most Western troops are withdrawn from Afghanistan in 2014.

But, although partially justifiable, Pakistani strategy carries with it an immense risk: that despite the genuine efforts of Pakistani intelligence, a Pakistani-based group will manage to carry out a major terrorist attack on the US mainland, leading to massive US attacks on Pakistan. One form of this US offensive would be missile strikes on real or suspected terrorist targets deep in Pakistan. The other would be ground raids into FATA and northern Balochistan, which would risk bringing US troops into direct conflict with the Pakistan Army and FC. Since the destruction of the existing Pakistani state is the goal of the Pakistani Taliban and their allies, they have an obvious motive to try to provoke such a US attack—which, by the same token, is why the United States should avoid attacks on Pakistan.

Should this occur, then the dilemma of the Pakistani state and military would become acute and quite possibly fatal: either fight back against the United States and suffer appalling damage from US attacks, or continue to cooperate and risk seeing the Punjabi sections of the military mutiny against their commanders and join the Islamist revolutionaries. At this point, the Pakistani state's efforts to defeat terrorism would then have been overwhelmed in their entirety, and the state itself would most likely be doomed, with all the horrors that would result for the people of Pakistan and the world.

Notes

1. See also "Path to Freedom: Timeline of Raymond Davis Case," *Dawn*, March 17, 2011, http://dawn.com/2011/03/17/path-to-freedom-timeline-of-davis-case/.

2. For the army's obsession with India, see Haqqani 2005, 267–47; and Jones 2009.

3. For the historical and cultural roots of Pashtun support for the Taliban, see Franco 2009 and Strick van Linschoten and Kuehn 2012. For the history of jihad among the Pashtuns of the Afghan frontier, see Haroon 2007.

4. Much of the analysis in this section is based on the author's interviews and informal opinion polls in Pakistan during the period 2008–11, which form much of the research basis for his book *Pakistan: A Hard Country* (London: Penguin, 2011).

5. For example, buying off tribal chieftains in Balochistan is a continuation of the British model. For the conflict in Balochistan and the Pakistani strategy, see PIPS 2008.

6. For an examination of the changing social character of the Pakistani officer corps, see Fair and Nawaz 2011.

7. For this critical distinction in several parts of the Muslim world, see Gellner 1981.

8. For the military's suppression of revolts in Balochistan, see Nawaz 2008, 332–35, 550–51.

9. "National Survey of Households on Political Issues," *Gallup Pakistan*, April 2013, Islamabad.

10. For military recruitment by province, see the official figures in ibid., 570–72. These figures show a drastic decline in the proportion of Punjabis in the army. However, military

acquaintances have described this trend as greatly exaggerated by official statistics—though a certain decline has undoubtedly taken place. For the historic pattern of Punjabi dominance, see Cohen 1983. For the present state of the military, see Lieven 2011, 161–203.

11. The term "long march" was coined to refer to a large number of Pakistani lawyers, later joined by political parties, who came out on the streets in 2008 to protest against then-president Musharraf's act of sacking the Supreme Court chief justice and a number of other senior judges. The "long march" finally succeeded in getting the government to buckle and reinstate the judges.

12. "Next Generation Goes to the Ballot Box," *British Council*, March 2013, www.britishcouncil.org/pakistan-next-generation-ballot-box-report.pdf. The voter turnout in the May 2013 elections topped 60 percent, considerably above Pakistan's traditional turnout, which hovered well below the 50 percent mark on average; "Voter Turnout Was 60 Percent: CEC Ebrahim," *Geo*, May 12, 2013, www.geo.tv/GeoDetail.aspx?ID = 100579.

13. For a discussion of the character of the PML-N, see Lieven 2011, 243–49.

14. For the LeT and the nature of its links to the Pakistani military, see Tankel 2011.

15. This description of Pakistani strategy is based on my off-the-record interviews with Pakistani military officers and officials between 2007 and 2011.

Conclusion

MOEED YUSUF

THE AUTHORS of this volume were tasked to examine Pakistan's Islamist militant challenge. The topics covered are not exhaustive; the focus was deliberately narrowed to counterterrorism (CT), defined strictly as actions intended to directly prevent or respond to outfits or individuals employing terrorist tactics. The contributions covered both the military and nonmilitary aspects of CT—political weakness, policing, legal and financial lacunae, and the use of cyberspace. The analyses produced some telling observations, not only on the monumental scale of Pakistan's CT challenge but also in terms of deeper structural issues that make these specific challenges all the more difficult to overcome. Five major trends emerged from the volume.

Lack of Clarity: Who Is the Enemy?

The Pakistani state is yet to fulfill the first prerequisite of tackling any challenge, let alone a violent one: clarity on what or who is to be targeted. The question, "who is the enemy" continues to lack an obvious answer, both for outsiders who largely believe that Pakistan continues to condone Islamists for strategic reasons and for the domestic audience, where views are polarized and conflicted. The lack of clarity is even reflected by the state's institutions that are responsible for tackling terrorism. It is obvious from the chapters focusing on the nontraditional force functions that key functionaries are often puzzled over just how widely they are to cast their CT net. A history of state support to militancy, a civil–military disconnect, a public discourse that allows Islamists to create ambivalence and conflate issues to their advantage, and an overall lack of direction all feed into this very evident sense of confusion.

The "capacity versus will" question raised in chapter 1 lies at the heart of this concern. Once the Pakistani state pledges lack of capacity, determining whether it has the resolve to go after militants of all shades becomes impossible. Is Pakistan really pursuing a sequential approach dictated by its capacity limitations, as it claims, or is the approach a selective one that aims to merely manage rather than eliminate Islamist militancy, as the Western world contends? From a Pakistani perspective, one may be able to argue that convincing the world of its sincerity is of secondary importance and that there is a limit to how much effort and resources it can expend on it. Not providing clarity domestically, however, could prove to be fatal. The Pakistani civilian and military leadership must clearly lay out for all its internal organs, most importantly the functionaries responsible for implementing any aspect of the CT effort, their outlook, and their vision on tackling militants. And if Pakistan is indeed committed to pacifying the entire web of militants, its domestic audience must be able to see a concrete, long-term, and holistic strategy, both militarily and in terms of addressing the nonmilitary issues examined in this volume. There are no signs of this yet.

The primacy of the domestic audience does not imply that the state can ignore the external, geostrategic factors when it comes to Pakistan's CT conundrum because these are also intrinsically linked to the future of Islamist militancy in the country. There is little doubt that the post-9/11 developments in Afghanistan have caused a backlash in Pakistan, and the militant enclave has cashed in on constant US pressure on Pakistan to "do more" in order to sow confusion in Pakistani minds about the Islamists' ultimate objectives. Lieven's analysis in chapter 9 crystallizes just how central the United States has become to this equation. While remaining upbeat about Pakistan's ability to prevent an Islamist takeover, the two tipping points he presents are both linked to provoking Washington to substantially expand the remit of direct military action against Pakistan, and to consequently overwhelming any possibility of the Pakistani state prevailing over violent Islamists.

The larger regional question is just as important: Pakistan's concerns about India are largely dismissed as paranoia by outsiders, but the Western world has failed to incentivize the Pakistani military's move away from its India obsession. Pakistan, for its part, professes to have realized that its number one threat is internal, but its policies in Afghanistan hardly reflect this change. The result may well be a continuing disproportionate focus on India that will distract the state from the internal threat and perhaps keep some of the militant groups attractive as policy tools. In essence, Pakistan will be consumed by its concerns about the growing regional imbalance—more than a country facing such a severe internal threat can afford.

All of this makes for extremely dismal reading. If the Pakistani view of capacity constraints is correct, we should expect a protracted period where the "capacity versus will" debate will linger inconclusively, thereby retaining the murkiness about who the enemy is. Meanwhile, if the Western world's view on Pakistan's "selective" outlook toward militancy is closer to reality, then we may be witnessing a replay of the complacency exhibited by Islamabad during the 1990s when it believed that Islamist outfits could serve a policy purpose, and that the domestic blowback could be curtailed at will. Pakistan, then, is either petrified of the Islamist challenge or complacent about it; neither is conducive to mounting a comprehensive CT effort.

A Disjointed Policy Space

Our authors have not left too much room for optimism in terms of the specific issues discussed in this volume, even going beyond the external geostrategic dimension. The norm in Pakistan seems to be the presence of articulate, well-designed, and rather comprehensive policy documents and laws that are seldom translated into an implemented reality. The second major point this volume makes is that the aspects of CT discussed in this volume do not even meet the "good policy / bad implementation" benchmark typical of a number of other Pakistani sectors. From policing that lacks a specific CT vision to the many legal lacunas highlighted by Soofi in chapter 6 to the virtual absence of any holistic policy or laws to deal with the use of cyberspace by Islamists, the gaping holes in CT-related policies are obvious. A collective read of the preceding chapters presents a tale of ambiguous missions and overlapping, contradictory, and dated laws and jurisdictions that directly affect outputs.

Absence of an Overarching Coordinating Mechanism

The third—and the most frequently highlighted—weakness within the CT domain is the absence of an overarching body that could coordinate the state's CT efforts, give it an overall mission and direction, and bring the various disparate efforts ongoing at present under a coherent umbrella. There is unequivocal support among the authors for the National Counter Terrorism Authority (NACTA) to be empowered to play this role. The urgency and importance for ensuring this is also underscored by another observation that is quite evident from the preceding analyses: the CT aspects we have covered are interdependent; addressing one without parallel attention to the others is unlikely to deliver results.

Improvement Nonetheless, but Much More Is Needed

On the positive side, none of these problems can take away from the fact that tangible improvements in the performance of the state over the past decade have been noted by the authors in virtually every area. Haider's assertion in chapter 3 that the military has gone through a learning curve but is now able to "clear" and "hold" areas far more effectively than its rather directionless beginning post-9/11 is a crucial one. The conclusion one can draw from this is more explicitly echoed in Lieven's chapter (9), when he suggests that the army's unified presence ensures that the militant encroachment in the Federally Administered Tribal Areas (FATA) and Khyber Pakhtunkhwa (KPK) province cannot translate into a threat of an Islamist takeover of the Pakistani state. Other authors, too, have pointed to progress even as they have maintained an overall pessimistic tone: for example, there is admission of improved police performance; the Aid in Action of Civil Power (AACP) legislation provides some legal cover, even if partial, to military operations in FATA and the Provincially Administered Tribal Areas (PATA); and the state has introduced laws aimed at curbing financial activities of militants, at least in the formal sector. A great deal more needs to be done, and this volume has pointed out specific actions that can be taken to improve CT performance in multiple sectors. In total, all of these actions can be a step in the right direction, helping Pakistan address its terrorism challenge holistically rather than disjointedly.

The analyses in the preceding chapters have highlighted a number of policy prescriptions that could be implemented in the short to medium term to improve the situation further. Pakistan's best chance of overcoming the Islamist militancy challenge lies in a government led by a dominant faction that is able to build consensus on a holistic CT policy. Civilian law enforcement needs nationwide constitutional writ, especially in areas that are infested with militants. Moreover, diverse law enforcement agencies—and military institutions that share the same mandate—must be unified to prevent overlapping jurisdiction. In addition, civilian law enforcement must be empowered legally and technologically to make them operationally autonomous from the military. Criminal procedural laws—including regarding cybercrime—must be revamped to give current law enforcement efforts real "bite." This will, in parallel, regulate the conduct of the military in CT efforts. Nontraditional sources of funding for militants remain a major gap in CT efforts and require the state to spread its focus beyond the formal sector. Media sources must be better regulated—as much as possible, in a context where religious idioms command respect and their opposition tends to quickly discredit voices.

The Underlying "Binding Constraints"

The final observation one can make on the basis of the analysis is that underpinning and constraining the emergence of this CT apparatus are two key factors: the civil–military imbalance that limits synergetic policymaking—especially security policy—and the need for public support for the CT vision and strategy put forth by the Pakistani state.

Civil–Military Disconnect

The widely recognized civil–military imbalance in Pakistan directly underpins a number of concerns highlighted in this volume. For example, for NACTA—as the coordinating body for the Pakistani CT effort—to transform into a truly empowered nerve center, the state apparatus would have to overcome the problem of political factionalism, as highlighted by Hussain and Zahra-Malik in chapter 4, that explains so many of the poor outcomes across various sectors in Pakistan. Recent political developments in the country present a mixed picture on the likelihood of the state being able to move beyond factionalism. On the one hand, Pakistan is transitioning from two-party dominance to a coalitional model of politics as epitomized by the Pakistan Tehrik-e-Insaf's rise as a genuine third force in national politics in the May 2013 elections. This has only encouraged more factionalism and intra- and interparty tussles. Moreover, as right-wing rhetoric has permeated mainstream public discourse, and as frustrations linked to poor governance outputs have grown, the society has become increasingly polarized, impatient, and intolerant of dissenting voices. On the other hand, however, Pakistan is moving to a new equilibrium as far as its institutional balances are concerned, and the military is gradually losing political space to civilian leaders. This may encourage the civilian dominance desperately required to bring greater control over national security policy and the Inter-Services Intelligence (ISI). Indeed, underpinned by the overall political context where the military has had a dominant role in national security policy formulation and where it has remained at the behest of the pre-and post-9/11 engagement with Islamists, the ultimate solution lies not in mere tactical changes but in the overall correction of the civil–military imbalance. This is where the institutional rebalancing, if it were to happen, will prove to be transformational. With a strong civilian government and a somewhat rebalanced civil–military equation, an empowered NACTA and an overarching CT vision can become a reality.

The possible reorientation of the civil–military equation is also a welcome development given that the lack of civil–military coordination seems to encroach upon every policy space examined in this volume. Haider strongly suggests in chapter 3 that there is little the military will be able to do in Pakistan's urban towns or even in the cleared areas of the FATA and KPK without a complementary civilian role. Specifically for the police, one of Tajik's main critiques in chapter 5 is the military and ISI's overreach into the civilian sphere and the inability of the police to bring clarity to its mission due to this disconnect. In chapter 6, Soofi points to civilian weakness as forcing the military to detain miscreants illegally and to shy away from presenting them for prosecution due to the problems associated with the criminal justice system.

The Importance of Public Opinion

Nothing, however, is perhaps more important for the Pakistani state than public support for its vision and strategy to tackle militancy. Unless citizens see the state as credible and have clarity on the state's short-, medium-, and long-term CT outlook, the militant enclave will likely succeed in continuously conflating narratives, thereby keeping the masses from standing behind the state as it pushes ahead to squeeze the enemy's space.

The Pakistani citizenry's outlook toward the militant challenge makes this variable an especially crucial piece of the policy puzzle. On the one hand, Pakistanis agree on the inadmissibility of extremism and terrorism as a whole; 93 percent believe terrorism to be one of the major problems facing Pakistan today, and the Pakistani Taliban—the most visible group threatening the country at the moment—has been rated negatively since 2009, when its unpopularity (it was then considered a "very serious threat") reached its peak at 57 percent in 2009 (Pew Research Center 2013, 2). This spike was linked directly to the exponential rise in acts of terrorism in Pakistani cities after the July 2007 Red Mosque incident in Islamabad. In previous years, a lower proportion took a hard-line view of the Taliban. For instance, in 2007, only 34 percent of Pakistanis viewed Islamist militants and the Pakistani Taliban as a threat to the country's vital interests (Ramsay et al. 2009); the numbers have been consistently lower for the Afghan Taliban and anti-India groups. That said, as Lieven points out in chapter 9, this does not imply a preference for Taliban rule in Pakistan. Political choices of Pakistanis do not even show much sympathy for Islamic political parties, let alone militant outfits. At the core, the Pakistani mindset remains conservative but mainstream. A less-than-total disapproval and concern about the Islamists targeting the state has more to do with the ambivalence about the agenda of the militant enclave and the conflation these outfits successfully created by portraying themselves as anti-American and pro-Muslim forces.

One consistent feature of Pakistani public opinion throughout has been preference for nonmilitary options to resolve the Islamist militancy. Jones and Fair (2010) demonstrate the propensity of the Pakistani public to prefer peace deals and other forms of nonmilitary action—80 percent initially supported a peace deal with the militants in Swat in 2009 and only backed Operation Rah-e-Rast once the deal went sour and the Taliban were blatantly exposed. But barring a few specific moments like this over the past decade, Pakistanis have not been taken in by the idea of state-led violence as the principal answer to Islamist militancy. Moreover, given the violence-induced trauma the Pakistani public has experienced over the past decade, it is unlikely that they will back repeated military operations that have not managed to provide permanent respite from militancy. A strategy that privileges nontraditional functions of force over military CT efforts is therefore likely to offer the greatest probability of ensuring popular support and, in turn, success of the state's bid to eliminate Islamist militancy. This further underscores the importance of the nonmilitary aspects of CT examined in this volume.

Neither weak civilian political coalitions that are the new political norm nor the country's image-conscious military are likely to take decisions without keeping an eye on the street sentiment. Without public support, the situation would be comparable to the 2004–8 period, when the state retreated in the face of public opposition generated by its early military failures combined with the ability of the militant enclave to present the state as the aggressor. The alternative of denting militant capabilities by focusing efforts on nonmilitary aspects would not only make the task of military operators less central and relatively easier; it would also do so while keeping public opinion supportive of the state's actions.

To be sure, none of the desired changes mentioned in this chapter are going to take place overnight; they will inevitably entail a lengthy and rather messy interim, as is usual for contexts seeking recalibration of long-held equilibriums. Whether Pakistan has the luxury to go through this period without losing further ground to Islamist militancy and radical thought remains to be seen. After all, the state is facing an agile and innovative enemy that has proven to be extremely flexible and accepting of new methods and tools. The regular use of suicide bombers after 2007, the militants' exploitation of the lacunas in the country's legal regime, the various channels militant organizations have developed to expand their financial flows in response to state-imposed bans on certain outfits and its efforts to curb financial flows to militants that used formal channels, and miltants' use of cyberspace even as they shun modernity are evidence of their shrewd capacity to evolve and capitalize on social space. Because of this, Pakistan is truly battling for its survival as a functional state and a moderate polity.

The task to ensure course correction is monumental—even more so than a reader may take away from this volume, given its focus on only a narrow part of the overall counterinsurgency (COIN) campaign. In reality, fixing the operational shortcomings in the military, policing, criminal justice, financial, and cyberspace aspects will only be the start to addressing the deeper structural concerns. Reasons for the lack of credibility of the state in the eyes of its citizens, the increasing resistance from society in terms of obeying rule of law, the immense expansion of Islamist rhetoric, the socioeconomic and educational failures that feed into the problem, and the ease with which militants can recruit foot soldiers, among many others, are areas that either fell outside the purview of this book or did not form the crux of the analyses, but these are all aspects that require just as much, if not more, attention. We have also not examined the non-Islamist violence that has become commonplace over the past decade and has exacerbated the challenge multifold.

In the long term, sustainable peace requires Pakistan to address the entire gamut of "supply" and "demand" factors that Yusuf and colleagues briefly note in chapter 1. Otherwise, even if Pakistan does exceptionally well on the issues focused on in this volume—by no means a given, as the authors have repeatedly emphasized—it is entirely possible for the state to win the CT campaign while losing on the broader COIN front. The result would still be a country that is riddled with violence and periodic acts of terrorism even as it remains strong enough to prevent any concerted insurgency that could lead to its collapse.

The Pakistani state, with the help of its citizens, must strive with a great deal of urgency to correct fallacies in the CT and COIN arenas. Meanwhile, the world, specifically the United States, must be careful not to push Pakistan over the edge. A collapsing or collapsed nuclear-weapon state with a united Islamist militant front is a nightmare scenario no one dare risk. Pakistani leadership and the world owe a sincere and concerted effort to the more than forty-seven thousand Pakistanis killed by terrorist violence over the past decade, and to the millions more who are desperate to see Pakistan emerge as a moderate, tolerant, and prosperous country.

References

Abbas, Hassan. 2005. *Pakistan's Drift into Extremism: Allah, the Army and America's War on Terror.* Armonk, NY: M. E. Sharpe.

———. 2008. "A Profile of Tehrik-e-Taliban Pakistan." *CTC Sentinel* 1, no. 2.

———. 2009a. "Deciphering the Attack on Pakistan's Army Headquarters." *Foreign Policy*, October 11. http://afpak.foreignpolicy.com/posts/2009/10/11/deciphering_the_attack_on_pakistan_s_army_headquarters.

———. 2009b. "Defining the Punjabi Taliban Network." *CTC Sentinel* 2, no. 4 (April): 1–4.

———. 2010. "Militancy in Pakistan's Borderlands: Implications for the Nation and for Afghan Policy." *Century Foundation*, http://tcf.org/assets/downloads/tcf-Militancy.pdf.

———. 2011. "Special Report: Reforming Pakistan's Police and Law Enforcement Infrastructure." Washington, DC: United States Institute of Peace.

Abbasi, Salaar. 2013. "Sleeping with the Enemy." *The News*, May 8. http://images.thenews.com.pk/08-05-2013/ethenews/e-176147.htm.

Abbot, Sebastian. 2012. "Pakistanis Divided on Army Offensive after Attack," *Associated Press*, October 17. http://news.yahoo.com/pakistanis-divided-army-offensive-attack-16 1235408.html.

Ahmad, Saghir. 1977. *Class and Power in a Punjabi Village*. New York: Monthly Review Press.

Ahmed, Aijaz. 1992. "The National Question in Balochistan." In *Regional Imbalances and the National Question in Pakistan*, edited by S. Akbar Zaidi, 193–225. Lahore, Pakistan: Vanguard Books.

Ahmed, Issam. 2011. "As US Troops Begin Drawdown in Afghanistan, Violence Threatens Pakistan Border." *Christian Science Monitor*, July 25. www.csmonitor.com/World/Asia-South-Central/2011/0725/As-US-troops-begin-drawdown-in-Afghanistan-violence-threatens-Pakistan-border.

Ahmed, Khaled. 2011. "A Most Dangerous Man." *Newsweek Pakistan*, July 29.

Ahmed, Shafiq. 2006. "Taliban-Linked Traders Found Involved in Illegal Sugar Sale." *Dawn*, March 11, 2006. http://archives.dawn.com/2006/03/11/nat17.htm.

Alavi, Hamza. 1972. "The State in Post-Colonial Societies: Pakistan and Bangladesh." *New Left Review* 1, no. 74: 59–81.

———. 1988. "Pakistan and Islam: Ethnicity and Ideology." In *State and Ideology in the Middle East and Pakistan*, edited by Fred Halliday and Hamza Alavi, 64–111. New York: Monthly Review Press.

Alavi, Hamza, and Fred Halliday. 1988. *State and Ideology in the Middle East and Pakistan*. New York: Monthly Review Press.

Ali, Imtiaz. 2009. "Militant or Peace Broker? A Profile of the Swat Valley's Maulana Sufi Muhammad." *Terrorism Monitor* 7, no. 7 (March 26).

Almeida, Cyril. 2010. "Kayani Spells Out Threat Posed by Indian Doctrine," *Dawn.com*, February 4. http://archives.dawn.com/archives/44561.

Alston, L. J., T. Eggertsson, and Douglass C. North, eds. 1996. *Empirical Studies in Institutional Change*. Cambridge: Cambridge University Press.

Ameen, Yasir. 2012. "Pakistan Has Highest Growth Rate of Internet Users in Region," *Weekly Pulse*, September 28. http://weeklypulse.org/details.aspx?contentID=2801&storylist=16.

Ayubi, Nazih N. 1996. *Overstating the Arab State: Politics and Society in the Middle East*. London: IB Tauris.

Azam, Muhammad. 2008. "Radicalization and Media: Who Influences Whom and How in Pakistan?" *Peace and Conflict Studies* 1, no.1 (October–December).

Azeem, Munawer. 2011. "Kidnapping for Ransom a Boon for Militants." *Dawn*, January 26.

Babar, Mariana. 2009. "Frontier Constabulary Jawans: Dying Comes Easy to Them, It's Living They Can't Afford!" *News Pakistan*, May 8.

Bajoria, Jayshree, and Jonathan Masters. 2011. "Pakistan's New Generation of Terrorists." Council on Foreign Relations, www.cfr.org/pakistan/pakistans-new-generation-terrorists/p15422.

Ball, Desmond. 1996. "Signals Intelligence (SIGINT) in South Asia: India, Pakistan, Sri Lanka (Ceylon)." *Canberra Papers on Strategy and Defence*, No. 117, 41–62. Canberra: Australian National University, Strategic and Defence Studies Centre.

Baloch, Farooq. 2012. "Mobile Number Portability Banned Permanently due to Security Fears." *Express Tribune*, November 15. http://tribune.com.pk/story/465855/mobile-number-portability-bann ed-permanently-due-to-security-fears/.

Balochistan Police. 2007. "Annual Policing Plan 2007–08," www.docstoc.com/docs/14576336/Annual-Policing-Plan-2007---Baluchistan-Police-Official-Site.

Behuria, Ashok K. 2007. "Fighting the Taliban: Pakistan at War with Itself." *Australian Journal of International Affairs* 61, no. 4 (December): 531–32.
Bellinger, John B., III, and Vijay M. Padmanabhan. 2011. "Detention Operations in Contemporary Conflicts: Four Challenges for the Geneva Conventions and Other Existing Law." *American Journal of International Law* 105, no. 2 (April): 201–11.
Bergen, Peter. 2011. *The Longest War: The Enduring Conflict between America and al-Qaeda*. New York: Free Press.
Blunt, Gary R. 2003. *Islam in the Digital Age*. London: Pluto Press.
Boone, Jon. 2011. "Taliban Join the Twitter Revolution." *Guardian*, May 12. www.guardian.co.uk/world/2011/may/12/taliban-join-twitter-revolution.
———. 2012. "Taliban 'Holy War' in Afghanistan Is Justified by Islamic Law." *Guardian*, October 14.
Boot, Max. 2013. *Invisible Armies: An Epic History of Guerilla Warfare from Ancient Times to the Present*. New York: Liveright/W. W. Norton.
Borger, Julian. 2012. "Pakistan Will Not Support Afghan Talks until Kabul Backs Them, Says Minister." *Guardian*, February 21. www.guardian.co.uk/world/2012/feb/21/pakistan-not-support-afghan-peace-talks.
Bose, Sarmila. 2011. *Dead Reckoning: Memories of the 1971 Bangladesh War*. New York: Columbia University Press.
Boyle, Michael. 2010. "Do Counterterrorism and Counterinsurgency Go Together?" *International Affairs* 86, no. 2: 333–53.
Brandt, Ben. 2010. "The Punjabi Taliban: The Causes and Consequences of Turning against the State," *CTC Sentinel* 3, no. 7: 6–9.
Brulliard, Karen, and Pamela Constable. 2010. "Militant Factions with Global Aims Are Spreading Roots throughout Pakistan." *Washington Post*, May 10. www.washingtonpost.com/wp-dyn/content/story/2010/05/09/ST2010050901487.html.
Bukhari, Irfan. 2011a. "Non-Functional NACTA Awaits Statutory Status." *Pakistan Today*, April 4. www.pakistantoday.com.pk/2011/04/04/news/national/non-functional-nacta-awaits-statutory-status/.
———. 2011b. "US Concerned over Pakistan's 'Ill-trained' Prosecutors." *Pakistan Today*, August 30. www.pakistantoday.com.pk/2011/08/30/news/national/us-concerned-over-pakistan%E2%80%99s-%E2%80%98ill-trained%E2%80%99-prosecutors/.
Burki, Shahid Javed. 1999. *Pakistan: 50 Years of Nationhood*. New York: Vanguard.
Candland, Christopher. 2006. "Religious Education and Violence in Pakistan." In *Pakistan 2005*, edited by Charles Kennedy and Cynthia Botteron, 230–55. Oxford: Oxford University Press.

Carment, David, and Yiagadeesen Samy. 2012. *Assessing State Fragility: A Country Indicators for Foreign Policy Report*. Country Indicators for Foreign Policy. Ottawa, Canada: Carleton University. http://reliefweb.int/sites/reliefweb.int/files/resources/1402.pdf.

Caroe, Olaf. 1958. *The Pathans: 550 BC–AD 1957*. London: Macmillan.

Cheema, Umar. 2011. "Arrested Helper of Militants Had Warned of PNS Mehran Attack." *The News*, May 26.

Cohen, Stephen. 1983. *The Pakistan Army*. Oxford: Oxford University Press.

———. 2004a. "With Allies Like This: Pakistan and the War on Terror." In *A Practical Guide to Winning the War on Terrorism*, edited by Adam Garfinkle, 103–16. Stanford: Hoover Institution Press.

———. 2004b. *The Idea of Pakistan*. Washington, DC: Brookings Institution Press.

———. 2011. *The Future of Pakistan*. Washington, DC: Brookings Institution Press.

Cole, Rob. 2010. "Dozens Dead in Lahore Mosque Attacks," *Sky News HD*, May 29. http://news.sky.com/story/782157/dozens-dead-in-lahore-mosque-attacks.

Coll, Steve. 2004. *Ghost Wars: The Secret History of the CIA, Afghanistan, and Bin Laden from the Soviet Invasion to September 10, 2001*. New York: Penguin Press.

Constable, Pamela. 2009. "Defiant Taliban Forces Advance to within 60 Miles of Islamabad." *Washington Post*, April 24. www.washingtonpost.com/wp-dyn/content/article/2009/04/22/AR2009042200863.html.

Cordesman, Anthony. 2006. *The Iraq War and Lessons for Counterinsurgency*. Washington, DC: Center for Strategic and International Studies.

Crilly, Rob. 2012. "Al Qaeda Leader Abu Yahya al-Libi Target of US Drone Strike." *Telegraph*, June 5. www.telegraph.co.uk/news/worldnews/al-qaeda/9312050/Al-Qaeda-leader-Abu-Yahya-al-Libi-target-of-US-drone-strike.html.

Dasgupta, Jyotindra. 2001. "India's Federal Design and Multicultural National Construction." In *The Success of India's Democracy*, edited by Atul Kohli, 49–77. Cambridge: Cambridge University Press.

Diamond, Larry. 2010. "Liberation Technology." *Journal of Democracy* 21, no. 3 (July): 69–83.

Eglar, Zekiye. 1960. *A Punjabi Village in Pakistan*. New York: Columbia University Press.

Ellahi, Abida. 2010. "Overview of Police in Pakistan." *Scribd.com*, December 13. www.scribd.com/doc/24031499/.

Elmusharaf, Mudawi Mukhtar. 2004. "Cyber Terrorism: The New Kind of Terrorism." *Computer Crime Research Center*, April 8. www.crime-research.org/articles/cyber_terrorism_new_kind_terrorism/.

Exum, Andrew. 2009. "On CT vs. COIN." *Small Wars Journal*, March 26. http://smallwarsjournal.com/jrnl/art/on-ct-vs-coin.

Fair, Christine. 2008. *The Madrassah Challenge: Militancy and Religious Education in Pakistan*. Washington, DC: United States Institute of Peace Press.

Fair, Christine. 2009. "Antecedents and Implications of the November 2008 Lashkar-e-Taiba Attack upon Several Targets in the Indian Mega-City of Mumbai." Testimony before the Committee on Homeland Security, Subcommittee on Transportation and Security and Infrastructure Protection, US House of Representatives, March 11. www.rand.org/content/dam/rand/pubs/testimonies/2009/RAND_CT320.pdf.

Fair, Christine, and Shuja Nawaz. 2011. "The Changing Pakistan Army Officer Corps." *Journal of Strategic Studies* 34, no. 1 (February): 63–94. doi:10.1080/01402390.2011.541765.

Fazl-e-Haider, Syed. 2011. "Pakistan's Military Budget Surges by 12 Percent." *Asia Times*, June 9. www.atimes.com/atimes/South_Asia/MF09Df02.html.

Fearon, James D., and David Laitin. 2003. "Ethnicity, Insurgency, and Civil War." *American Political Science Review* 97, no. 1 (February): 75–90.

Finer, Samuel E. 1962. *Man on Horseback: The Role of the Military in Politics*. London: Pall Mall.

Firdous, Kiran. 2009. "Militancy in Pakistan." *Strategic Studies* 39, no. 2–3: 112–29.

Fischer, Michael D. 1991. "Marriage and Power: Tradition and Transition in an Urban Punjabi Community." In *Economy and Culture in Pakistan: Migrants and Cities in a Muslim Society*, edited by Hastings Donnan and Pnina Werbner, 97–123. London: MacMillan.

Fishman, Brian. 2010. *The Battle for Pakistan: Militancy and Conflict across the FATA and NWFP*. Washington, DC: New America Foundation.

Franco, Claudio. 2009. "The Tehrik-e-Taliban Pakistan." In *Decoding the New Taliban: Insights from the Afghan Field*, edited by Antonio Giustozzi, 269–92. London: Hurst.

Friedman, Uri. 2011. "US Drone Attacks Resume after Release of CIA Contractor." *Atlantic Wire*, March 17. www.theatlanticwire.com/global/2011/03/us-drone-attacks-resume-after-release-cia-contractor/35908/.

Galula, David. 2006. *Counterinsurgency Warfare: Theory and Practice*. Westport, CT: Praeger.

Gan, Steven, James Gomez, and Uwe Johannen, ed. 2004. *Asian Cyber Activism: Freedom of Expression and Media Censorship*. Thailand: Friedrich Naumann Foundation.

Gannon, Kathy. 2008. "Pakistan's Militants Focus on Afghanistan." *Associated Press*, July 14. http://usatoday30.usatoday.com/news/world/2008-07-13-2315421363_x.htm.

Gardner, Frank. 2010. "Death of Mustafa Abu al-Yazid Setback for Al Qaeda." *BBC News*, June 1. www.bbc.co.uk/news/10206180.

Gayer, Laurent. 2007. "Guns, Slums, and 'Yellow Devils': A Genealogy of Urban Conflicts in Karachi, Pakistan." *Modern Asian Studies* 41, no. 3: 515–44.

Gellner, Ernst. 1981. *Muslim Society*. Cambridge: Cambridge University Press.

Ghauri, Irfan. 2006. "Government Will Stop Funding Seminaries." *Daily Times* (Lahore), May 4.

———. 2011a. "Fighting the Terrorists: Defense Body Looks to First Strike Policy." *Express Tribune*, May 26.

———. 2011b. "Moral Policing?: PTA Backtracks, Says List of Banned Words Not Final." *Express Tribune*, November 22, http://tribune.com.pk/story/295633/moral-policing-pta-backtracks-says-list-of-banned-words-not-final/.

Ghosh, Bobby. 2010. "Beyond Times Square: Pakistani Terrorism Targets US." *Time*, May 6. www.time.com/time/magazine/article/0,9171,1987578,00.html.

Gill, John H. 2003. *An Atlas of the 1971 India-Pakistan War: The Birth of Bangladesh*. Washington, DC: National Defense University Press.

Gishkori, Zahid. 2011. "Illegal Construction of Mosques on Rise." *Express Tribune* (Islamabad), April 15.

Giustozzi, Antonio. 2013. "Turmoil within the Taliban: A Crisis of Growth?" *Central Asia Policy Brief*, no. 7 (January). www.centralasiaprogram.org/images/Policy_Brief_7,_January_2013.pdf.

Godson, Roy, and Richard Shultz. 2010. *Adapting America's Security Paradigm and Security Agenda*. Washington, DC: National Strategy Information Center.

Goldman, Adam, and Matt Apuzzo. 2011a. "Osama Bin Laden Dead: How One Phone Call Led US to Bin Laden's Doorstep." *Huffington Post*, May 2. www.huffingtonpost.com/2011/05/02/osama-bin-laden-dead-one-phone-call_n_856674.html.

———. 2011b. "How bin Laden Emailed without Being Detected." *NBC News*, May 12, msnbc.com/id/43011358/ns/technology_and_science_and_gadgets/t/how-bin-laden-emailed-without-being-detected/#.UBcX7Y5nEyw.

Government of KPK (Khyber Pakhtunkhwa). 2010. "White Paper 2010–11." Finance Department, June 12. www.peaceandwomen.net/white-paper.pdf.

Grare, Frédéric. 2009. *Reforming Pakistan's Intelligence Agencies*. Washington, DC: Carnegie Endowment for National Peace.

Gul, Imtiaz. 2011a. "Performance on the Anti-Terror Front." *Friday Times*, April 1–7. www.thefridaytimes.com/01042011/page4.shtml.

———. 2011b. *The Most Dangerous Place: Pakistan's Lawless Frontier*. New York: Penguin Press.

Gunaratna, Rohan. 2007. "Strategic Counterterrorism: The Way Forward." In *Terrorism: What's Coming; The Mutating Threat*, edited by James O. Ellis III, 63–73. Oklahoma: Memorial Institute for the Prevention of Terrorism (MIPT). http://publichealthnursingprojects.pbworks.com/f/Terrorism-Whats-Coming-The-Mutating-Threat.pdf.

Haider, Ejaz. 2009. "Swat's Wicked Problem." *Indian Express*, April 14. www.indianexpress.com/news/swat-s-wicked-problem/446627/.

———. 2011. "The Curious Case of the Shamsi Airbase." *Express Tribune*, July 4.

Hameed, Zulfiqar. 2012. "The Need for Reform in Anti-Terror Law." *Friday Times*, January: 13–19.

Hamid, Zaid. 2009. "A Message from Zaid Hamid to All Pakistanis across the Globe." *Siyasat Aur Pakistan*, July 20. http://siyasipakistan.wordpress.com/2009/07/20/.

Hanauer, Larry, and Peter Chalk. 2012. *India and Pakistan's Strategies in Afghanistan: Implications for the United States and the Region*. Occasional Paper. Santa Monica, CA: Rand.

Haqqani, Hussain. 2005. *Pakistan: Between Mosque and Military*. Washington, DC: Carnegie Endowment for International Peace.

Haque, Jahanzaib. 2012. "The Great (Fire) Wall of Pakistan." *Tribune* (Pakistan), March 4. http://tribune.com.pk/story/345378/the-great-firewall-of-pakistan/.

Haroon, Sana. 2007. *Frontier of Faith: Islam in the Indo-Afghan Borderland*. London: Hurst.

Hasan, Syed Shoaib. 2009. "Video Shows Pakistan Army Abuse." *BBC*, October 1. http://news.bbc.co.uk/2/hi/8285564.stm.

Henckaerts, Jean-Marie, and Louise Doswald-Beck. 2005. "Study on Customary International Humanitarian Law: A Contribution to the Understanding and Respect for the Rule of Law in Armed Conflict." *International Review of the Red Cross* 87, no. 857 (March). www.icrc.org/eng/assets/files/other/irrc_857_henckaerts.pdf.

Hopkirk, Peter. 1992. *The Great Game: The Struggle for Empire in Central Asia*. New York: Kondansha International.

Howenstein, Nicholas. 2008. *The Jihadi Terrain in Pakistan: An Introduction to the Sunni Jihadi Groups in Pakistan and Kashmir*. Pakistan Security Research Unit (PSRU), Research Report 1. Bradford: PSRU.

HRCP (Human Rights Commission of Pakistan). 2010a. *Swat: Paradise Regained? Report of an HRCP Fact-Finding Mission*. Lahore: Human Rights Commission of Pakistan.

———. 2010b. "Constitutional Petition in Supreme Court—List of People Missing Who Have Been Traced."

Human Rights Watch (HRW). 2010. "Pakistan: Extrajudicial Executions by Army in Swat," July 16. www.hrw.org/news/2010/07/16/pakistan-extrajudicial-executions-army-swat.

———. 2011a. "Pakistan: Upsurge in Killings in Balochistan," July 13. www.hrw.org/news/2011/07/13/pakistan-upsurge-killings-balochistan.

———. 2011b. "We Can Torture, Kill, or Keep You for Years," July 28. www.hrw.org/reports/2011/07/28/we-can-torture-kill-or-keep-you-years.

Huntington, Samuel. 1958. *The Soldier and the State: The Theory and Politics of Civil-Military Relations*. Cambridge, MA: Belknap Press of Harvard.

———. 1968. *Political Order in Changing Societies*. New Haven, CT: Yale University Press.

Hussain, Chaudhry Fawad. 2010. "Why Terrorists Get Acquitted." *News* (Pakistan), June 22. www.thenews.com.pk/TodaysPrintDetail.aspx?ID=246494&Cat=9&dt=6/22/2010.

Hussain, Muhammad Samir. 2011. "Pakistan's Response to the Growing India-US Strategic Relationship." *Foreign Policy Journal*, October 14. www.foreignpolicyjournal.com/2011/10/14/pakistans-response-to-the-growing-india-u-s-strategic-relationship/.

Hussain, Mujahid. 2012. *Punjabi Taliban: Driving Extremism in Pakistan*. New Delhi: Pentagon Press.

Hussain, Syed. 2011. "Why Do Terrorism Cases Fail in Court? An Empirical Analysis." Paper Presented at the Annual Meeting of the ASAC, Washington DC, November 15.

Hussain, Tayyab. 2013. "Senate Passes NACTA, Electoral Laws Amendment Bills." *Pakistan Today*, March 13. www.pakistantoday.com.pk/2013/03/13/news/national/senate-passes-nacta-electoral-laws-amendment-bills/.

Hussain, Touqir. 2005. "US-Pakistan Engagement: The War on Terrorism and Beyond." United States Institute of Peace, Special Report 145.

Hussain, Zahid. 2007. *Frontline Pakistan: The Struggle with Militant Islam*. New York: Columbia University Press.

———. 2010. *The Scorpion's Tail: The Relentless Rise of Islamic Militants in Pakistan—And How It Threatens America*. New York: Free Press.

ICG (International Crisis Group). 2006a. "Pakistan: The Worsening Conflict in Balochistan." *Asia Report*, no. 119 (September 14). www.crisisgroup.org/~/media/Files/asia/south-asia/pakistan/119...pakistan_the_worsening_conflict_in_balochistan.ashx.

———. 2006b. "Pakistan's Tribal Areas: Appeasing the Militants." *Asia Report*, no. 125 (December 11). www.crisisgroup.org/~/media/Files/asia/

south-asia/pakistan/125...pakistans_tribal_areas___appeasing_the_mili tants.
———. 2009. "Pakistan: Countering Militancy in FATA." *Asia Report*, no. 178 (October 21). www.crisisgroup.org/en/regions/asia/south-asia/paki stan/178-pakistan-countering-militancy-in-fata.aspx.
———. 2010. "Reforming Pakistan's Criminal Justice System." *Asia Report*, no. 196 (December 6). www.crisisgroup.org/en/regions/asia/south-asia/ pakistan/196-reforming-pakistans-criminal-justice-system.aspx.
———. 2011. "Reforming Pakistan's Prison System." *Asia Report*, no. 212 (October 12). www.unhcr.org/refworld/pdfid/4e968f382.pdf.
———. 2013. "Pakistan: Countering Militancy in PATA." *Asia Report*, no. 242 (January 15). www.crisisgroup.org/~/media/Files/asia/south-asia/ pakistan/242-pakistan-countering-militancy-in-pata.pdf.
ICRC (International Committee of the Red Cross) 2004. "What Is International Humanitarian Law?" ICRC Resource Centre Legal Fact Sheet, July 31. www.icrc.org/eng/resources/documents/legal-fact-sheet/humanitarian-law-factsheet.htm.
———. 2008. "Procedural Safeguards for Security Detention in Known International Armed Conflict," Meeting proceedings. London: Chatham House, September 22–23.
Imran, Zafar. 2010a. "Al-Qaeda's Ambitions in Pakistan: Changing Goals, Changing Strategies." *Terrorism Monitor* 8, no. 31. www.defence.pk/ forums/pakistans-war/68500-al-qaeda-s-ambitions-pakistan-changing-goals-changing-strategies.html.
———. 2010b. "Hafiz Muhammad Saeed, Lashkar-e-Taiba's Unrepentant Leader." *Militant Leadership Monitor* 1, no. 6 (June 30): 7. http://mlm.james town.org/single/?tx_ttnews%5btt_news%5d=36549&tx_ttnews%5bba ckPid%5d=568&no_cache=1.
Imtiaz, Hussain. 2006. "Freezing the Accounts of Mullah Omer Aide." *Weekly Pulse* (Islamabad), March 10–16.
Innocent, Malou. 2009. "Pakistan and the Future of US Policy." *CATO Policy Analysis*, no. 636, April 13. www.cato.org/publications/policy-analysis/ pakistan-future-us-policy.
IPRI. 2009. "The Operation Rah-e-Rast." IPRI Fact File, June. www.ipripak .org/factfiles/ff111.pdf.
Iqbal, Shahid. 2013. "$48bn Remittances: Rupee Depreciates 58pc in Five Years." *Dawn*, January 13. http://dawn.com/2013/01/13/48bn-remittan ces-rupee-depreciates-58pc-in-five-years/.
IRIN. 2009. "Pakistan: Timeline on Swat Valley Turbulence." *IRIN*, February 11, www.irinnews.org/Report/82864/PAKISTAN-Timeline-on-Swat-Val ley-turbulence.

Jaffrelot, Christophe. 2002a. "Islamic Identity and Ethnic Tensions." In *A History of Pakistan and Its Origins*, edited by Christophe Jaffrelot, 9–38 (Anthem Press: London, 2002).

———. 2002b. "Nationalism without a Nation: Pakistan Searching for Its Identity." In *Pakistan: Nationalism without a Nation?*, edited by Christophe Jaffrelot, 7–50. London: Zed Books.

Jalal, Ayesha. 1990. *The State of Martial Law: The Origins of Pakistan's Political Economy of Defense*. New York: Vanguard.

———. 1995. *Democracy and Authoritarianism in South Asia: A Comparative and Historical Perspective*. Cambridge: Cambridge University Press.

Jamal, Arif. 2009. *Shadow War: The Untold Story of Jihad in Kashmir*. New York: Melville House.

Jamal, Asad, and Sanjay Patel, ed. 2010. *Police Organizations in Pakistan*. Lahore, Pakistan: Commonwealth Human Rights Initiative.

Jones, Owen Bennett. 2009. *Pakistan: Eye of the Storm*. New Haven, CT: Yale University Press.

Jones, Seth, and Christine C. Fair. 2010. *Counterinsurgency in Pakistan*. Santa Monica, CA: Rand.

Kaplan, Fred. 2009. "Counterinsurgenterrorism." *Slate*, March 27. www.slate.com/articles/news_and_politics/war_stories/2009/03/counterinsurgenterrorism.html.

Kepel, Gilles. 1986. *Muslim Extremist in Egypt: The Prophet and the Pharaoh*. Berkeley: University of California Press.

———. 2000. *Jihad: The Trail of Political Islam*. Paris: Gallimard.

Khaliq, Fazal. 2010. "For Men Fighting the War, Women Were 'Easy Targets'." *Express Tribune*, November 14. http://tribune.com.pk/story/77168/for-men-fighting-the-war-women-were-easy-targets/.

Khan, Hasan. 2010. "Pakistan Journalists Vow to Resist Media Regulation." *Central Asia Online*, July 7. http://centralasiaonline.com/en_GB/articles/caii/features/pakistan/2010/07/07/feature-01.

Khan, Ilyas M. 2004. "Profile of Nek Mohammad." *Dawn*, June 19. http://archives.dawn.com/2004/06/19/latest.htm.

Khan, Ismail. 2009. "Desperate Moves On to Secure Swat: The Lost Valley." *Dawn*, January 14. http://archives.dawn.com/archives/41410.

Khan, Mushtaq H. 1999. "The Political Economy of Industrial Policy in Pakistan 1947–1971." SOAS Department of Economics, Working paper no. 98. http://eprints.soas.ac.uk/9867/1/Industrial_Policy_in_Pakistan.pdf.

Khan, Mushtaq H., and Kwame Sundaram Jomo, ed. 2000. *Rents, Rent-Seeking, and Economic Development: Theory and Evidence in Asia*. Cambridge: Cambridge University Press.

Khan, Riaz M. 2011. *Afghanistan and Pakistan: Conflict, Extremism and Resistance to Modernity*. Washington, DC: Woodrow Wilson Center Press / Johns Hopkins University Press.

Khan, Sabina. 2011. "FATA's Political Status: What Are the Consequences and Options for Pakistan?" *Strategic Insights* 10, no. 2 (Summer): 35, 38.

Khan, Shahrukh Rafi. 2013. "Explaining the Puzzle of Pakistan's Lagging Economic Growth." In *Development Challenges Confronting Pakistan*, edited by Anita M. Weiss and Saba Gul Khattak, 23–42. Sterling, VA: Stylus Publishing.

Khan, Zafarullah. 2001. *Medieval Mindset, Modern Media*. Islamabad: Friedrich Naumann Foundation.

Khan, Zia. 2010. "The Fission of Lashkar-e-Jhangvi." *Express Tribune* (Islamabad), November 17. http://tribune.com.pk/story/78500/the-fission-of-lashkar-e-jhangvi/.

———. 2011. "Taliban Strapped for Cash as Funding Routes Blocked." *Express Tribune*, February 28. http://tribune.com.pk/story/124949/money-matters-taliban-strapped-for-cash-as-funding-routes-blocked/.

Khattak, Daud. 2012. "Reviewing Pakistan's Peace Deals with the Taliban," *Combating Terrorism Center* (West Point), September 26. www.ctc.usma.edu/posts/reviewing-pakistans-peace-deals-with-the-taliban.

Kilcullen, David. 2006a. "Counterinsurgency Redux." *Survival: Global Politics and Strategy* 48, no. 4: 1–15.

———. 2006b. "Three Pillars of Counterinsurgency." Remarks delivered at the US Government Counterinsurgency Conference, September 28, Washington DC. www.au.af.mil/au/awc/awcgate/uscoin/3pillars_of_counterinsurgency.pdf.

———. 2010. *Counterinsurgency*. New York: Oxford University Press.

Kohli, Atul, ed. 2001. *The Success of India's Democracy*. Cambridge, MA: Cambridge University Press.

Lalwani, Sameer. 2010. *The Pakistan Military's Adaptation to Counterinsurgency in 2009*. Washington, DC: New America Foundation.

Lamb, Robert, and Sadika Hameed. 2012. "Subnational Governance, Service Delivery, and Militancy in Pakistan." Program Report on Crisis, Conflict and Cooperation. Washington, DC: Center for Strategic and International Studies.

Lester, Tom. 2010. "Ilyas Kashmiri: Most Dangerous Man on Earth?" *CNN World*, November 12. http://articles.cnn.com/2010-11-10/world/pakistan.kashmiri.profile_1_ilyas-kashmiri-david-coleman-headley-pakistani-kashmir?_s = PM:WORLD.

Lieven, Anatol. 2011. *Pakistan: A Hard Country*. New York: Public Affairs.

Lister, Tim. 2010. "WikiLeaks: Pakistan Quietly Approved Drone Attacks, US Special Units." *CNN*, December 2. http://edition.cnn.com/2010/US/12/01/wikileaks.pakistan.drones/index.html.

Livingston, Ian, Heather Messera, Michael O'Hanlon, and Amy Unikwicz. 2011. "States of Conflict: An Update." *New York Times*, April 9. www.nytimes.com/interactive/2011/04/09/opinion/04102011_stateofwar.html.

LJCP (Law and Justice Commission of Pakistan). 2009. "Judicial Statistics for Pakistan, 2009," Islamabad. www.ljcp.gov.pk/Menu%20Items/Publications/Reports%20of%20the%20LJCP/Judicial%20Statistics/Judicial%20Statistics%20for%20Pakistan%202009.pdf.

Lodhi, Maleeha. 2009. "The Swat Operation: Possibility and Peril." *News International*, May 26.

———, ed. 2011. *Pakistan: Beyond the "Crisis State."* New York: Columbia University Press.

Lyon, Stephen M. 2002. "Power and Patronage in Pakistan." PhD diss., University of Kent, Canterbury. www.dur.ac.uk/s.m.lyon/Publications/Lyon.pdf.

MacDonald, Myra. 2010. "Lashkar-e-Taiba Cadres Sucked into Al Qaeda Orbit." *Reuters*, November 7. www.reuters.com/article/2010/11/07/us-security-lashkar-idUSTRE6A611Z20101107.

Malik, Shahzad. 2006. "17 Banned Groups Warned against Collecting Hides." *Daily Times* (Lahore), December 28.

Malik, Yaqoob. 2012. "Terrorists Attack Kamra Air Base: Nine Attackers Dead, Plane Damaged." *Dawn*, August 17. http://dawn.com/2012/08/17/terrorists-attack-kamra-air-base-%E2%80%A2-nine-attackers-dead-%E2%80%A2-plane-damaged/.

Manor, James. 2001. "Centre-State Relations." In *The Success of India's Democracy*, edited by Atul Kohli, 78–102. Cambridge: Cambridge University Press.

Maqbool, Arshad. 2004. "Al-Qaeda Wings in Pakistan." *Nida-e-Millat* (Lahore), December 2–8.

Markey, Daniel. 2008. *Securing Pakistan's Tribal Belt*. Council Special Report No. 36. Washington DC: Council on Foreign Relations Press.

———. 2009. "From Af-Pak to Pak-Af: A Response to the New US Strategy for South Asia." Policy Options Paper, Council on Foreign Relations, April. www.cfr.org/pakistan/afpak-pakaf-response-new-us-strategy-south-asia/p19125.

Mauro, Paolo. 1995. "Corruption and Growth." *Quarterly Journal of Economics* 110, no. 3: 681–712.

Mayar, Muhammad Riaz. 2010. "VC of Swat Varsity Shot Dead in Mardan." *News* (Pakistan), October 3. www.thenews.com.pk/Todays-News-13-1040-VC-of-Swat-varsity-shot-dead-in-Mardan.

McCormick, Gordon, Steven B. Horton, and Lauren A. Harrison. 2007. "Things Fall Apart: The Endgame Dynamics of Internal Wars." *Third World Quarterly* 28, no. 2: 321–67.

Mian, Asaf. 2009. "FATA: Tribal Economy in the Context of Ongoing Militancy." *Conflict and Peace Studies* 2, no. 3 (July–September). http://san-pips.com/download.php?f=24.pdf.

Mir, Amir. 2008. *The Fluttering Flag of Jihad*. Lahore: Mashal.

———. 2009. "Peace Deal to Legitimise TNSM." *News International*, February.

———. 2011. "Khakis Unhappy with ATC's Performance." *News*, February 21. www.thenews.com.pk/Todays-News-13-4120-Khakis-unhappy-with-ATCs%E2%80%99-performance.

Momein Fahad A., and M. Nawaz Brohi. 2010. "Cybercrime and Internet Growth in Pakistan." *Asian Journal of Information Technology* 9, no. 1: 1–4.

Mufti, Mariam. 2012. "Religion and Militancy in Pakistan and Afghanistan: A Literature Review." CSIS Program Report on Crisis, Conflict and Cooperation. Washington, DC: Center for Strategic and International Studies.

Mullick, Haider Ali Hussain. 2009. "Helping Pakistan Defeat the Taliban: A Joint Action Agenda for the United States & Pakistan." Washington, DC: Institute for Social Policy and Understanding, August. www.ispu.org/content/Helping_Pakistan_Defeat_the_Taliban_A_Joint_Action_Agenda_for_the_United_States_Pakistan#sthash.vLJZi0oa.dpuf.

———. 2010a. "Al Qaeda and Pakistan: Current Role and Future Consideration." Washington, DC: Institute for Social Policy and Understanding, October 7. www.ispu.org/GetReports/35/1879/Publications.aspx.

———. 2010b. "The Pakistani Surge: The Way Forward for Counterinsurgency in Pakistan." Hawthorn, Australia: Australian Strategic Policy Institute, June 10. http://apo.org.au/node/21994.

Munawer, Azeem. 2010. "Militants Have a Nexus with the Underworld." *Dawn* (Islamabad), December 27.

Murphy, Eamon. 2012. *The Making of Terrorism in Pakistan: Historical and Social Roots of Extremism*. London: Routledge.

Nagl, John. 2002. *Learning to Eat Soup with a Knife: Counterinsurgency Lessons from Malaya and Vietnam*. Westport, CT: Praeger.

Nasr, S. V. R. 1994. *The Vanguard of Islamic Revolution: The Jama'at-i-Islami of Pakistan*. Berkeley: University of California Press.

———. 2001. *Islamic Leviathan: Islam and the Making of State Power*. New York: Oxford University Press.

———. 2002. "Islam, the State and Rise of Sectarian Militancy in Pakistan." In *Pakistan: Nationalism without A Nation?*, edited by Cristophe Jaffrelot, 85–114. London: Zed Book Ltd.

Nawaz, Shuja. 2008. *Crossed Swords: Pakistan, Its Army and the Wars Within*. Oxford: Oxford University Press.

———. 2009. *FATA: A Most Dangerous Place*. Washington, DC: Center for Strategic and International Studies.

———. 2011. "Learning by Doing: The Pakistan Army's Experience with Counterinsurgency." *Atlantic Council*, February 1. www.acus.org/publication/learning-doing-pakistan-armys-experience-counterinsurgency,9–12.

Nayyar, A. H., and Ahmed Salim. 2005. "The Subtle Subversion: The State of Curricula and Textbooks in Pakistan." Sustainable Development Policy Institute. http://unesco.org.pk/education/teachereducation/reports/rp22.pdf.

NDTV. 2011. "Pak Counter-terror Measures Not Effective: Obama to Congress." NDTV, October 2. www.ndtv.com/article/world/pak-counter-terror-measures-not-effective-obama-to-congress-138035.

Negroponte. John D. 2008. "Pakistan's Fata Challenge: Securing One of the World's Most Dangerous Areas." Testimony before the Senate Foreign Relations Committee, Washington DC, May 20. http://2001-2009.state.gov/s/d/2008/105041.htm.

Niaz, Tahir. 2008. "ISI Back Under PM's Control." *Daily Times*, July 28. www.dailytimes.com.pk/default.asp?page = 2008]78‹tory_28-7-2008_pg1_1.

North, Douglass C. 1990a. *Institutions, Institutional Change and Economic Performance*. Cambridge: Cambridge University Press.

———. 1990b. "A Transaction Cost Theory of Politics." *Journal of Theoretical Politics* 2:355–67.doi:10.1177/0951692890002004001.

———. 2005. *Understanding the Process of Economic Change*. Princeton NJ: Princeton University Press.

Olson, Mancur. 2000. *Power and Prosperity: Outgrowing Communist and Capitalist Dictatorships*. London: Oxford University Press.

Open Society Foundations and Liaison Office. 2011. "The Cost of Kill/Capture: Impact of the Night Raid Surge on Afghan Civilians." September 19. www.opensocietyfoundations.org/sites/default/files/Night-Raids-Report-FINAL-092011.pdf.

PEMRA (Pakistan Electronic Media Regulatory Authority). 2010. Annual Report 2010, Islamabad: PEMRA.

Perlez, Jane. 2010. "Distrust Slows US Training of Pakistanis." *New York Times*, July 11. www.nytimes.com/2010/07/12/world/asia/12training.html?pagewanted = all.

———. 2011. "Report Says Militants in Pearl Killing Still at Large." *New York Times*, January 20. www.nytimes.com/2011/01/21/world/asia/21pearl.html?ref = danielpearl.

Peters, Gretchen. 2009. "How Opium Profits the Taliban." United States Institute of Peace, *Peaceworks*, no. 62, August. www.usip.org/files/resources/taliban_opium_1.pdf.

———. 2010. *Seeds of Terror: How Drugs, Thugs, and Crime Are Reshaping the Afghan War*. New York: St. Martin's Press.

Pew Research Center. 2009. "Mapping the Global Muslim Population: A Report on the Size and Distribution of the World's Muslim Population." *Pew Research Religion and Public Life Project*, October 7. www.pewforum.org/2009/10/07/mapping-the-global-muslim-population/.

———. 2012. "Pakistani Public Opinion Ever More Critical of US." Pew Global Attitudes Project, June 27. www.pewglobal.org/files/2012/06/Pew-Global-Attitudes-Project-Pakistan-Report-FINAL-Wednesday-June-27-2012.pdf.

———. 2013. "On Eve of Elections, a Dismal Public Mood in Pakistan: Rising Concerns about the Taliban." Pew Global Attitudes Project, May 7. www.pewglobal.org/files/2013/05/Pew-Global-Attitudes-Pakistan-Report-FINAL-May-7-20131.pdf.

Pion-Berlin, David, ed. 2001. *Civil Military Relations in Latin America: New Analytical Perspectives*. Chapel Hill: University of North Carolina Press.

PIPS (Pakistan Institute for Peace Studies). 2008. *Balochistan: Conflicts and Players*. Islamabad: PIPS.

———. 2010. *Pakistan Security Report 2010*. Islamabad: PIPS.

———. 2012. *Pakistan Security Report 2012*. Islamabad: PIPS.

Pollitt, Mark M. 1997. "A Cyberterrorism Fact or Fancy?" Proceedings of the 20th National Information Systems Security Conference, October 7–10, Baltimore, Maryland. http://csrc.nist.gov/nissc/1997/proceedings/,285–89.

Popalzai, Shaheryar, and Jahanzaib Haque. 2011. "Filtering SMS: PTA Nay Ban over 1,500 English, Urdu Words." *Express Tribune*, November 16. http://tribune.com.pk/story/292774/filtering-sms-pta-may-ban-over-1500-english-urdu-words/.

Qazi, Shehzad H. 2011. "Rebels of the Frontier: Origins, Organization, and Recruitment of the Pakistani Taliban." *Small Wars and Insurgencies* 22, no. 4: 574–602.

Quinn, Andrew. 2012. "Pakistan Dragging Its Feet on Mumbai Mastermind: Clinton." *Reuters*, May 7. www.reuters.com/article/2012/05/07/us-pakistan-us-militants-idUSBRE84604U20120507.

Rahman, Javaid-Ur. 2010. "PEMRA Lacks Clear Policy for Channels on Cable TV." *Nation*, April 9. www.nation.com.pk/pakistan-news-newspaper-daily-english-online/Politics/09-Apr-2010/PEMRA-lacks-clear-policy-for-channels-on-cable-TV.

Ramsay, Clay, Steven Kull, Stephen Weber, and Evan Lewis. 2009. "Pakistani Public Opinion on the Swat Conflict, Afghanistan, and the US." World Public Opinion.org. www.worldpublicopinion.org/pipa/pdf/jul09/WPO_Pakistan_Jul09_rpt.pdf.

Rana, Amir Muhammad. 2002. *Jihad-e-Kashmir-o-Afghanistan*. Lahore: Mashal Publishers.

———. 2003. "Living with the Faithful—a Neighborhood Choice." *Daily Times*, September 22.

———. 2005a. *Seeds of Terrorism*. London: New Millennium Publications, 171.

———. 2005b. *A to Z of Jihadi Organizations in Pakistan*. Lahore: Mashal.

———. 2008a. "Jihadi Print Media in Pakistan: An Overview." *Conflict and Peace Studies, A PIPS Research Journal*, no. 1.

———. 2008b. "Interview, Shahnawaz Khan, Crime Reporter." *Daily Times*, December, Lahore.

———. 2012. "Patterns of Violence." *News on Sunday*, November 11. http://jang.com.pk/thenews/nov2012-weekly/nos-11-11-2012/spr.htm#4.

Rana, Amir Muhammad, and Iqbal Khattak. 2004. "Afghan, Pakistani, US Forces Set for Spring Offensive." *Daily Times* (Lahore), February 21. www.dailytimes.com.pk/default.asp?page=story_21-2-2004_pg1_1.

Rana, Amir Muhammad, and Rohan Gunaratna. 2008. Al-Qaeda Fights Back: *Inside Pakistani Tribal Areas*. Islamabad: PIPS.

Rao, Shahid. 2009. "Terror Attack on GHQ." *Nation*, October 11. www.nation.com.pk/pakistan-news-newspaper-daily-english-online/Po litics/11-Oct-2009/Terror-attack-on-GHQ/.

Rashid, Ahmed. 2001. *Taliban: Militant Islam, Oil and Fundamentalism in Central Asia*. New Haven, CT: Yale University Press.

———. 2009. *Descent into Chaos: Afghanistan, Pakistan and the Threat to Global Security*. London: Penguin Press.

Rassler, Don, and Vahid Brown. 2011. "CTC: The Haqqani Nexus and the Evolution of Al-Qaeda." Combating Terrorism Center at West Point. www.ctc.usma.edu/wp-content/uploads/2011/07/CTC-Haqqani-Report_Rassler-Brown-Final_Web.pdf.

Record, Jeffrey, and W. Andrew Terrill. 2004. *Iraq and Vietnam: Differences, Similarities and Insights*. Carlisle, PA: Strategic Studies Institute.

Rice, Condoleeza. 2005. "Iraq and US Policy." Statement before the US Senate Foreign Relations Committee. US Senate, Washington, DC, October 19. http://2001-2009.state.gov/secretary/rm/2005/55303.htm.

Rizvi, Hasan-Askari. 1998. "Civil-Military Relations in Contemporary Pakistan." *Survival: The IISS Quarterly* 40, no. 2 (Summer): 96–113.

———. 2000. *The Military, State and Society in Pakistan*. London: Palgrave Macmillan.

Robertson, Nic, and Greg Botelho. 2013. "Ex-Pakistani President Musharraf Admits Secret Deal with US on Drone Strikes." *CNN*, April 12. http://edition.cnn.com/2013/04/11/world/asia/pakistan-musharraf-drones.

Rodriguez, Alex. 2010. "Pakistani Criminal Justice System Proves No Match for Terrorism Cases." *Los Angeles Times*, October 28. http://articles.latimes.com/2010/oct/28/world/la-fg-pakistan-acquittals-20101028.

Roggio, Bill. 2009a. "Sufi Muahmmad 'Hates Democracy' and Calls for Global Islamic Rule." *Long War Journal*, February 18. www.longwarjournal.org/archives/2009/02/sufi_mohammed_hates_democracy_and_calls_for_global_islamic_rule.php.

———. 2009b. "Terror Alliance Takes Credit for Peshawar Hotel Assault." *Long War Journal*, June 11. www.longwarjournal.org/archives/2009/06/terror_alliance_take.php.

———. 2009c. "Tahir Yuldashev Confirmed Killed in US Strike in South Waziristan." *Long War Journal*, October 4. www.longwarjournal.org/archives/2009/10/tahir_yuldashev_conf.php.

———. 2010. "Chinese Terrorist Leader Abdul Haq al Turkistani Is Dead: Pakistani Interior Minister." *Long War Journal*, May 7. www.longwarjournal.org/archives/2010/05/chinese_terrorist_le.php.

Roniger, Luis, and Ayse Gunes-Ayata. 1994. *Democracy, Clientelism, and Civil Society*. Boulder, CO: Lynne Rienner Publishers.

Rotella, Sebastian. 2010. "On the Trail of a Terrorist." *Washington Post*, November 14. www.washingtonpost.com/wp-dyn/content/article/2010/11/13/AR2010111304345.html.

Roul, Animesh. 2005. "Lashkar-e-Jhangvi: Sectarian Violence in Pakistan and Ties to International Terrorism." *Terrorism Monitor* 3, no. 11 (June 3). www.jamestown.org/single/?no_cache=1&tx_ttnews[tt_news]=497.

Roy, Olivier. 1994. *The Failure of Political Islam*. Translated by Carol Volk. Cambridge, MA: Harvard University Press.

Rubin, Barnett, and Ahmed Rashid. 2008. "From Great Game to Grand Bargain: Ending Chaos in Afghanistan and Pakistan." *Foreign Affairs*, November–December. www.foreignaffairs.com/articles/64604/barnett-r-rubin-and-ahmed-rashid/from-great-game-to-grand-bargain.

Sahi, Aoun. 2009. "Varied Motives: The Militants Are Better Trained Than the Police." *Jang*, May 10. http://jang.com.pk/thenews/may2009-weekly/nos-10-05-2009/spr.htm#7.

Sahl, Silke. 2007. "Researching Customary International Law, State Practice and the Pronouncements of States regarding International Law." *GlobaLex*,

June/July. www.nyulawglobal.org/globalex/Customary_International_Law .htm.
Sayeed, Khalid B. 1980. *Politics in Pakistan: The Nature and Direction of Change*. Westport, CT: Praeger.
Schmid, Alex P., and Albert J. Jongman. 2005. *Political Terrorism: A New Guide to Actors, Authors, Concepts, Data Bases, Theories, and Literature*. Amsterdam: Transaction Books.
Shah, Aqil. 2011. "Security, Soldiers, and the State." In *The Future of Pakistan*, edited by Stephen P. Cohen. Washington, DC: Brookings Institution Press.
Shahzad, Saleem. 2010. "Afghan War Moves Deeper into Pakistan." *Asia Times*, October 7. www.atimes.com/atimes/South_Asia/LJ07Df02.html.
———. 2011. *Inside Al-Qaeda and the Taliban: Beyond Bin Laden and 9/11*. London: Pluto Press.
Shapiro, Jason, and Christine C. Fair. 2010. "Understanding Support for Islamist Militancy in Pakistan." *International Security* 34, no. 3: 79–118.
Siddiqa, Ayesha. 2011. "Pakistan's Counterterrorism Strategy: Separating Friends from Enemies." *Washington Quarterly* 34, no. 1 (Winter): 149–62.
Siddique, Abubakar. 2010. "IMU Evolution Branches Back to Central Asia." *Radio Free Europe / Radio Liberty*, December 8. www.rferl.org/content/imu_evolution_branches_back_central_asia/22407 65.html.
Siddiqui, Naveed. 2007. "Govt Plans to Plug Jihadi Funds." *Daily Times* (Lahore), January 16.
Siddiqui, Salman. 2010. "Financing Terrorism." *Express Tribune*, November 10.
Sisson, Richard, and Leo E. Rose. 1991. *War and Secession: Pakistan, India, and the Creation of Bangladesh*. Berkeley: University of California Press.
Sivan, Emmanuel. 1990. *Radical Islam: Medieval Theology and Modern Politics*. New Haven, CT: Yale University Press.
Smith, Rupert. 2007. *The Utility of Force: The Art of War in the Modern World*. New York: Random House.
Strick van Linschoten, Alex, and Felix Kuehn. 2012. *Poetry of the Taliban*. London: Hurst.
Sweeny, Annie. 2011. "Mumbai Attacks: US Prosecutors in Chicago Charge 4 Men with Ties to Pakistani Terror Group." *Chicago Tribune*, April 25. http://articles.chicagotribune.com/2011-04-25/news/ct-met-new-defendants-terrorism-trial20110425_1_mumbai-attacks-david-coleman-headley-lashkar.
Talbot, Ian. 1991. "The Unionist Party and Punjabi Politics 1937–1947." In *The Political Inheritance of Pakistan*, edited by Donald A. Low, 86–105. Cambridge: Cambridge University Press.

Tankel, Stephen. 2010. "Lashkar-e-Taiba in Perspective: An Evolving Threat." *New American Foundation*, February. www.newamerica.net/sites/newamerica.net/files/policydocs/tankel.pdf.

———. 2011. *Storming the World Stage: The Story of Lashkar-e-Taiba*. New York: Columbia University Press.

Tellis, Ashley. 2008. "US–Pakistan Relations: Assassination, Instability, and the Future of US Policy." Testimony prepared for the Hearing of the Middle East and South Asia Subcommittee of the House Foreign Affairs Committee. www.gpo.gov/fdsys/pkg/CHRG-110hhrg40224/pdf/CHRG-110hhrg40224.pdf, 29–38.

Temple-Raston, Dina. 2013. "Pakistan's Ambitious Program to Re-Educate Militants." *National Public Radio*, April 1. www.npr.org/2013/04/01/175706661/pakistans-ambitious-program-to-re-educate-militants.

Thatcher, Margaret. 1985. "Speech to the American Bar Association," July 15, London. www.margaretthatcher.org/speeches/displaydocument.asp?docid = 106096.

Thier, Alexander J. 2008. "A Toxic Cocktail: Pakistan's Growing Instability." United States Institute of Peace, Peacebrief, February. www.usip.org/publications/toxic-cocktail-pakistans-growing-instability.

UN (United Nations). 2008. *United Nations Peacekeeping Operations: Principles and Guidelines*. New York: UN Department of Peacekeeping Operations.

———. 2010. "Report of the United Nations Commission of Inquiry into the Facts and Circumstances of the Assassination of former Pakistani Prime Minister Mohtarma Benazir Bhutto," Report No. 15, April.

UNODC (UN Office of Drugs and Crime). 2009. "Addiction, Crime and Insurgency: The Transnational Threat of Afghan Opium," October. www.unodc.org/documents/data-and-analysis/Afghanistan/Afghan_Opium_Trade_2009_web.pdf.

Van Creveld, Martin. 2008. *The Changing Face of War: Combat from the Marne to Iraq*. New York: Ballantine.

Walsh, Declan. 2009. "Video of Girl's Flogging as Taliban Hand out Justice." *Guardian*, April 2. www.guardian.co.uk/world/2009/apr/02/taliban-pakistan-justice-women-flogging.

———. 2011. "WikiLeaks Cables: The US Aid Will Not Stop Pakistan Supporting Militants." *Guardian*, November 30. www.guardian.co.uk/world/2010/nov/30/wikileaks-us-aid-pakistan-militants.

Waseem, Mohammad. 2002. "Causes of Democratic Downslide." *Economic and Political Weekly* 37, no. 44–45: 32–38.

Weinbaum, Marvin G. 2010. "Bad Company: Lashkar-e-Taiba and the Growing Ambition of Islamic Militancy in Pakistan." Testimony before the

House Committee on Foreign Affairs, Subcommittee on the Middle East and South Asia, March 11.

Weiner, Myron. 1989. *The Indian Paradox: Essays in Indian Politics*. London: Sage Publications.

Weingast, Barry R. 1993. "Constitutions as Governance Structures: The Political Foundations of Secure Markets." *Journal of Institutional and Theoretical Economics* 149, no. 1 (March): 286–311. www.jstor.org/stable/40751603.

Wilder, Andrew. 2005. "Islam and Political Legitimacy in Pakistan." In *Islam and Democracy in Pakistan*, edited by M. A. Syed, 31–88. Islamabad: National Institute of Historical and Cultural Research.

Williams, David. 2011. "Pakistan to Overtake Britain as World's Fifth Largest Nuclear Power." *Daily Mail*, February 21. www.dailymail.co.uk/news/article-1359231/Pakistan-overtake-Britain-worlds-fifth-largest-nuclear-power.html.

World Bank and Asia/Pacific Group on Money Laundering (APGML). 2009. "Anti-Money Laundering and Combating the Financing of Terrorism: Pakistan." https://openknowledge.worldbank.org/bitstream/handle/10986/12243/700310ESW0P1110an0MER0final0version.pdf?sequence = 1.

Yousaf, Kamran. 2011. "Denying WikiLeaks Disclosure: Kayani Sought US Drone Support only for Surveillance." *Express Tribune*, May 21. http://tribune.com.pk/story/172573/ispr-denies-kayani-asked-us-for-more-drone-strikes/.

Yousafzai, Sami, Ron Moreau, and Christopher Dickey. 2010. "The New Bin Laden." *Newsweek*, November 1, 38.

Yusuf, Huma. 2010. "Funds for Terror." *Dawn*, November 7.

Yusuf, Moeed. 2009a. "Rational Institutional Design, Perverse Incentives, and the US–Pakistan Relationship Post-9/11." *Defense against Terrorism Review* 2, no. 1 (Spring): 15–30.

———. 2009b. "Taliban Have Been Fooling Us All Along." *Friday Times* 21, no. 12 (May 8–14).

———. 2011a. "A Society on the Precipice? Examining the Prospects of Youth Radicalization in Pakistan." In *Reaping the Dividend: Overcoming Pakistan's Demographic Challenges*, edited by Michael Kugelman and Robert M. Hathaway, 76–105. Washington, DC: Woodrow Wilson Press. www.wilsoncenter.org/sites/default/files/ReapingtheDividendFINAL.pdf.

———. 2011b. "Getting Pakistan to Act against Militant Sanctuaries: Helping Pakistan to Help Itself." *Journal of International Peace Operations* 7, no. 4 (July–August): 15–16.

———. 2013a. "Decoding Pakistan's 'Strategic Shift' in Afghanistan." *Stockholm International Policy Research Institute*, May.

———. 2013b. "The Intersection of Development, Politics, and Security." In *Development Challenges Confronting Pakistan*, edited by Anita Weiss and Saba Gul Khattak, 239–66. Sterling: Kumarian Press.

———, ed. 2014. *Insurgency and Counterinsurgency in South Asia*. Washington, DC: United States Institute of Peace Press.

Yusuf, Moeed, and Anit Mukherjee. 2007. "Counterinsurgency in Pakistan: Learning from India." Outlook Series, American Enterprise Institute, September. www.academia.edu/493935/Counterinsurgency_in_Pakistan_Learning_from_India.

Yusuf, Moeed, Huma Yusuf, and Salman Zaidi. 2011. "Pakistan, the United States, and the End Game in Afghanistan: Perceptions of Pakistan's Foreign Policy Elite." Jinnah Institute and United States Institute of Peace. www.usip.org/publications/pakistan-the-united-states-and-the-end-game-in-afghanistan-perceptions-pakistan-s-forei.

Zahab, Mariam Abou, and Olivier Roy. 2004. *Islamist Networks: The Afghan-Pakistan Connection*. New York: Columbia University Press.

Zaidi, Akbar. 1992. "The Economic Bases of the National Question in Pakistan: An Indication." In *Regional Imbalances and the National Question in Pakistan*, edited by S. Akbar Zaidi, 90–138. Lahore: Vanguard Books.

———. 2012. "The Strongest Institution?" *Dawn*, July 2. www.beta.dawn.com/news/731118/the-strongest-institution.

Zaidi, Syed Manzar Abbas. 2010. "Understanding the Appeal of the Taliban in Pakistan." *Journal of Strategic Security* 3, no. 3: 1–14.

Zani, Ubaidul Islam Syed. 1988. *Islami Sahafat* (Islamic Journalism). Lahore: Idara Muarif-i-Islami.

Zengerle, Patricia. 2013. "Top General Says US to Assess Afghan Troops Level after Summer." *Reuters*, April 16. www.reuters.com/article/2013/04/16/us-usa-afghanistan-troops-idUSBRE93F10S20130416.

Ziring, Lawrence. 1980. *Pakistan: The Enigma of Political Development*. Boulder, CO: Westview.

———. 1997. *Pakistan in the 20th Century: A Political History*. Oxford: Oxford University Press.

Contributors

Ayesha Chugh is a researcher, writer, and editor based in Washington, DC. Currently a research coordinator at the International Foundation for Electoral Systems, Chugh recently earned a master's degree in democracy and governance studies at Georgetown University. She frequently contributes to Muftah .org, a digital foreign policy magazine.

Stephanie Flamenbaum is a graduate student at The Fletcher School of Law and Diplomacy, where she currently serves as the managing print editor of the *Fletcher Forum of World Affairs*. Prior to attending Fletcher, she worked on Afghanistan and Pakistan issues at the United States Institute of Peace. She graduated summa cum laude from Boston University with a BA in international relations and a BA in history.

Ejaz Haider has been a journalist since 1991, starting his career at *The Frontier Post*, Lahore. During his career, he has held several editorial positions and was the news editor of *The Friday Times* and executive editor of the *Daily Times*. He is currently editor for national security affairs at Capital TV and hosts a program called "Bay-laag" ("Straight Talk"). Haider is also a Visiting Fellow at the Sustainable Development Policy Institute in Islamabad and writes a weekly column for *Express Tribune*.

Savail Meekal Hussain is an economist and entrepreneur. He runs Pakistan's largest stationery manufacturing firm and has been on the adjunct faculty at the Lahore University of Management Sciences. He has also served on the prime minister of Pakistan's economic panel as its youngest member. Hussain holds a master's degree from the University of Sussex.

Zafarullah Khan is an Islamabad-based civic educator and researcher. Presently he is the executive director of the Centre for Civic Education Pakistan, a research and training organization in the field of social sciences recognized by the country's Higher Education Commission. Khan has previously worked with leading newspapers and occasionally contributes to *The Friday Times*, *Newsline*, and *News on Sunday*. He holds a master's degree in media and communication from the London School of Economics and a master's of philosophy in Pakistan studies from Quaid-i-Azam University, Islamabad.

Anatol Lieven is a professor in the War Studies Department of King's College London and a senior fellow of the New America Foundation in Washington, DC. He is a former senior associate at the Carnegie Endowment for International Peace, and previously covered central Europe for *The Financial Times*; Pakistan, Afghanistan, the former Soviet Union, and Russia for *The Times* (London); and India as a freelance journalist. His book *Pakistan: A Hard Country* was published in 2011 by Basic Books in the United States and by Penguin in the United Kingdom.

Megan Neville is an associate project manager at Control Risks in London. She focuses on risk mitigation solutions for clients who are operating in complex areas. Previously, Neville acted as a research analyst at Integrity Research and Consultancy and the United States Institute of Peace. She earned an MA in conflict resolution from Georgetown University and a BA in anthropology and peace studies from the University of Notre Dame.

Muhammad Amir Rana is a security and political analyst and the director of Pakistan Institute for Peace Studies (PIPS), an independent Islamabad-based think tank. He worked as a journalist with various Urdu and English daily newspapers from 1996 until 2004. Additionally, he has been affiliated with the Institute of Defence and Strategic Studies, Singapore, as a visiting fellow. He is also the editor of the Pakistan annual security report, the English-language research journal *Conflict and Peace Studies*, and the Urdu monthly magazine *Tajziat*.

Ahmer Bilal Soofi is an advocate of the Supreme Court of Pakistan and an experienced litigation attorney. In Pakistan, he is a leading expert of international law and is a founding president of the Research Society of International Law, through which he has advised the Pakistani government on various international legal issues. Soofi is also a member of the UN Advisory Committee on Human Rights. He served as federal minister for law, justice, and human rights during the caretaker administration that supervised the transition to the elected government in Pakistan in 2013.

Suhail Habib Tajik is a police officer who studied for six years in Waziristan, and then served in Khyber Pukhtunkhwa and South Punjab. He worked with the United Nations in Kosovo, Rwanda, and Liberia. He was a member of the teams that investigated high-profile cases, such as the 2008 Mumbai attacks and the Benazir Bhutto assassination case. He is a recipient of the government of Pakistan's highest civil award, Tamgha-e-Imtiaz. He has also been a Hubert Humphrey Fellow. Habib holds a master's degree from the London School of Economics and Political Science.

Marvin G. Weinbaum is professor emeritus of political science at the University of Illinois at Urbana–Champaign, and previously served as an analyst for Pakistan and Afghanistan in the US Department of State's Bureau of Intelligence and Research from 1999 to 2003. He is currently a scholar in residence and director of the Pakistan Center at the Middle East Institute in Washington, DC.

Moeed Yusuf is the director of South Asian programs at the United States Institute of Peace. He is responsible for managing the institute's Pakistan program. A native of Pakistan and a political scientist by training, prior to joining USIP, Yusuf was a fellow at the Frederick S. Pardee Center for the Study of the Longer-Range Future at Boston University and concurrently a research fellow at the Mossavar-Rahmani Center at Harvard Kennedy School. His co-edited volumes, *South Asia 2060: Envisioning Regional Futures* and *Getting It Right in Afghanistan* were published, respectively, by Anthem Press (UK) and United States Institute of Peace Press in 2013. He is also the editor of a forthcoming book, *Insurgency and Counterinsurgency in South Asia*, to be published by United States Institute of Peace Press in 2014.

Mehreen Zahra-Malik is currently a Pakistan special correspondent for Reuters and an assistant editor at *The News*, Pakistan's largest English-language daily. She previously worked as news editor for *The Friday Times*, she writes a weekly column for *The News*, and her articles have also appeared in *Newsweek*, *Al Jazeera English*, *Express Tribune*, *Indian Express*, *Tehelka*, and several other international newspapers and magazines.

Index